A Question of Honour

LORD MICHAEL LEVY

SCRIBNER
New York London Toronto Sydney

SCRIBNER
A Division of Simon & Schuster, Inc.
1230 Avenue of the Americas
New York, NY 10020

Originally published in Great Britain in 2008 by Simon & Schuster UK Ltd,
a CBS Company

First Scribner hardcover edition June 2008

For information about special discounts for bulk purchases,
please contact Simon & Schuster Special Sales:
1-800-456-6798 or business@simonandschuster.com

Manufactured in the United States of America

1 3 5 7 9 10 8 6 4 2

ISBN-13: 978-1-4165-9824-4
ISBN-10: 1-4165-9824-3

To my wife Gilda – for all her love and support.

To my children, Daniel and Juliet – for always being there for me.

To my parents, Annie and Samuel – for teaching me the meaning of life.

To Gilda's parents, Mimi and Bruno – for bringing Gilda into this world.

Contents

A Question of Honour

CHAPTER 1

Summer Storm

On a gloriously sunny afternoon in July 2006, my world suddenly fell apart.

It was my sixty-second birthday. My wife Gilda and I, with her 83-year-old cousin, Erika, visiting from America, drove up to Oxford early in the morning to spend the day with our daughter Juliet and her partner, Phil. It was a welcome retreat from weeks of fevered headlines about 'cash for peerages'. For the media, it was a 'scandal' that threatened to drive Tony Blair – and me, his trusted 'Lord Cashpoint' – off the political stage, and quite possibly into the dock. To me, it still all seemed almost surreal, and the notion that as the Labour Party's 'high-value' fundraising chief I had conspired to trade lordships for contributions, frankly ludicrous. The furore had begun in earnest in January, following a sting operation by the *Sunday Times*. A woman reporter posing as a businessman's representative hinted that he was interested in giving money for one of the new 'city academies'. The academies programme had been conceived by the Downing Street education adviser Andrew Adonis, with Blair's blessing. It was aimed at getting successful business figures to help build model institutions as an alternative to Britain's most badly failing state secondary schools. Since I had raised record sums for Labour, I was asked by Tony to take the lead in bringing in academy sponsors, and dozens of new schools were now in the pipeline. Clearly charmed by the *Sunday Times* reporter over drinks and dinner at a London hotel, a veteran headteacher named Des Smith was taken in. We were working in totally different areas of the academies programme, and I had never even met him. But he claimed – rashly, inaccurately, and tragically for a model teacher who had dedicated much of his life to educating young people – that the *Sunday Times*'s 'academy sponsor' could expect to be nominated by Downing Street for 'an OBE, a CBE or a knighthood'. According to the newspaper, Smith 'went on to explain how donors could be put forward for honours and how, if they gave enough money, even get a peerage'.

A media frenzy erupted, with the press ultimately accusing Labour of having dangled promises of peerages in order to bring in millions of pounds in emergency loans to fund the 2005 election campaign. But the most damaging blow came from within, when Jack Dromey, the party's treasurer, went on television in mid-March and indignantly insisted that he had been in the dark about the loans. He added that Downing Street 'must have known' about the arrangement and said he was ready to question even the prime minister to 'get to the bottom' of the affair. Tony was furious, especially since he was convinced that a bit player like Dromey could never have fired such a broadside on his own. Lurking somewhere in the background, Tony believed, was the hand of a one-time friend and colleague who now desperately coveted his job: Gordon Brown. Yet neither of us had time to brood about party-political implications. In the wake of Dromey's statement, a little-known Scottish Nationalist MP saw a golden opportunity to inflict embarrassment, if not worse, on Blair and the government. He demanded a criminal investigation under a 1925 law barring the sale of political honours, and the Metropolitan Police obliged. In April, Des Smith himself was rousted out of bed shortly after dawn and, despite protesting his innocence, arrested.

Still, as we drove up the M40 from London early on 11 July, any Westminster worries gradually receded as they always did when I was in the cocoon of my family. With my wife of nearly forty years beside me, we were on our way to see Juliet – thirty-six, bright, pretty, but above all blessed with a sense of what truly mattered in life. She had a wonderful gift for helping people that had shone through in her voluntary work with disadvantaged children, drug addicts and asylum seekers. To the extent that 'cash for peerages' was on my mind at all as we headed for Oxford, I assumed that, before long, a sense of political sanity would reassert itself. Des Smith would no doubt be cleared – with apologies, for whatever they would be worth – and allowed to get on with rebuilding his life. Maybe, I dared to hope, the commentators who were grandly pronouncing on the 'ethics' of Labour fundraising might even get round to asking similar questions of the reporter who had passed herself off as an academy supporter and wrecked Smith's career.

As for my own role, though naturally upset at being a target of choice for the newspapers, I was confident that the police would soon recognise I had done nothing wrong. 'Cash for honours', it seemed to me, had been a fact of life for ever – whether in the arts, or in the world of charity, or in political parties. Over the years, long before I met Tony Blair and began helping Labour in the mid-1990s, I had raised tens of millions of pounds for charities, persuading dozens of wealthy people to give money to a range of causes in which I passionately believed. They gave out of genuine generosity. But very few of them were Mother Teresas. They hadn't amassed enormous personal wealth without also having a well-developed sense of their own accomplishments, a fierce competitiveness, a desire to get ahead, and usually the hope of some form of recognition or validation as well – their name on an old people's home, a school or an opera house, or perhaps the chance to let drop across the dinner table that they'd met a prime minister or leader of the Opposition. That was simple human nature. It was also a key part of the process through which all voluntary organisations secured the funding – the financial oxygen – without which they could not survive. Still, that was quite different from suggesting a direct trade-off: give money and you'll get an honour in return. I had never done any such thing. Never. Full stop. And crucially, I *couldn't* have done, even had I been minded to do so. Only one person in Labour decided whose names went on the lists for peerages: Tony Blair. Only a core Downing Street team of which I was not a part – in Blair's final years, mainly his chief-of-staff Jonathan Powell and top political aide Ruth Turner – sat in on the meetings where the peerage lists were discussed, debated and finalised. 'Michael,' Tony had joked to me after the police probe was first announced, 'if you're in trouble, I'm in trouble.' It was meant, no doubt, as reassurance. But on some level, he must also have recognised that it was true.

As we drove into Oxford, I spoke to my office on the car-phone and told them I was taking the rest of the day off. We picked up Juliet and Phil, and with a sense of liberation, I turned off my mobile. We headed for Le Petit Blanc, the popular brasserie in the centre of Oxford – Raymond Blanc's food but without the rather fancy prices of his Manoir aux Quat' Saisons in Great Milton just outside the town. We had a lovely, lazy family lunch, capped by a delightful surprise birthday cake. Then we set out for several hours on foot in the summer sunshine to show the indomitable Erika Oxford's famous dreaming spires – Balliol College, Magdalen, Christ Church, the Bodleian Library – before finally dropping Juliet and Phil back home at the end of the afternoon. But when we were saying goodbye and I instinctively switched my mobile back on, it erupted in a cascade of jarring beeps as voicemail alerts appeared one after another. Please call the office as soon as you can, said successive messages, which was mildly worrying. Then, more ominously: 'It's urgent. Please call Neil O'May.'

Neil, a dazzlingly bright but softly spoken man in his mid-forties, was the senior criminal-law partner at the London solicitors' firm Bindmans. When the police investigation was announced, I had taken the precaution of going to see him to get his view on the rash of allegations and innuendo appearing in the press and ask him what, if anything, I should do in response. As I explained my fundraising role, and my relationship with

Blair and his aides and the Labour Party, Neil was reassuring. Once the police understood the true picture, he was certain, they could only conclude there was simply no case to answer. Still, to speed things along, we decided to take the initiative of writing to Scotland Yard and offering to send over any and all material they might want in order to help their inquiries. For weeks, we had heard nothing back. No news, we both assumed, was good news.

Now, as I dialled Neil from Juliet's front hall, I figured we had at last got an answer. Perhaps it was the all-clear. Much more likely, I suspected, given the rash of text messages on my phone, it was a request to send over the files we had offered. That would mean that things might well drag on for some time. Still, nothing prepared me for Neil's message when he answered the phone. 'Michael,' he said, 'the police have told us that we are to report to Colindale police station at ten o'clock tomorrow morning. You are going to be arrested.'

I was horrified. I literally broke down. 'What?' I shrieked into the phone, as Neil and Gilda and Juliet sought to calm and reassure me. 'How can this be happening? I'm being *arrested*?' For years I had worked hard, in business, in community life and charity, now in politics – not just for myself, but for those who worked alongside me, for people in real need, for a prime minister whom I had befriended and a vision of Britain I believed in. And above all, for my family. I felt tears welling up in my eyes, all the more painful because I felt powerless to stop them. Partly, it was raw anger: at the police, whom we had offered everything they might need, but who seemed intent on grandstanding; and, I suppose, at the Labour Party, at Blair and the Downing Street insiders who took the real decisions on both funding and honours. But mainly it was from a terrifying sense of injustice, and of helplessness.

And of shame. Not because I had the slightest doubt that even if, God forbid, my arrest somehow led to charges or even a trial, I would be vindicated. But because everything I had fought so hard for on my journey from a one-room flat in an impoverished corner of east London to improbable reaches of comfort and success and contentment seemed suddenly – and very, very publicly – about to be torn away.

CHAPTER 2

The Journey

It is barely ten miles from 'Chase House' – the 'north London mansion' to which I returned to find a phalanx of TV cameras after my questioning by the police – to the one-room flat that I shared with my parents for the first eight years of my life. But it was, I could not help reflecting as I navigated the media scrum with a false, forced smile of self-assurance, a world away.

On a map of London, the universe of my childhood occupies the tiny, crowded rectangle of streets where Hackney meets Stoke Newington and Clapton – a few miles away from the old Jewish East End of Whitechapel, Commercial Road and Brick Lane. It was bounded on the south by the riotously colourful stalls of Ridley Road market with its fishmongers, its bakers, its kosher butchers and pavement vendors (none more vivid in my memory than the self-styled 'Prince Honolulu', a West Indian who was always festooned in full tribal regalia). On the north, it stretched to Cazenove Road, home to the Bnei Akiva Orthodox youth movement, where my oldest childhood friend, Barrie Berns, and I used to engage in marathon table-tennis battles during the school holidays. Its western boundary was what I still think of as 'my father's synagogue' – on Walford Road, a few blocks from Bnei Akiva, just the other side of Stoke Newington High Street. And it reached on the east to Cleveleys Road, in Upper Clapton, where Gilda and her family lived.

In some ways, it is all unrecognisable today. Synagogues have been replaced by mosques; kosher bakers and butchers by halal shops as a vibrant and thriving Muslim community follows in the footsteps of earlier groups of immigrants. Most of the large Jewish community of the post-war years, which shared the area with thousands of newly arrived Caribbean families, has moved on. Yet many of the landmarks are remarkably familiar. My first school, Colvestone Primary, still stands (though Fleetwood Primary, where I went from age nine, a half-mile to the north, off Stoke Newington High Street, is identifiable only by a gateway with a now-incongruous inscription: 'Boys'). The imposing red-brick building of Shacklewell Lane Synagogue, where I attended Hebrew classes until my barmitzvah, is still unchanged from the outside (although a sign identifies it as a mosque and the base for 'UK Turkish Islamic Funeral Services'). The Lea Bridge Road synagogue in Clapton, where I led the children's service – and first met Gilda – has given way to a temporary hostel for immigrants. But a surviving rectangle of red bricks salvaged from the synagogue building is a reminder of the deeply etched set of shared experiences, and shared values, without which I doubt either of us could have survived the days and months following my arrest. The Hackney Downs Grammar School, where I spent my teenage years, whose teaching also famously inspired the likes of Harold Pinter and Michael Caine, is gone. Having degenerated by the mid-1990s into a badly failing school, it was forced to close. But in its place stands 'Mossbourne'. It is a flagship city academy, designed by Richard Rogers and endowed by one of my closest friends, the Stoke Newington-born businessman and philanthropist Clive Bourne, during the final years of his sixteen-year battle with cancer.

I was born to Samuel and Annie Levy in July 1944. But I did not live with my parents in our rented, top-floor room at Number 48 Alvington Crescent – just around the corner from Colvestone Primary and Ridley Road market – until months later. My mother had struggled to have children. She had undergone an operation to be able to conceive, and she remained in hospital, desperately ill, after I was born. My father's sister, Aunt Cissie, cared for me at first, in his parents' small flat on the other side of Alvington Crescent. Still, my first memories are of the rented room at Number 48. There was a toilet, but no bath. Once a week we would make our way up Shacklewell Lane to the public baths. Every weekday morning from when I was five, my mother would walk me to school. When she collected me in the afternoon, we would often stop at Ridley Road market, where she would buy whatever provisions we could afford and, occasionally, a bit of cake or a piece of fruit as a treat for me.

We were, I suppose, poor. We lacked almost all of the creature comforts I now take for granted – even after we moved, shortly before my ninth birthday, to a narrow, three-storey home a mile away on Brooke Road in Stoke Newington. There, although half of the house was rented out to tenants with whom we shared a bathroom, we had our own small bedrooms, and a kitchen – which my mother invariably called our 'scullery'. Still, we did not get a television, a tiny black-and-white one, until my late teens. We never had a record player, or a clothes-washing machine, and we never took a family holiday. Still, I had no sense of deprivation. My life revolved around my parents, highlighted by what even now seems to me the emotional luxury of Friday-night dinners at home; around school; and around the matrix of synagogues and clubs that defined the Jewish community. It was a small, somehow safe, world, in which I thrived. I did well in my Hebrew studies at Shacklewell Lane and, after my barmitzvah, in the more advanced religious teaching down the road that equipped me to teach and to lead services. I excelled not only at table tennis, but in our Sunday football matches on Hackney Marshes, and above all at athletics. I was headboy at Fleetwood and went on to join the academic 'Alpha-stream' at Hackney Downs. And I sensed then, but I know even more deeply now, that whatever it was that allowed me to achieve these things began with my parents – with a father whose irrepressibly sunny disposition conveyed a certainty that good things would somehow happen, but above all with my mother. That was due in part, no doubt, to her near-fatal illness after my birth, which meant that I grew up as an especially cherished only child.

Both my parents were the children of East European Jewish immigrants – on my father's side from Poland, and on my mother's from the Russian–Polish border area of Lomza. My mother's parents had ended up in Wales (because, according to family lore, they had got off the boat in Cardiff, believing it to be

New York) and my mother was born there. But her father, the Reverend Abraham Birenbaum, moved the family to Victoria Park in Hackney in the early 1930s. He became a much-loved *magid*, one of the powerfully eloquent preachers who used to go from synagogue to synagogue in the East End. A rarity among Orthodox Jewish clergy at that time, he also preached support for a Jewish state in Palestine, although both he and his wife died before I – and four years later, the State of Israel – was born. My dad's father was an East End tailor, although he was more often than not out of work during his and my paternal grandmother's final few years in Alvington Crescent.

My father and mother met in their late twenties, in a coffee shop, no longer there, called Goides. It was near the Petticoat Lane market in Whitechapel, and my mother worked there. My father used to come in for coffee, and after many months of courtship he persuaded her to marry. Not long afterwards, having scraped together enough money for the room in Alvington Crescent, he began what would be his life's work – as the *shammas* of Walford Road synagogue. The word translates literally as 'beadle'. But it is a role which, particularly in the immigrant Jewish synagogues of inner London after the war, involved nothing less than holding the synagogue and its community together. The rabbi, who preached on the Sabbath, was indisputably the senior partner. I have vivid memories of our venerable Rabbi Len Spector holding forth on the relevance of the week's Torah reading for the congregants' everyday London lives. But it was the *shammas* who kept the records, paid the bills, ensured that the synagogue functioned, and who, crucially, made a point of knowing, caring for, and communicating with every last one of the congregants. At any time of day or night, he would rush off to visit a synagogue member who was ill, or more urgently, a newly bereaved family in need of help in making funeral arrangements for a loved one. Still, I can rarely recall my father without a smile on his face. My most treasured memories of him are of when we would walk home from synagogue along Stoke Newington High Street after services on Saturday – a high point of my week until my mid-teens, when I began to take the Sabbath children's service at Lea Bridge Road. The shopkeepers would come out on to the pavement. They were members of the synagogue, but they had to work rather than go to the service on the Sabbath, simply to eke out their existence. Grinning in greeting, they would shout as he walked by: 'Hello, Sam! Good *Shabbas*, Sam!'

My mother always hoped I would become a rabbi. And there were times, when I was very young, at Hebrew classes at Shacklewell Lane or on the Sabbath walk home from synagogue with my father, when it was a dream I almost felt able to share. By the time I was fifteen or sixteen, however, I knew that I wanted a quite different future. This was no act of adolescent rebellion – against my parents, or the Jewish atmosphere in which they had raised me. I loved both far too much for that. Nor was it the allure of some wide, wild world beyond synagogue, school and youth clubs. I knew far too little of what lay beyond my east London life to be tempted. To the extent that I ventured out, it was only for a weekly two-hour train and bus journey south of the river to Croydon Synagogue to teach Sunday morning Hebrew classes there – courtesy of my mother's brother-in-law, the Reverend Samuel Michlewitz, or, as he later Anglicised his name, Reverend Michaels. He was the headteacher there.

Still, my horizons were inevitably widening as I grew older. At Hackney Downs, though about half the students were Jewish, I was exposed to classmates of different cultures and different backgrounds. Quite literally exposed, in one sense: I still remember the shock of our first swimming session where, by school tradition, everyone bathed in the nude. It was a practice whose origins I never fathomed. On a deeper level, however, my identity and loyalties were for the first time being tugged at by influences outside the familiar environment of home and synagogue. I still felt very much a member of the Jewish community of my parents. Every day at school, I would join other observant students and walk the ten minutes to Shacklewell Lane synagogue, where kosher lunches were provided. The kind and welcoming woman in charge was the appropriately named Mrs Angel. But the noontime ritual left me with a lifelong taste for desserts – rice pudding, sponge pudding, treacle tart – since they were usually the only items on offer that could be described as edible. On Saturdays, after leading the children's service at Lea Bridge Road and joining my parents for Sabbath lunch, I would almost always head for an afternoon of Orthodox youth activities – discussions, learning, tea and comradeship – at Bnei Akiva on Cazenove Road. And since I was lucky enough to have been favoured with a key, Barrie Berns and I would spend hours there playing table tennis during term holidays, when we usually had the premises pretty much to ourselves. But Barrie – by far my closest friend almost from the day both of us started at Hackney Downs as eleven-year-olds – came from a non-observant family. Increasingly inseparable, we spent far less of our time at Bnei Akiva than with another, far less religiously centred, Jewish youth group. The Clapton Club was run by a kindly, devoted and endlessly energetic couple named Lou and Celia Rose. It was based at Lea Bridge Road synagogue, which was Orthodox – in fact, in the same premises where I led the children's service on Saturdays. But its focus was on social and sporting activities – table tennis, cricket, football, athletics, and occasional group days outside London. And crucially, it included girls. Even with the dawn of the swinging sixties, it was not a haven for sex and drugs and rock 'n' roll. But there was the occasional adolescent kiss. And there were dances. It was there that I first encountered the excitement of Elvis Presley, and learned to jive. And it was one of many reasons that I began to realise that although I valued and wanted a life that was rooted in Judaism, I did not want to – could not – embrace a life that was exclusively defined by it.

The main catalyst, however, probably came at home. I not only loved, but truly admired, my mother and father. Yet as I grew older, I saw how hard both of them had to work to make a life and a home for our family. Their shared commitment to Judaism was, and remains, an inspiration to me. They of course kept a kosher home, and even had they been able to afford a car they would not have dreamed of driving on the Sabbath – a stricture that I keep to this day. But of the two, my mother's Jewish faith seemed somehow deeper, more emotional, instinctive. Although my father would never have said so, his Judaism was necessarily coloured by the fact that it was not only his faith, but his job. It was a job that he loved. But the older I got, the more I came to realise that only my mother's hard-headed housekeeping and budgetary genius ensured that our Sabbath meal would be on the table. I began to chafe at the demands of his all-consuming synagogal duties, and at the meagre rewards, beyond the fulsome greetings of members on Saturdays and an occasional word of thanks, which he received in return. I did not know exactly what I would do with my life. But I was determined that one way or another I would secure a much greater sense of control over my own destiny. Part of this was a desire for material success. I did not crave money for money's sake. Even when, years later, I had become very successful in business and, as the key figure in the Labour Party's 'high-value' fundraising operation, was hobnobbing with multimillionaires, I was never dazzled by the size of a bank balance. But I wanted a future in which I could afford to live in an attractive home, dress well, go on exotic holidays – and above all, provide financially for a wife and children, and for my own parents, who had struggled heroically to give me my extraordinarily fortunate start in life. And of one thing I was certain: I could accomplish none of this by working for a synagogue as my father had. Not even as a rabbi.

The urge to make a future life different from my parents also partly explained, I think, an increasingly competitive streak. For almost as long as I remember, I have felt the urge to succeed, no doubt reinforced by my mother's unquestioning belief that I would triumph at whatever I did. At Fleetwood, I took huge pleasure in being headboy. At Hackney Downs, I took pride in being not only in the academic 'Alpha-stream', but consistently among the top five in my year. Both at Clapton Club and at Hackney Downs, where I competed for my house, Richards, in an array of intramural competitions, I was always fiercely determined to win – that fire, as much as any natural ability, helped me finish as a teenage Jewish youth-club champion in the 100-yard dash. Even when Barrie and I would face up in our table-tennis battles, I would insist that if he somehow emerged victorious in our agreed best-of-three-game match, we kept going – best-of-seven, best-of-nine, whatever it took – until the tally ended up in my favour. It was all done in good fun, but there was beneath it all a serious need to compete, and to prevail, that stayed with me long afterwards.

As I neared the end of my time at Hackney Downs, the issue of my future could no longer be finessed. I entered the sixth form in 1960 at the age of sixteen, hoping and intending to go on to university at the London School of Economics. My results were good enough, and years later I would sometimes regret not having gone on to higher education. My parents not only accepted, but supported, my desire to go to the LSE. But I began to feel it would be unfair to spend a further five or six years engrossed in classwork, athletics and table tennis before beginning in at least some small way to contribute financially to the home they had made for me. I did not need to tell my mother that I was not going to enter the rabbinate. She was too wise not to have sensed this – and too kind, too devoted to supporting me in whatever I chose to do, to have protested in any case. Why not medicine, then? she suggested. Or accountancy? Or law? I explained that in order to become a doctor I would have to go on for years of university and further study. But at that time, one could become a lawyer or an accountant by working a five-year period of articles – and she was enthusiastic when I said that I would try to do so. The only question was which, since I had not the slightest idea of what either law or accountancy entailed. I would in later years make crucial decisions in my life – a change in professional direction, moving home – with an almost whimsically irrational sense of self-confidence. But nothing compared to this first, critical step in my professional life. Law or accountancy? With my bemused parents standing beside me as the decision was made, I quite literally flipped a coin. Heads for law. Tails for accountancy.

It was tails.

CHAPTER 3

Articles and Faith

It was my mother, through the Reverend Michaels at Croydon synagogue, who got me my position as an articled clerk at the accountants Lubbock Fine just off Holborn, a minute's walk from the tube station, on Red Lion Street. One of the senior partners, Stanley Prashker, was originally from Croydon and had been a member of the synagogue. He agreed to take me on at the princely sum of £5 a week – which barely covered my bus fare, though it was boosted by the few pounds that I still made by taking children's services at Lea Bridge Road and teaching Hebrew classes in Croydon.

I felt a mix of anticipation, excitement and fear as I donned my synagogue suit and tie to set off for my first day of work shortly before my seventeenth birthday. Lubbock Fine was a 'Jewish' firm, or at least had started that way. Stanley Prashker, a boss who would also become a mentor, was very much part of the Jewish community in which I'd grown up. But my years on Red Lion Street opened up a much wider world. The Lubbock of Lubbock Fine was Harry, who with his younger brother Reggie had set up the firm in Whitechapel a quarter of a century earlier. He was nearing retirement, rarely dropped in, and was too far above my pay-grade for me to have so much as said hello. But still a legendary presence, he was a vintage East End Jewish working-class man, whose politics would make Tony Benn look like Tony Blair. Harry was a proud, card-carrying Communist, and among his legacies was the fact that one of our clients was the party's official organ, the *Daily Worker*. Another was Copes, the football-pools business and one of Harry's early labours of love. The client list, however, had branched out from the original mix of politics, pools and small Jewish businesses. It included Scotts, purveyors of the finest cooked ham – I was one of very few on the team of auditors not tempted to sample the wares. And, in a first taste of an area that would later become a life-changing part of my career, there were also entertainment clients – Tommy Steele, the Cockney boy who became one of Britain's first pop idols, and Mantovani and his string orchestra.

The mechanics of accountancy – the maths and bookkeeping, the rules and regulations – were the easiest part of my apprenticeship. I found I had a natural ability for numbers. Hackney Downs had given me a sense of academic discipline that, along with the constant encouragement of parents whom I was determined not to let down, made me confident that I would emerge successful from my five years in articles. But the experience was both challenging, and eye-opening, in countless other ways. Within days of my arrival, I began to feel the tug of an entirely new culture. Even my fellow junior clerks wore silk ties, and some even bowler hats, and it was not long before I dipped into my pitifully meagre savings to purchase my own. An early run-in with another clerk, who at eighteen was barely older than me, captured the mix of ambition and insecurity with which I entered this unfamiliar new world. We were sent out to visit a client. The other clerk paused to fix his bowler just right, straighten his tie, and then turned to me, held out his briefcase, and said: 'Carry this.' I refused, and added in a threatening whisper that if he had any problems we could meet outside after work and 'I would sort him out'. It was partly a pre-emptive truculence, a Hackney-sized chip on my shoulder, which has stayed with me always. And partly, it was that I had been raised, nurtured, to feel pride in who I was and where I came from and was not about to carry around some other boy's bag. That feeling, too, has stayed with me.

As has another lesson, which I think is why the people who knew me the longest and best stood by me unswervingly during the 'cash for peerages' ordeal. As I settled in at Lubbock Fine, I was given increasingly serious work, even going out on my own for audits. A few months after joining, I was sent back across London to Stratford, at the eastern reaches of the East End, to audit a garment-manufacturing firm. As I went through the figures – gross salary, net salary, tax deducted, national insurance deducted – they just didn't add up. No matter how often I calculated and recalculated the sums, the salary amounts seemed to be overstated. I approached the kindly looking woman who did the internal accounts and suggested something was wrong.

No, she assured me, everything was fine. Feeling sure of my maths, but nowhere near sure enough of my junior position to take things further on my own, I phoned Stanley Prashker and explained what I had found. He was sceptical at first, but he agreed to come and take a look. Barely had he arrived, when the bookkeeper broke down and admitted that she had been overstating the salaries and pocketing the difference. The startled company bosses called in the police. For me, still not eighteen, it was a traumatic experience – not only the idea, so foreign to my childhood world, that a trusted employee would cook the books; but the prospect of this middle-aged woman's life being wrecked as a result. In my later life, whether in business or politics, close friends would remark on the fact that my determination to get ahead was tempered by an almost obsessive insistence on 'playing by the rules'. They were right. It was an instinct that probably began at home, but which took on a sudden new seriousness for me in the crucible of a garment factory in east London.

The job also took me outside London, and not to the heritage sites I'd occasionally visited on day-trips with Barrie with Clapton youth club, but to what seemed to me exotic 'business' trips to places like Bletchley and Birmingham, Manchester and Cardiff. In Cardiff, to audit a company called Tuf Abrasives, I remember being literally open-mouthed on arriving by taxi at my hotel for the night: the St Mellons Country Club, on the Newport Road. For the first time, I had a sense that I might really be heading for a future free of the material insecurities my parents had endured. It was an impression reinforced, or perhaps more accurately a dream reinvigorated, by the ever-present examples of Stanley Prashker and the firm's other leading partner, Phillip Fine – both of them full of self-confidence, immaculately dressed, living in spacious homes in London's growing northern suburbs, and utterly at ease with clients and the world of business.

My own world, of course, was still very much centred on the inner city of my childhood. Shortly before I took – and with relief, and not much cramming, passed – the 'intermediate' exams two years into my articles, we again moved house. It was the final few miles in my parents' northward migration from Alvington Crescent, past Stoke Newington and into Stamford Hill – then, as now, home to tens of thousands of ultra-Orthodox Chasidim. We took a small but comfortable ground-floor family flat in what was at the time one of the area's nicest blocks, Stamford Lodge, on Amhurst Park, from where my parents and I would make our slightly longer way on foot to synagogue every Saturday morning. While the world of work dominated my life during the week, I still spent many weekend hours with Barrie and our group of friends, still played table tennis and went to Clapton Club, and still – if inevitably less often – joined them for football on Sunday afternoons.

The games were exhilarating – I was a scrappy right back, though my failure to take my talents further was not exactly a fatal loss to England's national side – but they were less important than the lasting love of football, and in particular one brand of football, which they gave me. Barrie, like most of our other friends, was an obsessive supporter of the Arsenal, and it was a passion I soon adopted as my own. Since he was not Orthodox, he would happily board the bus to Highbury to watch the team every Saturday that they were playing at home. My Orthodox Judaism – preventing me from travelling, or carrying money, on the Sabbath – meant that I couldn't join him. But that didn't stop me altogether. I would set out on foot, while Barrie or another of our friends would wait for me outside the stadium and pay my way in for the match. For months, the arrangement worked fairly well. Yet since the walk from Stamford Hill was long, and the end of our Sabbath meal unpredictable, it sometimes meant my friends ended up missing a good chunk of the first half of the game. So with trepidation, I embarked on a first – and I told myself, harmless – act of rebellion against the religious strictures I had always quite easily and happily accepted. I began carrying just enough money for my Arsenal ticket and making my own way into the ground – until on one fateful Saturday evening, for reasons I never discovered, my parents asked me point-blank whether I'd been to watch the football on the Sabbath. It never occurred to me to lie, but they were angrier than I could ever recall and, I think, genuinely and understandably hurt. It was some years later that, no longer living at home, I next went to Highbury.

Football also played a part in cementing my relationship with Stanley Prashker as the end of my articles drew near. It was 1966, England's World Cup summer. In July, Stanley called me into his office for what I assumed would be a routine chat ahead of my crucial final exams. Though he recognised, and I think appreciated, the dedication I brought to my work, he knew that I'd been somewhat less diligent in keeping up with the correspondence course I'd been taking to prepare for the qualification test. But instead, after asking me in uncomfortably stern tones to take a seat, he declared: 'Michael, you have one last challenge here at Lubbock Fine before you finish your articles.' When I asked, puzzled, what it was, he smiled and said: 'Get two tickets for the football final.' To which I replied, censoring out a somewhat coarser expletive: 'How the heck am I going to do that?' He said that was up to me. When I asked how much I could pay, he said: 'I'm going to pay. You just get the tickets!' For many hours, beginning that very evening, I called what few useful contacts I could think of – I was too junior to contemplate phoning any of our clients – and finally, through a friend of a friend of a friend, struck gold. Gold, in fact, might have been cheaper: the total price tag of several hundred pounds was more than my yearly salary. But Stanley was delighted, and I am certain far more impressed with my World Cup triumph than anything I'd done in the realm of double-entry bookkeeping. I had not become friends with Stanley Prashker, since he was, after all, my boss. But I genuinely liked him, I had learned from him, and I admired him. On the most superficial level, I envied his sense of style, his self-confidence, his success. Yet much more important, and much more lasting in its effect on me, was the emphasis that he placed on human relationships. Our clients, he always said, were not just names on balance sheets, but people with whom we had to build a genuine bond of trust. He also extended that respect to the people he worked with – even mere articled apprentices. It was an example that would guide the rest of my working life – a lesson in the need to value people I worked with or for, no matter the size of their bank balance, their rank or their job.

But another experience, as the end of my articles approached, changed my life much, much more dramatically. It occurred not on Red Lion Street, nor at a garment business in Stratford, a luxury hotel in Cardiff or at Highbury – but at the synagogue on Lea Bridge Road. After leading the Sabbath children's service, we would join the whole congregation in the synagogue hall for the traditional *kiddush* – small beakers of wine raised for the rabbi's blessing followed by bite-sized sandwiches and small talk. For weeks, I had noticed a girl in her late teens – with long hair, a beaming smile, and looks that reminded me of a movie star – emerging from the main service. Finally, I built up the courage to approach her. In my Lubbock Fine bowler, I must have cut a fairly ridiculous figure. And despite my Clapton Club level of proficiency in the jive, I had no real idea how to proceed once we'd exchanged names between nibbles on our smoked-salmon rolls. Still, I somehow marshalled enough self-confidence to volunteer that I led the weekly children's service, and to invite her to look in on it the following Sabbath. She did.

Her name was Gilda. She was, I would very soon discover, a mix of seriousness, sharp intelligence, and sudden, sunny mirth. She was a local girl. She had gone to school at the nearest female equivalent of Hackney Downs grammar – the Skinners' Company's School for Girls – and was about to embark on a university course in English and drama. She was also passionately political – though, as she insisted on adding, 'political with a small "p"'. She had little time for, or interest in, the major parties, beyond an instinctive inclination to support Labour. But she was a fully fledged member of the CND, and even attended their rallies in Hyde Park. She had also been her school's sixth-form representative to the Council of Education and World Citizenship, an earnestly idealistic UN-sponsored organisation that did what it said on the tin – and that hosted annual London conferences at County Hall for hundreds of like-minded student leaders from around the country.

She was one of two daughters of a successful market trader and an extraordinarily strong, supportive mother. They had both escaped Vienna literally in the shadow of the Nazi Holocaust – thanks to the fact that Gilda's father, although raised in Austria, had been born in London and had a British passport. Her mother's family was not so lucky. Her maternal grandparents, along with three of their other seven children, were murdered in the death camp of Auschwitz. The other children – Gilda's mother, Mimi, her uncle Peter, aunt Lottie and uncle Pepi – survived through a mix of luck, raw desperate intelligence, and human kindness. Peter was only three when he was among the handful of children taken by the Red Cross from the concentration camp at Theresienstadt, in Czechoslovakia, on a *Kindertransport* evacuation to Sweden. Lottie, the eldest, was heroically hidden by her husband's non-Jewish family in the countryside outside Vienna for the duration of the war. Pepi banded together with several other boys and bribed a Czech guard to help them escape from Theresienstadt. He made his way first to Italy and finally to Palestine, where he joined the pre-state Haganah – and died fighting in Israel's 1948 war of independence. That all this should have given Gilda a sense of seriousness, of purpose, about life was hardly surprising. But she also had – and conveyed with her wonderfully unpredictable bursts of humour and her entrancing talk of a happier future for herself and others – an irresistible joy for life.

I was, at first hopefully and soon helplessly, in love. I found myself looking forward to Sabbath services with a whole new sense of anticipation, a feeling that only intensified after our first real 'date'. I was confident that, if only because of Gilda's love for stage shows, my invitation would be difficult to resist: an excursion to the West End to see the hit comedy revue with Peter Cook and Dudley Moore, *Beyond the Fringe*. She accepted, and even volunteered to look into getting tickets, and phoned me the next afternoon to ask, not unreasonably: 'How much should I spend?' To which I replied – my excitement getting the better of my few pounds in savings: 'Don't worry about the price. Get the best tickets!' Barrie loaned me the money. It was the rashest, wisest excursion into debt that I ever made.

In the weeks that followed, we spent almost every evening together. After work, I would head from our flat in Stamford Hill to Gilda's home in Cleveleys Road. The first time I opened the small, black iron gate outside Number 31, where she and her parents lived, I remember marvelling at what to me seemed the luxury of the place. In fact, it was a small two-storey home, no bigger than the one we had lived in on Brooke Road. But it had bright red paint and bay windows, a small garden, and a lived-in sense of permanence and ownership because there were no tenants or lodgers to share it with. There was even a car – belonging to Gilda's father, Benjamin – parked out front. Gilda and I would sit talking in the front room, or sometimes walk for hours along the streets where we had both grown up. A real closeness developed. It was rooted in a shared background and deepened by a sense that we both wanted broadly the same things for our lives – personal success, a happy marriage, children, and the ability to repay in some small measure the sacrifices our own parents had made for us. In those first few weeks, of course, we never spoke of marriage. Although I must confess that the idea crossed my mind almost from the moment I set eyes on Gilda; she was still young, I was too nervous of rejection, and I think we both figured there would be time enough for such talk in future.

However, I had known her for all of three weeks when I

mentioned that since my qualification exam was coming up, I had arranged to go away for an extended pre-test course in Wales to make up for the relaxed approach I'd taken to my distance-learning studies. 'You won't suddenly start going out with someone else,' I said with what I dared to imagine was a suitably self-confident smile. After a few moments, she replied mischievously: 'But why not?' I must have known, or at least hoped, this moment would come. My reply was instantaneous: 'Because,' I said, 'I want you to marry me.' She looked shocked, not I think because either of us doubted the seriousness of the relationship that had grown, but because of the suddenness of it all. Still, after a painfully long pause, she smiled, and replied: 'Yes.'

I still recall the ashen look on the face of Gilda's mother when she opened the door and I blurted out the news of our engagement. I don't think my future mother-in-law's reaction was a reflection on her daughter's choice of partner. It was the idea that Gilda – in a sense, still the baby, eight years younger than her sister, Miriam, who was long married, with three children – would be leaving home. Besides, Gilda had always been so immune to frippery and flattery, so unfailingly *sensible*. Now, she had decided to spend the rest of her life with a boy she had known for only a matter of weeks! Prudently, I left Gilda with her mother, while her father and I retreated to the kitchen and I formally, fearfully, asked for her hand. Once their initial astonishment had passed, both her parents – and mine – were not only supportive; they were soon sharing their, and our, excitement. The final, practical hurdle came a number of weeks later, when I sat my exam. I felt fairly confident I had passed, but still remember spending the morning that the results were due to arrive closeted in our bathroom in Stamford Lodge and, when the post finally arrived, asking my mother to slip the letter under the door. I literally shrieked in relief when I opened it.

As our marriage approached, Gilda's parents moved to a modest semi-detached home in the increasingly popular north-west suburb of Edgware, near where Gilda's sister, Miriam, lived. Yet there was never any doubt about where the wedding would take place. With Barrie as best man and my parents beaming with pride beside me, we were married on 20 August 1967 – a month after my twenty-third birthday and three months before Gilda's twenty-first. The ceremony took place in the synagogue that had for so long dominated my father's life, and mine, on Walford Road.

It was just one of a series of seismic changes in my life, and Gilda's, within a period of a few months. Both of us had grown up in extraordinarily close-knit families, I as an only child and Gilda with a married sister who was nearly a decade older. Now we were setting out on our own. The extent of the change was evident literally from the moment we were married. It was Gilda who chose our honeymoon destination, having come across a sheaf of tourist brochures extolling the virtues of Napoleon's one-time place of exile, the island of Elba off Italy's Tuscan coast. It was the first time either of us had been on an aeroplane.

When we got back, we pooled our wedding gifts and our tiny shared savings. With the encouragement of Stanley Prashker's brother, a successful estate agent who had Anglicised his name to Ronnie Preston and would become a friend and colleague in Jewish charity work, we managed to scrape together the £1,000 deposit for our first home. It cost £6,000. It was small but solid-looking two-storey home of red brick, with a garage and a small garden, on a quiet road called The Ridgeway, in the north-west

London suburb of Stanmore. It was barely a mile from Gilda's parents. The building society owned most of it – the mortgage was £5,000. Yet to us it was, and remains, the embodiment of the life and the family we were setting out to build together.

Our new life began with a change of professional direction that was so rash and risky that it seems in retrospect only slightly less impetuous than the coin-toss with which I'd chosen accountancy over law barely six years earlier. But Gilda, who surely must have harboured doubts, was supportive. I had successfully completed my articles, and was now a fully qualified chartered accountant, and had every prospect of beginning a path towards partnership at Lubbock Fine with Stanley Prashker's guidance and support. But I decided instead to opt out, and to strike out on my own. I was driven, I think, by the same urge to control my own future, to work for myself, that had made it so hard for me to imagine life as a communal rabbi. Now, with no office and no capital and not a single client, I decided to set up an accountancy practice. In the early months, I worked from the Ridgeway – though 'work' is the wrong word, since I in fact *net*worked, fishing and hoping for business and answering dozens of newspaper adverts placed by small-time companies in need of freelance help. Finally, a first potential client phoned. I had met Ray Chettur several years earlier, when I was auditing a client at Lubbock Fine and he was installing an intercom system there. He had heard I had started on my own. He had done the same, setting up a company called Highams Electrical Contractors, and asked whether I would do the books. Needless to say, I accepted. When he asked me how much I would charge, I was left to reply: 'How much are you happy to pay?' The answer was not that much, but it was fair, and it was a paycheck.

It was a timely boost. Within weeks of our wedding, Gilda was pregnant with our first child. We were both overjoyed, but not so starry-eyed that we didn't grasp the new changes and challenges that lay ahead. Gilda was by now nearing the end of her studies at the New College of Speech and Drama, the former Guildhall drama department that had broken off on its own and affiliated to London University. Having got engaged in her first year, and married in her second, she now had to juggle the final year of her course with approaching parenthood. But she completed the requirements for her diploma in dramatic arts, as well as a teaching diploma in English and drama. I surely would have had to phone Stanley Prashker and ask for my old desk back had it not been for Highams Electrical Contractors. Yet after that first breakthrough, a slow but steady stream of further clients appeared as Gilda's delivery date, in the summer of 1968, drew nearer.

One client in particular – though neither he nor I could know that at the time – would ultimately lead to my big break, and to an entirely new direction in my life. He did not come to me, as much of my early business did, through word of mouth, but through one of my seemingly endless responses to newspaper adverts. Barry Class wanted to hire an in-house accountant. I called the number listed in the advert and explained that I was not looking for a staff job but that I had qualified at Lubbock Fine, had recently gone into practice on my own, and was confident I could help him out. Clearly used to making on-the-spot decisions, he paused for a moment and replied: 'Let's give it a go.' We did. The result was a relationship that worked wonderfully for both of us. Barry had got a dedicated – and grateful – young accountant without having to add to his staff overheads. And he soon became not only my most important client, but a source of support as I expanded my practice. Within a few months, I took a small office one floor above his, in Westbourne Grove in Bayswater. The move was not only convenient; it proved to be the first step on a professional path that I had never imagined, and which over a period of two decades brought me a level of fulfilment and success that was, at the start, only a distant dream.

CHAPTER 4

Foundations, and Beyond

To say that Barry Class was in the music business when I began working for him early in 1968 is a bit like saying a travel agent is in the airline business. Barry didn't run a record company. But he did own a chain of six London record shops, called Disci. And he had the natural salesman's mix of ambition, street smarts and charm that suggested he would not remain just a record-shop owner for long. It was through Barry that I first met a fellow Hackney boy who had recently left the secondary modern near Lea Bridge Road to start a business selling television aerials. Years later, I would get to know him as a hugely successful entrepreneur – as well as a generous donor to Jewish and other charities, and to Labour. Back then, Alan Sugar was one of Disci's suppliers. He was cheery, reliable, resourceful and was clearly destined for bigger things.

Barry, too, was heading upwards. The first clue came on the record-shop floor. Not only did Disci sell records and record-players, but also radios, Alan Sugar's aerials – and just about anything that Barry thought his customers might want. It was the audio-visual equivalent of Ridley Road Market. More importantly, being in the record-store business in the late sixties meant being part of a larger, pulsating music scene. There were no iTunes downloads. These were the days of vinyl, when teenagers would wait for the chart shows, then rush into Disci or rival shops to be the first to buy the new singles. Crucially, the artists themselves were part of that culture. The Beatles' legendary manager, Brian Epstein, also got his start running a music store. Barry was not quite so lucky as Epstein in his choice of performing friends. But he did get to know some genuine stars and, like Epstein, he began to manage them professionally. I was fortunate enough to have started handling Barry's accounts just as one of his first musical discoveries was achieving success. They were called the Foundations – a mix of West Indians and Londoners led by a talented Trinidadian singer named Clem Curtis – and they became the closest thing Britain produced to a winning Motown-style act. Not long before I joined Barry, they had reached number one on the British music charts with a song called 'Baby, Now That I've Found You'. Their big breakthrough, however, came in 1968. It was called 'Build Me Up Buttercup' and it climbed to number one in America.

It was a breakthrough for me as well. 'I have this guy who is good with numbers,' Barry told the group. 'We'll get him to help me with your affairs on the financial side.' I did, and was soon not only advising him on the Foundations' accounts, but absorbing every bit of information that I could on the intricacies of licensing and copyright. Just months later, I boarded a flight for my first overseas business trip – to New York and Los Angeles, to help Barry negotiate deals for the group. I was mesmerised. I won't claim to have been a natural Foundations fan. I'd never even heard of the group before he introduced me to them. But it proved to be a life-changing introduction, if only because it soon brought me into contact with people like Russ Regan – a huge figure in the music business who was then head of the MCA division that handled the Foundations in the States, and remains a close personal friend to this day. From that very first overseas visit, as a young accountant in my early twenties struggling to set up on my own, I could not help but be excited by the lure of a career a world away from auditing Tuf Abrasives in Cardiff. Returning from the States – where I'd stayed in hotels that made the St Mellons Country Club on the Newport Road seem almost modest – I remember thinking: This is a lucrative business – and fun as well!

Still, when I was jotting down my initial notes for this chapter – and had instinctively sprinkled in phrases like 'hitting the big time', 'going gold' and 'top of the charts' – Gilda read them and remarked: '*That*'s not how you speak. That's not even how you spoke back then!' She was right. And as so often, her comment hit at a deeper truth. For while I enjoyed – and was sometimes, I admit, seduced by – the raw energy of the music scene, I was never fully a part of it. I am convinced that one main reason I clicked so well with the Foundations was that I always looked on them as just part of my professional responsibilities to Barry, and treated the music business as just that – a business.

Even back then, long before my Labour Party fundraising days, people whom I worked with remarked on my back-slapping, shoulder-grabbing flair for the social side of doing business. And that was undeniably an advantage when I was helping negotiate the best possible terms for a new recording deal. But Barry and the Foundations valued my work above all, I think, because I provided capable, honest, no-nonsense help on financial issues. They trusted my expertise and my judgement. They trusted *me*. And they were soon telling others in the music industry that they should trust me, too.

Within a period of barely a year, my professional life was transformed. And I soon outgrew the quarters I was renting from Barry. In early 1970, I seized on the opportunity to team up professionally with a fellow Lubbock Fine alumnus – though a much more senior one. Sidney Wagner was ten years older than me and had been a manager at Red Lion Street when I was in articles. Now, he also brought in a seasoned veteran named Leslie Prager, who was nearing retirement but provided our partnership with the imprimatur of his former City firm, Lovegrove Prager. And thus, a new London accountancy firm – Wagner, Prager, Levy – was born. My name may have come third on the letterhead. But at the tender age of twenty-six, I was a 50:50 partner – Leslie Prager came in only as a consultant – in a serious practice, with spacious new offices at Number 6 Porter Street, just off Baker Street.

A string of new clients – at first artists, then producers, and managers – came my way. And some of the most successful of my new clients taught me an early lesson in the perils of succumbing to the attractions of reflected stardom. They had begun as a small-time Kent schoolboy band called the Avengers. But at the urging of their producer Roger Easterby, they rebranded themselves – as 'Vanity Fare' – and recorded a string of hits including 'I Live for the Sun', 'Early in the Morning' and 'Hitchin' a Ride'. On a hitch-hiking mission of my own, I went with them to New York in 1970. Stepping off the plane alongside these budding pop idols at Kennedy airport, I told the immigration inspector, in my best big-shot's voice: 'I'm with the group.' For the next hour, Vanity Fare's vanity, and mine, were trampled in a humiliatingly thorough – yet thankfully fruitless – search for drugs. I would, in the twenty years that followed, make dozens of overseas trips with a range of well-known performers. But after that first experience, I always went through customs separately. I identified myself as a 'chartered accountant in business', which is, after all, what I was.

Still, it was not accountancy as I knew it. It was not only about audits but auditions. It strayed into areas – copyright and contracts, demo discs and distribution – that were also the province of lawyers and managers. And as I built a reputation as a specialist music-industry accountant, my client list changed. I was still auditing a few companies like Highams Electrical Contractors, and doing Barry Class's books. And over the next several years, I went on to work for clients ranging from what was then a small start-up company called Pizza Express, to Hartsbourne Country Club and the retail group Susan Handbags. Increasingly, however, I shifted to representing or doing specialist work for artists, from the Drifters' lead singer Clyde McPhatter to Tony Bennett, as well as producers like Easterby and songwriters such as Roger Greenaway, who with his former bandmate, Roger Cook, wrote a string of major hits, including the New Seekers anthem 'I'd Like to Teach the World to Sing'.

Life at home had changed dramatically as well, beginning on a warm June evening in 1968 when our first child was born, at Bart's Hospital, near the old Smithfield market, in central London. Both Gilda's mother and mine were with her on the maternity ward. Although in those days mere men were not allowed to be on hand for the birth, I paced nervously outside. Every ten minutes or so, as the crucial moment approached, I would sprint down four flights of stairs to report to the two grandfathers, who were parked in Gilda's father's car, and then sprint back up again. Finally, my shirt by now drenched in sweat, I was able to make a final dash, and report: 'Gilda's fine. It's a boy!' Both of us had settled quickly on a name: Daniel. Then, as now, it was a popular choice with parents, but seemed also somehow distinctive, resonant. It was also, of course, Jewish.

And Judaism, despite my budding professional success in the most worldly of industries, still mattered deeply to me. Though I had begun to work long hours and travel regularly – not only to the States but around Europe – only on very rare occasions was I not home by late afternoon on Fridays. At sunset, we would light the Sabbath candles for the traditional Friday-night meal, and on Saturday mornings I would walk the mile and a half to Stanmore synagogue for the morning service. The familiar, familial rituals, at home and in synagogue, were a comforting island of retreat from a working life which, though increasingly successful and at times exhilarating, was also draining.

The local synagogue, as it turned out, made living in Stanmore in the first years of our marriage a decidedly mixed experience. We loved our home, and had extended the lounge and dining area and the kitchen in the expectation of staying there for many years. It was certainly big enough for our family, even after we returned to Bart's in May 1970 for the birth of our second child, Juliet. This time, Gilda chose the name, the Shakespearean choice reflecting an artistic side that our daughter has inherited. But while I made a number of friends at Stanmore synagogue, the membership tended to be slightly older, set in its ways, and not particularly welcoming to new arrivals. If synagogue hadn't mattered so much to me – and there were times during my later period in the music business when I would lead a less Jewishly centred life – none of that might have mattered. But it did. And one of the first things I noticed as Gilda and I began tentatively looking into moving – to nearby Mill Hill – was the welcoming warmth of its Jewish community. Several members of the local synagogue heard that I had taken the children's services at Lea Bridge Road and said that if we moved into the area they would be delighted if I'd do the same. The local rabbi – his name was Shlomo Cutler; he and his wife Judith would become our close friends, but we never called them anything but Rabbi and Mrs Cutler – made a point of phoning to follow up the suggestion.

Our move to Mill Hill was yet another exercise in wild optimism over common sense. It cost us nearly £30,000, money that we didn't have. Still, even in the few years we spent in Stanmore, our home had risen in value – to about £10,000. We used the windfall to put down a deposit in Mill Hill, and took out a mortgage for the rest. Gilda was initially, and quite rightly, worried about the risk. Yet both she and I fell in love with a large family home at 78 Uphill Road, which was barely a mile from the synagogue, and still near her parents in Edgware. It was a three-storey, four-bedroom house with a large garden in the back and a rambling den area on the top floor – perfect for two growing children. We would spend the next twenty years there – until, during a life-changing period of personal crisis mixed with sudden personal wealth at the end of 1980s, we, unwisely, decided to move again.

Fortunately for the building society, in the years after our move to Mill Hill a mixture of my own raw ambition, the support and vision of others around me, and timely good fortune brought me extraordinary success at work. With a growing music-industry portfolio at the Porter Street practice, I was soon helping clients with deals worldwide, and meeting some of the top record-company executives in the process. I tried always to keep my feet firmly on the ground, to remember that while Gilda and I now lived in an impressive home in the north-west suburbs our roots were in humbler Hackney. One particular visit to the United States, barely a year after we had moved to Mill Hill, conveyed with a frightening suddenness both the attractions of the glitzy world in which I now operated, and the dangers of assuming that it would necessarily last. Arriving in New York in the afternoon, I took a taxi to my hotel – the glamorous Pierre on the edge of Central Park – and prepared for a meeting with one of the real giants of the music industry. Clive Davis remains a major figure today: having launched Whitney Houston's career in the 1980s, he has recently taken Britain's *X Factor* winner Leona Lewis under his wing. When I flew in to see him in 1972, he was the head of CBS/Columbia Records and I was representing Easterby, on the cusp of his Vanity Fare success, and Roger Greenaway. All the major American music companies were anxious to sign them.

Davis had made his company a major force in the sixties and early seventies with a string of successful artists, including Janis Joplin, Santana, Bruce Springsteen, Blood, Sweat & Tears and Pink Floyd. When I went to see him at Black Rock, CBS's skyscraper headquarters in Manhattan, he was disarmingly friendly. He showed me around the building, spoke enthusiastically about the potential for our doing business, and took me to see his head of international music Walter Yetnikoff, who some years later became the head of CBS, to discuss details before excusing himself and saying: 'I have to be off for a board meeting, but let's have dinner later in the week. I really want to close this deal.' Feeling flattered by the attention, and optimistic about the CBS tie-up, I walked back to the Pierre. Barely an hour later, however, a producer friend who knew that I'd been meeting Davis phoned and said: 'Did you hear the news? Clive Davis has been fired!' It was true – over accusations, which he absolutely denied, that he had used company funds for private expenses, including his son's barmitzvah. We never had that dinner. But I made a point of going to see him several days later at his apartment on Central Park West. It had the atmosphere of a house of mourning. I told him that I was sure that he would bounce back – a remark that was meant as an attempt at reassurance, but within several years turned out to be true. Still, it was for me a sobering reminder of the fragility of wealth and power in the music world.

I did, in fact, go on to do deals with CBS and to become friendly with its top executives. And the following spring, one of the most senior of them, Dick Asher, played a crucial role in what would turn out to be the most important business decision of my life. It is a measure of how well I was doing as a specialist accountant that our conversation took place in the south of France, where Gilda, the children and I had flown for a first European family holiday. When I met up with Dick, who was also on holiday, he mentioned a writer and producer whom I represented named Peter Shelley – eccentric but talented – who had been trying to get taken on by a number of record companies. CBS, like the others, had turned him down. But Dick said to me: 'I think our music people were wrong on this one. I think he is really talented. Why don't you back him and set up a small company – and we'll do the distribution for you?' When I replied, laughing: 'Dick, I don't have any capital,' he said: 'Borrow some money, and we'll try to help you out.' Coming so soon after we had overextended ourselves to buy our new home, his words frankly frightened me. I felt this would be one risk too many. But as we returned home, I found it hard to put the idea out of my head. Had Gilda objected, I am sure I wouldn't have taken it further. But as we talked, she felt it was a risk I might regret not taking. 'Why not have a go?' she said. As a hedge against failure, we both agreed that I'd keep the day job – staying on at Wagner, Prager, Levy until this new gamble actually paid off.

I was doing well enough there to convince my bank to loan me £15,000, and used the first chunk to rent a small basement room on York Street, thirty seconds' walk across Baker Street from the accountancy practice. We had no artists at first, just an idea for a logo and a company name: Bullet Records. That name, however, turned out to be registered to someone else. It was my secretary Jean Cobb – who had only recently started, but who would become an indispensable part of my working life over the following three decades – who rescued us from this first, inauspicious setback. Our logo, she said, 'really looks like a magnet as well'. And so it did. We named the company Magnet Records. I owned most of it, but Peter Shelley took a small share as well. Peter later recorded Magnet hits of his own – including 'Gee Baby' and the predictably quirkish 'Love Me, Love My Dog'. But first, he played an essential role in a critical early breakthrough, without which the company might well have been stillborn.

He had written a song called 'My Coo-Ca-Choo' and we advertised for someone to sing and record it. I had mixed feelings when a flamboyant, blond-haired 31-year-old knocked on our basement door a few days later and said he was our man. Auspiciously I suppose, his real name was Bernard Jewry, but he was better known as Shane Fenton. With his band, the Fentones, he had a few hits in the 1960s, but was not exactly a star. We explained to him as politely as possible that we had in mind someone with a 'harder, rock-type image' to front the song. He was utterly unfazed. A day later he returned – with his hair dyed black, black leather jacket, and wearing one black glove. We were instantly won over, the only remaining problem being the name. For a new company, and a new song, we needed at least the appearance of a new talent. It was Peter and he who came up with the name, which I thought was frankly nuts. They decided to call him Alvin Stardust. Though Alvin could clearly sing, as his great live performances proved, it was Peter's voice on that first record – fairly standard industry practice at the time. We cut the record late in 1973, just weeks after having set up the company. Dick Asher kept his word: CBS distributed it in Britain. Then, we waited. Our stroke of fortune came when Radio Luxembourg played, and raved over, the new single. By

Christmas, it was number two in the British charts. We had a genuine hit.

Which meant that I also had a genuinely difficult decision to make. Over the next eighteen months, I continued to work as hard as I ever had at the accountancy practice. But with Alvin emerging as a major star in performances in Britain and abroad, I was travelling the world, bleary-eyed, to tie up international distribution deals. Something obviously had to give. Magnet had started astonishingly well: Alvin followed up his single with a successful first album, and we had a further hit single called 'There's a Whole Lot of Loving' by the group Guys 'n' Dolls. However, if the company was to survive in the longer run, it clearly needed my full-time attention. Sidney Wagner also recognised this, and we both also feared that my Magnet role risked a conflict of interest with my accountancy clients in the music business. We agreed a deal under which I sold him my half of the accountancy practice. In return, Sidney took a financial interest in Magnet, which I eventually purchased back from him.

Suddenly, I was no longer an accountant. I owned a business of my own. It was a tiny one, off to a good start, but still with only a handful of successful artists on its books. With no guarantee we would find others, the prospect of building the company was daunting. But it was also exhilarating – especially during the first, difficult, five years. Slowly, we added to our stable of successes. In addition to Alvin, Guys 'n' Dolls and Peter Shelley, we had hits with the groups Silver Convention, Matchbox, the hugely talented band Bad Manners and, perhaps most satisfyingly, a librarian from Jamaica named Susan Cadogan. She had recorded a song called 'Hurt So Good', which her producer brought in for us to hear. We loved it, signed her on the spot, and brought her over to Britain, where the record became a major hit. And in 1977 – four years after setting up the company and barely two years after I had moved from my accountancy work into Magnet full-time – we managed to beat competition from larger and better-established record companies to sign up a talented doo-wop revival band called Darts. There were times, during those first extraordinary years at Magnet, when it was difficult to remind myself that the music business was in fact 'just a business' – perhaps none more so than when we rented the penthouse suite at the Montcalm Hotel, in Cumberland Place, to celebrate the gold-disc Darts single we released at the end of 1977 – with 'Daddy Cool' and 'The Girl Can't Help It'. The dinner started tamely enough, but ended with me literally losing my shirt. It began going wrong over dessert, strawberries Romanov, at which point the band members and their producers decided that rather than eat the ornately assembled mix of ice cream, strawberries and whipped cream, they preferred a good old-fashioned food fight. First they targeted each other, then me, and finally the walls of the suite. The hotel was not best pleased, though once they had been paid for the damage, they seemed prepared to forgive and forget – or at least to forgive. As for me, drenched in the dessert, I found myself walking back to the office in the small hours of the morning bare-chested.

But Magnet's big breakthrough really came nearly a year later – thanks to a quiet, thoughtful singer-songwriter whom we had signed almost at the beginning. He was from Middlesbrough and his grandparents came from Italy, and one of the few arguments we ever had was over his name. Having learned the magic of finding the right stage name through our experience with

Alvin Stardust, I told him we'd have to drop his real name, which was Chris Rea. 'It'll be a disaster,' I told him. 'Can you imagine the jokes: diar-*rhoea*, gonorr-*rhoea*?' Besides, I had the perfect solution, with the added bonus of being true to his Italian roots: Benny Santini. Chris, however, was having none of it. 'I am *not*,' he replied, '*fooking* changing my *fooking* name!' So we didn't. In Magnet's first few years, Chris had been one of the dozen-or-so artists on our books who were not doing all that much. Still, none of us had any doubt that his songwriting talent, his wonderful voice, his flair on the guitar, and his determination to succeed would eventually make him a star. It was a judgement that others in the music business whom I respected shared. It was, we were sure, just a matter of time – and of getting exactly the right sound. By 1977 we had recorded a first Chris Rea album, but still felt that it didn't come close to capturing his huge talent. So we literally burned the tapes and started over – after hiring Elton John's legendary producer Gus Dudgeon to handle the project. By early 1978, he had worked his magic and the debut album – which Chris mischievously insisted on calling 'Whatever Happened to Benny Santini?' – was ready. The single we released from it, 'Fool (If You Think It's Over)' became Magnet's first top-ten success in America, and the album was nominated for a Grammy Award. It was a worldwide hit, and made Chris by far our biggest artist. Only the fact that he was more of a thoughtful, introspective poet than a natural pop performer prevented him becoming not just the major star he clearly was, but a megastar.

I went on to run Magnet for a total of fifteen years, building it up into a 'mini-major' status that other independent companies could only envy. At one point, we had four singles in

Britain's top-ten chart. But though I was not fully aware of this until the very end, my success in the business, and the dazzling array of characters I met along the way, sometimes blinded me to the things I'd been raised to believe mattered most in life. I remain truly grateful for the opportunity to have met and worked with a group of gifted and good people at the company, and to have helped them achieve a success they fully deserved – whether key members of the management team including Graham Mabbutt, John Knowles, Ceri Ellis, and fellow Hackney Downs graduate Brian Reza, or singers like Alvin and Chris, and bands like Darts, Guys 'n' Dolls and Bad Manners. And another Magnet discovery, too, who didn't sing but has gone on to become a music star of another sort: Pete Waterman. In Magnet's early days, he was working in local radio in Birmingham, one of a string of DJs around the country with whom we stayed in close touch. We called them our 'field promotion team'. But Pete clearly had talent and flair that set him apart, and we soon persuaded him to move to London and join our A&R department. The abbreviation stood for 'artists and repertoire'. Essentially, the department was in charge of spotting new talent. Pete, the future Pop Idol judge, was even then uniquely gifted at doing so – if not yet the slick, sophisticated industry figure he would become. I remember his joining us shortly after we hired him, on a trip to MIDEM, the annual music-industry trade show in Cannes. We checked into our luxury hotel and agreed to meet in the lobby twenty minutes later – at which point Pete came down from his room, bubbling with excitement. 'This place is unbelievable!' he said. 'They even have footbaths in the rooms!' We couldn't help laughing – and pitying the next hotel guest to use the bidet.

The characters I got to know on the American music scene had a much rawer edge, and the one who epitomised this best was a successful, irresistibly charming promoter named Charlie Minor. Four years younger than I was, he had been born in Georgia but lived in a beautiful beach house in Malibu, California. From the start of Magnet, I saw a great deal of him, worked with him and couldn't help liking him – or marvelling at the rota of usually blonde, always beautiful, women he had on his arm. Gilda found him charming, too, although a visit to Uphill Road in early 1975 by Charlie and his girlfriend of the moment brought home how different my personal and professional worlds had become. Charlie and his companion had flown in from Los Angeles and they took a taxi from Heathrow to join us for dinner. Then – after excusing themselves and briefly visiting our bathroom with what proved literally to be their 'drug kits' – suggested that we all go out clubbing. Gilda, typically generous, said fine, if that was what our guests wanted we would go. But she turned to me and whispered in astonishment as we left: 'How can they want to go out?! They've just arrived on a long flight. And they've obviously got terrible colds. Look at how they are sniffling – and their noses are running!'

Two decades later, Charlie was relaxing at home in Malibu with his latest girlfriend when the latest-but-one – whom he had reportedly met in a topless club – burst in, fired nine times, and shot him dead. I couldn't get to his funeral. But my friend Russ Regan, who was by then head of 20th Century Records, phoned me the next day to tell me he had never seen so many beautiful women crying their eyes out. It was, he said, 'a send-off Charlie would have loved'.

In a way, my work with personalities like Charlie – with his open womanising and drug use – were the least draining on my personal life during my long period at Magnet. They had the merit of being so blatantly, blazingly different from Sabbath evenings on Uphill Road that I could hardly have failed to be conscious of the gap. Especially in the early days, such 'wake-up call' moments had a major effect on me. I recall one evening, for instance, shortly after I started Magnet when I went out for dinner in Los Angeles with some of the real heavyweights in the American recording industry. Over coffee, these dozen-or-so company executives and their wives started talking quite matter-of-factly about the delights of what they clearly considered fairly harmless recreational drugs. I instinctively interrupted and by the time I registered the mix of blank incomprehension and polite forbearance on my dinner companions' faces I was in too deep to stop. 'Why do you need to take such things?' I said. 'Surely one can find fulfilment in life in other ways, without drugs – through business and family and other things.' Back in my hotel room by about ten – six in the morning, London time – I remember phoning Gilda in a panic. 'I've just made a complete idiot of myself!' I told her. 'These were some of the biggest people in the American industry and I was telling them what they should do with their lives. It was none of my business! These are people I'm going to need to make Magnet succeed, and here I was telling them how to lead their lives!' Gilda was used to such agonised confessionals and the insecurity that they revealed just beneath the surface of all of my professional successes – but not at six a.m. 'Go to bed,' she said. 'It's done. There's nothing you or I can do to change what you said . . . It will all be fine.'

And it was, I suppose. Certainly I was never interested in, much less tempted by, the personal excesses of the music business. Yet in ways that for years I did not recognise, or at least admit – something that I find surprising now that I am older, more battle-scarred, and I hope slightly wiser – the music business itself began to hold an almost drug-like attraction for me. Each hit gave me a further buzz. And because of our improbably early success with Alvin Stardust I think I began to believe my own hype, and to feel I was on an inexorable path to the very top. Looking back recently at the first of a series of annual Magnet supplements we published in a leading music magazine, I could not help marvelling – and smiling with a sense of distance I didn't have at the time – at a constellation of black-and-white photos of the stars of the young company. I was in the centre, positively oozing the confidence of the boss of an impressively successful start-up company, with a perfectly coiffed mane of thick dark hair. Three of the photos – mine, Peter Shelley's and Alvin's – are distinguished by long, trendy Identikit sideburns. Following my progress through photos in supplement after annual supplement, the hair has thinned only slightly, but the image changes dramatically – gone is the casual pop-star look and in its place the immaculately tailored sports jacket, and the matching dark tie and pocket handkerchief, of an increasingly well-off business executive. Of course I worked hard for my success. It was at Magnet that I began a habit that has stayed with me ever since – through my entire business life, my first years with Tony Blair, and the brutal ordeal of 'cash for peerages'. Every night before bedtime I would go over in my head all of the day's meetings, phone calls, everything I'd done, and write down notes on things to be followed up, fixed, taken forward the next day. It was a habit partly rooted in my determination to control events rather than have them control me, but partly in that feeling's flipside: the ever-present fear that something was bound to go wrong. But at the height of my Magnet success, the paranoia was somehow in abeyance, overshadowed by a sense that nothing at all had the power to throw me, or my upward trajectory in business, off course.

Not even an extraordinary week in February 1975 that began with a distraught phone call from my mother early on Monday morning.

I was leaving for the office when she called. I had been due to take an afternoon flight to Los Angeles. 'Your father isn't well,' she said. She didn't say what was wrong with him, but I sensed from her tone of voice that it was serious. For Dad to be ill was a rare enough occurrence. I couldn't recall the last time it had happened. But for him to stay at home, or admit that things weren't right, was even rarer. I phoned the office and told Jean to cancel my trip to the States, and went straight over to the Stamford Lodge flat. By the time I got there, Dad was vomiting blood. Shocked and confused and frightened, I phoned our family doctor and close friend David Myers, and he rushed over. After examining my father briefly, he asked me to join him outside, where he said: 'Michael, I have to be honest – I don't think your father is going to make it to the hospital. We have to get him out of here, particularly since this is going to be upsetting for your mother.' He phoned an ambulance and accompanied my father to University College Hospital on Euston Road, where he knew the head of emergency medicine. I drove my mother separately, and when we arrived he was already in intensive care. He was alive, holding on, fighting. But as David explained to me that evening, he was bleeding internally – a complication from a liver ailment that had gone unnoticed, unmentioned, undiagnosed. 'There is nothing to be done,' David said. And on Friday, my father died. He was sixty-five. He never made it to retirement, although with the longer Sabbath walk to his synagogue from Stamford Hill, he had begun in recent months to talk about the prospect. We took my father, in his coffin, for one last time to Walford Road, placed him in front of the synagogue ark and said prayers and then went on to the Jewish burial ground in Streatham for the funeral.

In the week that followed, in keeping with Jewish tradition I sat *shivah* – receiving, in a chair alongside my mother's, streams of family friends and well-wishers in the Stamford Hill flat. And over the year that followed I regularly recited Kaddish, the prayer for the dead, in synagogue. But as with the loss of Gilda's father three years earlier, also at age sixty-five, it was a blow that was deeply and gnawingly upsetting without, somehow, being devastating. Yes, the loss of our fathers left a painful void, a vacuum. It was a reminder of our mortality – something for which Gilda in her late twenties and I, having barely turned thirty, were not prepared. But perhaps the suddenness of my dad's death – and the structure which was provided by *shivah*, and in the months that followed by reciting Kaddish – helped me to cope. And I am sure that the narcotic effect of my business life was also equally at work. I was getting ahead, on overdrive, moving from success to success, not only believing in but living off my own hype. Against this background, the death of my father seemed ultimately just a part of growing up. Or so I told myself.

Gilda also coped without any major upheaval. She was

always the steadier, more centred, of us. And besides, she had a full-time job with demands that were every bit as taxing, if sometimes less obvious, than mine: the primary role in raising two children. There were, increasingly, more creature comforts added at Uphill Road. The first was a tennis court in the back garden, where I took up the game that would later cement my relationship with Tony Blair, under the tutelage of an accountant neighbour, Michael Braham, who lived down the road. Later, we also put in a swimming pool. But the main focus – Gilda's and mine – remained on the less visible and more lastingly important aspects of creating a loving, nurturing home for ourselves, Daniel and Juliet. As I'd sensed almost from the start of our whirlwind courtship, we agreed on all the big issues. The only, brief hiccup came in deciding where to send the children to school. Gilda very much wanted them to be educated in the state system. I felt the same way, but with two major reservations. The first was that, at kindergarten and primary level, I wanted the kids to have a grounding in Jewish learning and Judaism. And as we talked it through, Gilda fairly quickly came to the same view – not least in order to remove the need to send them to the after-school Hebrew classes which both of us in retrospect felt had been useful, effective but uninspiring. When it came to secondary education, however, she felt more strongly that they should go to state schools. I said that while in principle I agreed – and would have had not even a moment's hesitation about sending them to a local equivalent of my own Hackney Downs grammar or Gilda's Skinners' Company's School – I wanted above all to ensure our children got a sufficiently good foundation to give them the option of going on to university. In the end, it was

Gilda's training as a teacher that won her over to my view. Today, Mill Hill has an excellent state secondary: Mill Hill County High School. Then, the local school was called Moat Mount and, on visiting and observing and asking local parents, Gilda pronounced it, with her gift for getting to the nub of the matter, 'awful, absolutely awful'. Both Daniel and Juliet ended up at an independent school, both thrived, both went on to university – and Gilda compensated with a determination, from which she never wavered, to make sure that the children also recognised the need to engage with, function in, and care for a much wider world.

As did I, but again in ways that I now see were coloured by my infatuation with my spiralling success in business. Particularly with Daniel as he grew older, I seemed to feel a need to provide an environment that was less physically and socially constricted, less narrow, than the one in which my parents had raised me. This was not a conscious decision. After all, I had succeeded beyond my wildest dreams on the foundations my parents had provided. But, as I explained it at the time to close friends, I wanted to live more 'outwardly'. I still went to synagogue, and was actively involved there. Gilda and I still kept a home steeped in the traditions and teachings of Judaism. But we – and particularly I – got increasingly comfortable socialising with the kind of people I'd met on my way up the business ladder, people whose focus tended to be much more on present diversions than past anchors, people more concerned with where they had got to, than where they'd come from. For the first time in my life, this meant dining in restaurants where I couldn't – and thus didn't – always eat foods that fell within the kosher dietary laws. For a while, I even began involving Daniel in a decidedly untraditional Sabbath rite – the one I had briefly adopted but then abandoned, as a teenager, in deference to my parents. We began going to Highbury to watch Arsenal on Saturday afternoons. In the end, I stopped doing so all over again, but only because I was spending so much time looking over my shoulder to see whether friends were there who might mischievously report on my lapse in observance, that I ceased being able to enjoy the games.

Still, by the mid-eighties – my own early forties – this new, delicately balanced lifestyle was, I felt, sorted. Despite the occasional excesses I found in the music business, and the occasional tensions they caused in my life, I was also careful to remain focused on the things that really mattered to me. During my final years in the music business, for instance, I was the founding chairman of the annual Music Industry Trust Awards. The scheme's public face is to honour a leading figure in the industry – most recently, Kylie Minogue – at a glittering London dinner. But its real work included financial support for the industry's Brit school in Croydon, which has helped develop extraordinary talents ranging from Katie Melua to Amy Winehouse, and for charities like Nordoff-Robbins music therapy, which uses music and sound to help special-needs children.

And I might well have happily, and very successfully, continued to thrive at Magnet – and never met or worked with Tony Blair, never raised money for him – had it not been for a further, sudden, unanticipated jolt in my life. I was, I now see with the benefit of hindsight, beginning to have the first serious misgivings about my work. A lot of record companies were by the 1980s starting to be affected by the kind of rot that now blights

Premiership football. Some of the most successful artists – like record-company bosses, and politicians – began to believe their own press cuttings. Losing touch with the skills, values and people that had helped them up the ladder, many were increasingly interested only in themselves, and how they could add to their own fame and fortune. Having recorded great songs by other writers, for instance, they would suddenly decide they could do it better themselves. Or, like today's football stars, they listened to agents who told them to shop around, to leave whatever mentor or manager or company that had made them a star in favour of a sweet new contract with someone else. Magnet was, thankfully, unaffected. It really did retain a sense of family. This was in large part because of my conscious decision to resist what I used to call the major companies' 'mud-on-the-wall' philosophy of signing and promoting dozens of artists each year in the expectation that at least one or two might make it. We handled a much smaller number, nurturing and supporting them in the confidence that their talent would eventually shine through. Chris Rea's success would never have come had we not given him the space, encouragement and financial backing to grow in his first five years with Magnet. And I look back with immense pride on the fact that we never lost a single one of our artists. It was impossible, however, not to feel the building gusts of change in the industry.

Nevertheless, in the end, I am fairly sure I would have stayed the course if events – or more accurately, a single event – hadn't intervened. Certainly, we could have held on to Chris and our other established artists, and we would have found and nurtured new talent. I was simply too focused, and surrounded by too many good and similarly dedicated people, not to have been able to cope. Until that further, fearful jolt in my personal life. As with the news about my father's illness, it came in the form of an unexpected early morning telephone call. Only this time, the call was not *from* my mother. It was about her.

CHAPTER 5

Shock Therapy

When the phone rang at 8.30 a.m. on Saturday 4 October 1986, we were getting ready to go to synagogue. It was the first day of the Jewish New Year holiday. Along with Yom Kippur the following weekend, it was always the most crowded service of the year, when even the least observant families invariably attended and reconnected with the community. 'I'll get it!' I shouted downstairs to Gilda and the kids, who were finishing breakfast. 'It may be about Mummy.' It was the name by which I still instinctively referred to my mother – and still think of her as today. Two days earlier, I had rushed her into University College Hospital, the same place where my father had spent his final days, but without any real sense of apprehension. She was at

UCH for what she, and I, assumed would be the latest of several brief hospital stays over a period of years to deal with a circulatory problem that had occasionally caused blood clots – previously in each of her legs, now in her right arm. If the doctors kept to their earlier routine, they would free the clot by thinning my mother's blood and giving her anti-coagulants, hold her for a few days' observation, and send her home again. I'd visited her on the previous afternoon, assuring her that I'd be back immediately after the New Year, and she had seemed in good spirits.

It was a UCH doctor who came on the line. After a perfunctory 'good morning' he said: 'Mr Levy, we need to see you. It's to talk about your mother's case.' I was, to put it mildly, puzzled at the apparent urgency of the request. The doctors had been reassuring when my mother was admitted. And given the pattern of her previous treatment, I had assumed there was nothing particularly serious to worry about. 'Today is not a good day to meet. It's the Jewish New Year,' I explained. 'Can't we speak on Monday morning?' When he said it would be 'much better' if we could meet as soon as possible, I asked why: was something wrong? His reply still chills me today. 'It's not the kind of thing that I had wanted to talk about on the phone,' he said. 'But we are going to have to amputate your mother's arm – today. If we don't, we fear she will die.'

I phoned David Myers and asked if he could meet me at the hospital, but first went with Gilda to synagogue – where we explained to Rabbi Cutler the sudden emergency and joined him in the traditional prayer of *refuah shlemah* for my mother's recovery. Then, for the first time in my life driving on a Jewish holy day, we sped off towards UCH. By the time we'd arrived, with

David waiting for us outside, it was clear there was very little to discuss. My mother's fingers had already begun to turn gangrenous, and she was taken straight into the operating theatre, where she was sedated and her arm amputated. I was stunned. The doctor gently explained there had been no other course, reminding me that when my mother had been admitted he had 'mentioned' amputation. And I realised he was right – but only to say: 'Don't worry. Your mother will be fine. We won't have to amputate, or anything like that.' It had barely registered at the time. Now, as she emerged from the operation, I was simply thankful that she was alive – so thankful, and perhaps so dazed, that it is only now, years later, that I recoil at the thought of the ritual performed, according to Orthodox tradition, after her ordeal. Two days later at the Jewish cemetery in Streatham, the local rabbi formally washed and buried my mother's severed arm. It was, it seemed to me at the time, just what had to be done. My focus, in any case, was on the life – still, I hoped and prayed, a long life – that lay ahead for my mother.

I was determined to do whatever was possible to help her to re-establish the fulfilling existence that she had built in the eleven years since my father had died. It had not been easy at first. The sheer suddenness of his death – the abruptness with which she was cut loose from the man who for three decades had been her soulmate – left a yawning hole in her life. But gradually, we had managed to help her fill the void. Many days, above all during the early months when she felt the loss most deeply, she would spend at Uphill Road. Although still single-mindedly fixated on Magnet, I managed to travel a bit less for a while, and come home a bit earlier, to help her to cope. But Gilda was magnificent in making her feel part of a loving and supportive family. And crucially, Gilda's mother and mine became extraordinarily close. Almost from the moment we had got engaged, the two of them hit it off – united at first, no doubt, in an all-embracing love of their own children, but strengthened as our own marriage flowered and with the birth of our children. Now, with both of them also widowed, they did far more than merely support one another. Though Gilda's mother was almost a decade younger, and more naturally independent, they both clearly and obviously enjoyed each other's company – whether shopping, chatting, or simply spending time together on Uphill Road, or at Gilda's mother's house in Edgware. They became friends, although I think even that word doesn't quite capture their partnership. 'Pals' somehow seems better.

They also became part of a family wider than themselves, wider even than just Gilda and me and Daniel and Juliet. There were three others, especially, whom we all felt were very much part of our own family – Steve, Ruth and Judith, the grown children of Gilda's older sister. Steve, though nearly a decade older than Daniel, became almost like an older brother to him. They bonded not least because they were both hopelessly devoted to football in general, and to Arsenal in particular. (So much so that Steve, who began his working life as my director of music at Magnet, has gone on to become one of the country's top football agents – the only mark against him being that he represents not only Gunner greats but the likes of Chelsea's Frank Lampard, and even the occasional Spurs star. When I've challenged him on 'crossing the line' by dealing with Tottenham, he simply smiles and replies: 'As you taught me, Uncle, business is business!') Steve, Ruth and above all Judith also became very close to Juliet. Gilda and I looked upon them, and still do, almost like our own children. Crucially for my mother, there was also steady support from the more extended family of Mill Hill synagogue – from our closest friends in the congregation, a young successful lawyer named Michael Goldmeier and his wife, Philippa, as well as from Rabbi and Mrs Cutler. The Cutlers became so warmly protective that for several years they even invited her to join them during Succot, the autumn festival that comes two weeks after the Jewish New Year, for their annual visit to a kosher hotel in Bournemouth.

In the years immediately after my father's death, my mother had remained in Stamford Hill. Despite the fact that the once-sought-after block of flats on Amhurst Park was becoming increasingly, distressingly dilapidated, she refused to entertain talk of moving. But the focus of her life was shifting away from her and my father's friendships of my childhood years. Gradually, she began to accept my view that she would be happier and less isolated if we could find her a place closer to us, to the Cutlers and her Mill Hill friends, and to Gilda's mother in Edgware. Finally I persuaded her to move – into a well-staffed building of warden-managed flats run, mostly for elderly people, by the Jewish charity B'nai B'rith in Willesden. It was wrenching for a while. She felt, I think, that at some level she had abandoned my father by leaving the final home she had shared with him. But before long, she was settled, and genuinely happy, with her new home in Willesden and the many days she spent with us in Uphill Road.

Now, it was to Willesden that she returned – thankfully alive, but with part of her life literally cut away. In one, narrow sense, I felt I knew what had to be done to make the loss less painful. She needed full-time nursing care, and with the savings built up through Magnet I was able immediately to provide for it. But it was soon clear that my mother's sense of loss and of pain was far more than physical. Unsure how to help her – and, I see now, myself – deal with this less visible trauma, I got in touch with a larger communal charity called the Jewish Welfare Board, which ran a network of homes for the elderly and vulnerable. I arranged to go and see its chief executive, Melvyn Carlowe. It was a meeting that would, within a few years, dramatically change my life. But now, more importantly, it helped educate me in the emotional and social-care issues that we would have to address if we were to help my mother recover. Melvyn, through the Welfare Board, arranged for some short-term care in one of its homes, and also helped provide for a social worker to drop in on my mother in Willesden. With Gilda, Gilda's mother and our children always keen to visit – and for Mummy to spend many hours of her time with us in Uphill Road – I began to feel as the months passed that we were managing to help build at least some sense of 'normal' life for her. Still, painful though it was for me to acknowledge, I could see that she remained badly weakened in a whole range of ways from the amputation. To speak of 'recovery' in any real sense was unrealistic. But at least, I felt, she had a real measure of life back again, and that the worst effects of her ordeal were over.

But then, in October 1987, almost exactly a year after the Saturday-morning phone call about her emergency operation, everything changed. Perhaps I should have seen the weather as an omen, for it was on the morning of the sixteenth – with London and southern England battered by the most destructive storm in nearly three centuries – that Gilda and I were setting off from Gatwick for Tokyo. It was one of few times she had accompanied me on a work trip – to sign a distribution deal for Magnet with JVC/Victor Records on the back of Chris Rea's burst of popularity in Japan – and we planned to spend a few extra weeks on holiday there. Somehow we made it to Gatwick, but our flight had been cancelled, and my initial impulse was to call JVC and suggest we delay for a few weeks. But Singapore Airlines had an indirect flight, through Hong Kong, and in the end we decided to go. On landing in Tokyo, we met briefly with the Japanese company executives to work out details of a formal signing later in the week, and then took the bullet train from Tokyo to Osaka, where Chris was giving a concert. But when we got to our hotel, an urgent message was waiting – from David Myers. It was about my mother, he said, and the news was only slightly cushioned by the fact that David was not only our doctor but our friend: 'Michael,' he said, 'she has had a massive stroke. She is in a coma, and I doubt she will last through the night. You must get back as soon as you can.'

In a mix of shock and confusion, I phoned JVC. Their chief executive was magnificent – he got us booked on the first flight back, over the North Pole with a stopover in Alaska. Gilda was at her strongest, gentlest and most reassuring on the seemingly interminable final leg of the flight into Heathrow, saying she was sure Mummy would hold on. I was less certain, but have never prayed for anything so passionately in my life. And when the car had sped us directly from the airport to UCH, David had at least one bit of good news: my mother was, 'amazingly', still alive. Even more amazingly, she would survive until the first days of December – six weeks that proved to be the most painful and potent of my life. For hours on end, day and night, I sat by her bedside, hoping for a further miracle – praying that somehow she would regain consciousness. She never did. Nor, of course, could she speak. But during those weeks of vigil, I sensed more and more powerfully that I was being given a message. 'Michael,' I was certain I could feel her saying to me, 'you've done well, but now is a time to look again at your life, and to change it.'

It has often been said that the genius of *shivah* – the Jewish rite of mourning in which close family, seated on low chairs and wearing clothes that have been symbolically torn, receive streams of well-wishers every evening for the week after their bereavement – is that it helps cushion the immediate blow and starts a process of coping and recovery. And I suppose that when my mother and I sat *shivah* for my father a dozen years earlier, that had been the case. Yet this time was agonisingly different. No longer in the role of supporting my grieving mother, I was relying on the support of others – on Gilda, Daniel, Juliet and many, many close friends. When Dad had died, I had barely turned thirty and was enjoying the first dizzying fruits of success at Magnet. Moreover, the fact that his passing had been so quick and apparently painless somehow also cushioned its impact on me. Mummy's death was different. She had died twice, in a sense – the 'burial' of her severed arm seemed suddenly appropriate – and I had watched first-hand the terrible year's decline until her second, protracted, final passing. An only child, I was now not only fatherless but without the mother to whom I had always been especially close. And I could not get the message that I was sure she had wanted me to hear in her final weeks out of my head.

During Judaism's formal month-long initial period of mourning for a loved one, I rarely went to the office. For a few weeks afterwards, I went through the motions of running the day-to-day business of Magnet. The company was still going strong. Chris Rea had released his *Dancing with Strangers* album not long before my mother's death, and was beginning work on what would prove to be one of his most well-received albums, *The Road to Hell*. Looking back, the title seems somehow to sum up my own agony at the time – until, very soon, I recognised that the only way I could regain any sense of purpose or stability in my life was to act on my mother's silent plea, to change direction, and that the first and most important change would have to involve Magnet.

I was literally in pain – not just from the sense of loss from my mother's death, but the realisation that none of the outward and visible signs of success I had accumulated in business were of any help at all. I am not a naturally reflective person. Or at least I hadn't been, until this first experience, at the age of forty-three, of a problem in my life that I simply couldn't beat. I did not at first talk about this sense of crisis with anyone but Gilda. But Barrie soon sensed it, as did other of my closest friends. And so, eventually, did the people I worked with – if only because I was less engaged, more impatient, distracted, sometimes volcanically short-tempered. I imagine that if I'd gone to see a therapist – an admission of weakness that it was not in my nature to contemplate – I'd have been told I was suffering from the classic signs of depression. Or perhaps even that the message I was – and absolutely still am – convinced my dying mother had delivered to me was in fact coming from somewhere inside myself. Yet all I knew, with more and more certainty as each week passed, was that the message felt irresistibly powerful and rang irrefutably true. I know it sounds trite, but those last intimate, silent weeks at her bedside acted as a kind of shock therapy. They led me to question everything in my life, my work, my accomplishments – and, within months of my mother's death, to set off in a dramatically different direction.

The change began at Magnet. I could still occasionally summon up bursts of energy at the office. Yet now they were not directed towards planning our next record launch, but at devising an exit strategy. I'd had a series of heavyweight suitors for the company over the years, perhaps most memorably the legendary Lew Grade, who invited me over to his office at the crack of dawn to make his pitch. Though it was barely six in the morning, he was smoking a huge cigar and offered me one as well. Feeling I had made the big time, though I think both he and I knew I was too wedded to Magnet to sell, I accepted the Havana, lit up and puffed away. I managed somehow to keep up the charade just long enough to finish the meeting, leave the building, and dart around the corner before being sick on the pavement. A few years later, the German media giant Bertelsmann also made an offer, and I had a few meetings with them – before again deciding that I was doing too well, and enjoying my success too much, to sell. Now, however, I began actively seeking potential buyers, and soon settled on the major American record company Warner Brothers as the most likely candidate. They were not only willing, but eager, to get hold of the 'mini-major' success that Magnet had become. For weeks, initially telling only Gilda, we gradually began working out the details of a deal. As it began to take shape, I phoned the lawyer we used at Magnet, Tony Russell, who was also on our board, and arranged to see him for dinner. I told him there was 'something private' I wanted to discuss. When we'd sat down, and I informed him that I had decided to sell the company, he looked literally stunned.

'You're nuts!' he said. He argued that even if I was determined to go ahead, this was 'absolutely the wrong time' to do so. Our series of separate licensing arrangements for distributing Magnet records around the world worked on a three-year term, and the current one was only just nearing the end of its first year. By waiting just two years more, he insisted, we could renegotiate the entire catalogue. The new deals would inevitably bring in much more money if by then I'd decided to hang on to the company. And even if I still wanted to sell, the fact that a buyer would have a free hand to do what he wanted without the trouble and expense of negotiating separate deals with the assortment of current distributors meant the price tag would be much higher. 'Tony,' I replied, 'don't you think I know all that? This is not about getting every last million out of this deal. It's about getting out. It's something that I know that I have to do.'

Within days, as he joined me in a series of final meetings with Warners' negotiators and lawyers, he recognised and accepted that this was no ordinary business deal for me. As the details were worked out, I naturally felt a sense of sadness that my Magnet days were drawing to an end. But there was also a strange, and more powerful, feeling of liberation. One of the final sticking points involved defining the so-called *de minimis* provision – the level of risk that we would agree was too low to be covered in any of the contract provisions. For hours, it seemed, the discussion went back and forth with no end in sight, and I finally said to the Warners team: 'Guys, this is mad! Let's just toss a coin. If I win, our proposal is accepted. If you win, we'll accept yours. No questions asked.' I remember the look of astonishment on the face of their principal accountant, no doubt trying to imagine how he would explain this back in New York. But they agreed – and as it happened, we won. Still, there were no hard feelings on either side. From the start, the talks had been unfailingly amicable: I wanted to sell, Warners wanted to buy, and I'd established a very good relationship with them during my years building up and expanding Magnet. In fact, the final issue involved their wanting me to stay on as a global consultant. Flattered though I was, I said no – explaining to them, as I had to Tony Russell, that I felt a need for a clean break from a business that had not only dominated but often defined my life for the past decade and a half. When I gathered my Magnet 'family' to deliver a similar message, they were at first shocked into silence, then sad, finally accepting – with just one exception. Chris Rea was abroad with our head of international business at the San Remo festival in Italy, so I phoned to tell them the news. Chris was so upset that he refused to talk to me for weeks afterwards, although it was clear to me that this was out of astonishment and a sense of abandonment, not any unkindness. He simply couldn't believe I would walk away from all that I – and he, and others – had built.

But I did. I felt emotionally that I simply had to. The sale was completed in the spring of 1988, within months of my mother's death. Tony Russell was right – the 'price tag' was much lower than it would have been had I decided, or felt able, to hold on for another two years. It was still, however, a sum that would have caused my parents to gasp in disbelief had they only survived for me to tell them – £10 million, far more than I had earned in my entire working life. Yet the money itself wasn't the issue. In fact, one irony – given the media battering I would take as Tony Blair's 'Lord Cashpoint' a decade later over utterly groundless allegations of tax avoidance – is that I shrugged off suggestions from my financial advisers that I 'go offshore' for a year and reduce the amount of tax I would have to pay on my windfall. The capital-gains rate was then far higher than it is now. What mattered, I felt, was that the money I was left with still offered me the possibility to reorder my priorities and to change the very focus of my life. Money, it seemed to me more than ever, was only important or useful as a means to an end – a way of securing not just the necessities of life but genuine quality of life.

I was, needless to say, not used to this size of bank balance – which was probably for the best, since it didn't last for very long. Within a period of months, I used a large chunk of it – more than £3 million in all – on not one, but two, family homes. The first was the more opulent. It was also – both Gilda and I would later come to realise – an ill-advised surrender to ego and hubris that almost certainly also owed something to my state of inner turmoil at the time. It was called The Warren, and although only a few miles from our Uphill Road home in Mill Hill it was utterly different. Tucked off Totteridge Common, it had a small pond in front, and a stately half-mile-long driveway – bordered by open fields where horses could be seen grazing – which led to a sprawling white estate. Gilda's nephew Steve lived across the road (and though I didn't know it at the time, Arsenal's David Dein just next door) and when he had heard us talking about the prospect of using part of the Magnet proceeds to move house, mentioned that he'd seen it was for sale. We were, I think, taken in by its countryside feel, and the impressive drive, more than anything. And by the time we had put in additional money, and more than two more years, to renovate it and add a tennis court, it was undoubtedly full of creature comforts. But because

Uphill Road had been so perfect a family home, and perhaps also because by the time we moved in Daniel was away at Cambridge University and Juliet at Manchester University, it seemed somehow to lack the very thing I'd hoped our more than £2 million would buy: warmth, a sense of family, real quality of life. Instead, it always had something more of the feel of a boutique hotel.

The second home that we purchased with the Magnet earnings was much more of what I'd hoped for. It was in Israel, in the beachfront suburb of Herzliya Pituach, north of Tel Aviv. When Daniel was twelve – and Magnet only about half that age – we had bought a small flat in the area. Now, we purchased a piece of breathtakingly beautiful land – perched on a cliff above the Mediterranean, next door to the US ambassador's residence – on the northern edge of the town. We built the house from scratch: modern, luxurious, Mediterranean-style, with a TV and table-tennis room in the basement, and a lovely pool and garden looking out over the sea. We came to love going there with the children during their university holidays. And Daniel in particular went on to use it as a home from home when – to his surprise, I think, and certainly to ours – he eventually settled in Israel after his graduation, with a double first, in his tripos course of archaeology, anthropology and social and political science, from Cambridge.

But by far my most significant major use of the money from Magnet – in the sense that it summed up my mindset at the time – was to set aside nearly £1 million for charitable causes and to establish the Levy Family Charitable Trust. It seemed to me a natural, and crucially important, part of my conscious decision to leave the pace and pressures of the music business for a new and more meaningful path. I had no idea where it would lead nor, to be honest, how long the process would last. In the first few weeks without my daily commute into central London, I felt such a sense of relief that I never gave such questions any thought. I did know I was not about to retire for good. I was just entering my mid-forties, after all, and sufficiently self-aware to recognise that the ambition and energy that had been with me since childhood meant that I would always be on the lookout for new challenges. Yet what I couldn't have foreseen is that the five years I would now devote to the world of charity and Jewish community life would, with its small-scale politics and large-scale fundraising, mark a first step on to a much larger, national stage – as Tony Blair's friend and financial right-hand man.

The focus of the first, but to me most meaningful, initiative of the Levy Family Charitable Trust was Mill Hill synagogue. A decade earlier, I had helped to finance the refurbishment of the main meeting hall in my father's memory. Now, we enlarged and remodelled it – and rededicated it as the Annie and Samuel Levy Hall. But at the same time, I began meeting with a range of charities, many of them with a Jewish focus, to consider larger contributions. The aim was simple: to give back some of the fruits of my good fortune to the community whose traditions and values had helped me achieve success. Even while at Magnet, I'd given hundreds of thousands of pounds, both through the company and from my own bank account, to a number of community charities. Along the way, I had also emerged as a leading figure in one of them: the Joint Israel Appeal. From the postwar years, in which the state of Israel was established, through the 1980s, the JIA had become by far the dominant charity in the British Jewish community. A huge number of Jewish families, like Gilda's, carried with them the raw scars of the Holocaust, and Israel was viewed both as a potential redemption for those who had survived and a potential haven if, unthinkably but not impossibly, some future threat to the very existence of Jews were to arise.

My own views on Israel and the broader Middle East were then very much part of that conventional mainstream – forged in Mill Hill on the autumn day in 1973 when the armies of Egypt and Syria launched a surprise attack that at least briefly seemed set to destroy Israel only twenty-five years after its foundation. It was Yom Kippur, the holiest day on the Jewish calendar, and I was in charge locally of the JIA's annual synagogue appeal for contributions for Israel. I had jotted down notes the day before on what I would say, but as word filtered into the synagogue that the Arab armies had attacked I delivered a much more personal and impassioned message – about Gilda and her family of Holocaust victims and survivors, about what defeat would mean not just for Israel but for the dreams of a new and hopefully peaceful haven for Jews, and about how the prospect of an Israeli 'war for survival' transformed all the clichés about our responsibility for fellow human beings into a real-life challenge to help. My words had an extraordinary, galvanising effect – not only attracting tens of thousands of pounds in emergency donations but inspiring some in the congregation to travel to Israel to do volunteer work to compensate for young reservists called up to fight. It also taught me two important and related lessons: that you don't have to be a seasoned politician in order to deliver a powerful message, only to believe genuinely and deeply in what you are saying; and that fundraising is a noble calling – again, if the cause is worthy and heartfelt. Over the next several years, I went on to do more and more of it for the JIA, rising from Mill

Hill appeal chairman to London-wide chairman and eventually to its national fundraising chair.

It was also an unexpected introduction to the world of politics. Nominally, leadership in the Jewish community has resided with a communal body modelled on the House of Commons, known as the Board of Deputies, and with the chief rabbi. But in fact, the key figures have for decades been an array of successful business or political personalities who organised British Jews' involvement with, and support for, the infant state of Israel. When Arthur Balfour, the then Tory Foreign Secretary, committed Britain in 1917 to the eventual establishment of a Jewish state, significantly he addressed his famous declaration not to the Board of Deputies or the chief rabbi, but to Lord Rothschild. By the time I became involved with the JIA in the 1970s and 1980s, it was the province mainly of the successful businessman Sir Trevor Chinn, who had built his father's network of London garages, called Lex, into a multimillion-pound motoring business that would eventually acquire the RAC. I was very much a new kid on the block. And though Trevor recognised and promoted my fundraising talents and we have since become friends, the initial and obvious reluctance to give up space at the top table was an early lesson in politics and power that made the battles I witnessed within New Labour a decade later at least slightly less difficult to navigate and understand.

In both cases, it was the simple fact that I was extraordinarily good at raising badly needed funds that made the difference. And a related fact: most other people in most charitable or voluntary organisations positively detest raising funds. Some are dismissive and cynical about it, preferring to take credit for charitable *work*, as if any charity could run without the money to fund its good deeds. Others are simply uncomfortable with asking for money, particularly approaching their friends or colleagues, or perhaps scared of rejection if they do. Yet I soon found that I was good at it, that I liked doing it, and was – and very much still am – proud of doing it well. At the height of the 'cash for peerages' controversy, even media profiles that touched on my talents as a fundraiser often implied there was something not quite wholesome about it – portraying me as some kind of confidence trickster who would manipulate hapless donors into parting with their cash. Very few things during the entire ordeal upset me so much, I think mainly because these slightly sneering portrayals missed the absolutely central point about fundraising, why I excelled at it, and why it mattered to me. It is this: having made money for myself during the Magnet years, my fundraising was for *other* people, other causes, in which I believed and which simply couldn't have operated without the contributions I helped to bring in.

Inevitably, I began before long to sense what worked and what didn't in raising money, and I suppose to develop a method – rules, even. But far from being an exercise in confidence trickery or manipulation, the 'rules' reflected a mix of simple common sense and my own personality and values. Crucially, none of it would have worked if I hadn't begun with a genuine fondness for dealing with people, and a belief in the causes for which I was raising funds. Beyond that, I recognised the central need to get to know people – those who weren't already friends – and to understand what they cared about and what made them tick before asking them for help. Rule two was that I would never run down other charities or causes but would passionately explain the needs and interests, and the strengths and virtues, of the organisation I was promoting. And I was never, ever scared of approaching anyone. I began with an understanding that most people who have the resources to give to charity ultimately feel good about doing so – and so they should. Moreover, I was not asking for money for myself, but for what I felt to be a genuinely good cause. The worst thing that could happen was that they would say 'no', or agree to give less that I had hoped or expected. But particularly if this was because the person had fallen on hard times, it never occurred to me to respond by hectoring or pressure. Fundraising, I found, was like so much else in life – it was about human relationships, building them, nurturing them, valuing them. On more than one occasion, a person who had said 'no' later became a valued supporter, and someone who had given very little eventually gave much more. And far from finding my fundraising dispiriting or draining, in those months after leaving Magnet it was an invigorating shift towards concentrating not on my own company's profit-and-loss statements but on charities dedicated to helping others.

One charity, however, soon became central to my life after Magnet – and helped propel me to an influential leadership role in the wider Jewish community. And it was not the JIA. Israel in the late 1980s was dramatically different to the beleaguered state whose cause I had argued in synagogue on the first day of the 1973 war. In 1982, the government of Menachem Begin had launched the country's first 'war of choice', invading Lebanon in an effort to defeat Yasir Arafat's PLO by force of arms. It ended in a humanitarian and diplomatic disaster, when Israel's Lebanese Christian militia allies murdered hundreds of people in the Beirut refugee camps of Sabra and Shatila, and in domestic division. Begin retired into reclusion. He was succeeded by a coalition of his right-wing political ally Yitzhak Shamir and Labour's Shimon Peres – increasingly strained as Peres pushed for, and Shamir resisted, a plan to join Jordan's King Hussein in promoting a regional peace conference. I remained an active and involved member of the JIA's leadership. Like the great majority of British Jews, I retained – and still do – an instinctive sense of commitment to supporting Israel's existence and doing all I could to help it secure a thriving, stable and peaceful future. But, again like many others, I began to recognise that the issues involved were more complicated than they had been when Israel had been forced to fight against enormous odds merely to survive. And much closer to home, another 'Israel issue' began to take on growing importance. For a community of only several hundred thousand, by no means all of them well-off, the Jews of Britain gave disproportionate millions each year to charity. But the great majority of it went to the JIA and to other Israel-related initiatives. The result was that domestic Jewish charities had to survive on the leftovers, struggling to provide for the needs of an increasingly ageing population, not to mention education, or extending help to orphaned or troubled children, the disabled and others with special needs. My mother's death, and my experience of the caring and professionalism of the Jewish Welfare Board, had given me a first-hand look at the scale of the needs which the home charities answered. Dedicating a synagogue hall in the name of my mother was one way to honour her. But I felt that a more fitting, lasting memorial would have to involve not just a plaque on a wall but a reflection of the values she had worked so hard to pass on to me. So I phoned Melvyn Carlowe and suggested we meet, and asked how I could help the Welfare Board help others as it had helped her.

My offer could hardly have come at a better time. The Welfare Board and another long-established home charity, the Jewish Blind Society, were deep in talks on a merger to form a larger unit – to be called Jewish Care. Though I remained involved in the JIA, I began to raise funds for the Welfare Board and, once the merger happened in 1989, for Jewish Care. For me, the mission was a bit like that first synagogue appeal for Israel back in 1973. It came from the heart, from my own and my family's experience – in this case, from having witnessed my mother's final year of decline and death after her amputation. Melvyn and I made a perfectly complementary team – crucially strengthened by the head of the charity's campaign department, Jeff Shear, whose expertise and commitment would also later prove crucial to overhauling Labour's fundraising. The three of us shared a no-nonsense talent for getting to the core of a problem – and a belief that what mattered in fundraising was the ability to convey to donors the critical value of the work the charity was doing and the real difference in human lives that a generous donor could make. The Welfare Board, of necessity, was a tightly run ship and the new charity formed with the Blind Society was, if anything, more so. Overheads were kept low. The focus was on the facilities and services provided. And when I, or the back-up team that I built with Melvyn, sought support, we did not just ask for a cheque. We involved would-be supporters in Jewish Care's work, took them to see first-hand the difference it made to people's lives. Very little in my life has made me more proud than the transformation I helped make possible in Jewish Care. Within five years, we were raising more than £15 million a year in donations, very much higher than the sums raised separately by the Welfare Board and the Blind Society. Jewish Care's annual income rose to tens of millions of pounds, as the work of our residential and day homes was also boosted by national and local-government contributions and fees. It was an extraordinary achievement, not just because of the sums raised, but because the quality of hands-on assistance that it allowed us to provide made Jewish Care a model for other charities both in Britain and abroad.

Personally, it had another effect as well. During the first two years of the new charity, it was run in rotation by the outgoing heads of the Blind Society and the Welfare Board: two gifted philanthropists who had long been involved in their work, David Lewis and Jeffrey Greenwood. But in 1992, the organisation chose the first chairman of its own – honouring me with the job, which I would hold until 1998, when I became the charity's president. Building further on Jewish Care's early successes – first alongside Melvyn and then, after he retired, with the extraordinarily able Simon Morris – became not only a major focus of my Jewish community activities but a personal passion. And though at first I was every bit as much the brash outsider on the community stage as I had been with Magnet in the music industry, I now found myself very much part of the community's leadership establishment. It was not a position I'd actively set out to achieve – except in the sense that the competitive streak and urge to be in control of circumstances rather than controlled by them had, since my teens, made it difficult for me to operate as a mere foot soldier. Yet I took satisfaction from it, and pride too. I felt that in playing a central role in Jewish Care's growth and success I had done well by doing good.

My expanding community role was brought home to me when, shortly after I had been made chairman of Jewish Care, the recently installed chief rabbi, Jonathan Sacks, got in touch to see whether I would turn my mix of fundraising, organisational and music-industry skills into setting up a community-wide awards scheme to recognise 'unsung heroes' in charity, education and other spheres. I had got to know his predecessor, Lord Jakobovits, following my mother's death. He was a rabbi of the old school, of my father's generation, a softly spoken, deeply spiritual man who retained the accent of his native Germany. His presence was humbling and powerful, perfectly balanced by the flair, charm, generosity and grace of his French-born wife, Amelie. Jonathan, by contrast, was slightly younger than me, British-born, with a first in philosophy from Cambridge. He had a sharp mind and was an accomplished writer. But he also struck me as extraordinarily shy and unself-confident. Our collaboration on two Chief Rabbi's Awards schemes seemed to prove something of a turning point for him. He became more self-assured in public – though still sometimes agonisingly uncomfortable in private conversation. It also seemed to encourage in him a growing enjoyment of the public stage, and an appetite to play a wider role in Britain's national political life.

Ironically, given the turn which my own life was about to take, that was certainly not my ambition at the time. I didn't see myself as a political figure. Yet while I continued to feel jabs of pain over my mother's death – especially on visits to Jewish Care homes, when I'd chat with women of her generation who were clearly in the throes of a difficult, final decline – I felt for the first time since my retreat from Magnet that I had regained the strength, energy and desire to take on new projects. In 1990, I even put a toe back in the music business. Backed by Polygram Records, and with a few members of the old Magnet team, I founded a small record label called M&G – which stood for Michael & Gilda. The company did well – achieving a top-five hit with Zoë's 'Sunshine on a Rainy Day'. But my heart wasn't in it, and barely five years later I sold it on, for a very small profit, to Bertelsmann. My time away had given me a sense of distance, perspective, on my music-industry years. They had been fun, and I had succeeded beyond my imagination. But I now felt the need for a genuinely new challenge – almost certainly in business, perhaps, I imagined, something based in the United States or in Israel.

Yet then came the unexpected catalyst of a brief conversation at a cocktail party in the spring of 1993. It propelled me in an utterly different direction – ultimately into the inner circle of Tony Blair and the very heart of British politics and power.

CHAPTER 6

New Life in New Labour

The cocktail party was in a large residence in St John's Wood, and Tony Blair wasn't even there. But it marked the first stage in an involvement with the Labour Party that would, within a few years, change my life beyond recognition.

The first step really came almost exactly a year earlier, on the evening of 10 April 1992, over a Friday-night dinner with friends at The Warren. I'm certain of the date, because it was the day after John Major had somehow led his divided and discredited Tories to victory over Neil Kinnock. Inevitably, the talk turned to politics. Gilda had always been the more politically engaged of the two of us. But while her CND days were by now well behind her, I don't think I had ever heard her more passionate, more disillusioned, or more determined than when one of our guests suggested offhandedly that the election result probably didn't matter much anyway. On the big issues, he argued, Major and Kinnock were not all that different. Besides, as he put it, Major seemed to lack the extremist zeal of Margaret Thatcher while still being reassuringly 'conservative – with a small "c"'. He was a 'safe pair of hands'. Gilda didn't raise her voice in reply: that wasn't her style. But I knew her well enough to recognise the real anger she felt over the election result – and over our friends' failure to grasp its significance. 'It is about a vision for the future of the country,' she said. Maybe Kinnock had failed to convey what was at stake. But surely it was time to turn back the Thatcher years' focus on dog-eat-dog individualism and restore a sense of shared responsibility in society – most of all, for those who were left behind. It was an outlook both of us shared. I, like Gilda, had always voted Labour, even when many British Jews were flocking to pay homage to the Conservatives during the rise of Mrs Thatcher. But in the years since selling Magnet and redefining my life around my community responsibilities, especially Jewish Care, I had become more personally interested and involved in social and political issues. My JIA role had for the first time brought me into direct contact with politics, and top-level leaders, in Israel and the Middle East. At Jewish Care, I had become engaged in political issues much nearer home, and met a range of government ministers and other politicians along the way. I, like Gilda, had felt a genuine sense of despondency, almost a sense of personal defeat, as we'd watched the BBC coverage of yet another Tory triumph. Particularly after hearing our friends' dispiriting response to Major's victory, I think that both of us felt a growing determination to do whatever we could – very little, we presumed – to help ensure that next time around, the long years of Tory rule would end.

Still, when we attended the annual Israel Independence Day reception at the ambassador's residence in St John's Wood in April 1993, neither of us imagined that a two-minute chat with one of the hundreds of invited guests would mark the beginning of that process. By the time we arrived, Kinnock's recently crowned successor, John Smith, had already greeted the ambassador, and smiled and handshaken his way through dozens of other notables. He was holding a sandwich in one hand and a drink in the other when I approached him and introduced myself. 'I have always voted Labour,' I said, 'and I'm ready to do anything I can to help you get back into power.' That, Smith replied with an engaging grin, was an aim he happened to share. He suggested I call his office, and within the week I did.

Any expectation I had of making an early impact evaporated with the first of what proved a series of conversations with his chief-of-staff, Murray Elder. He was aptly named, not because he was old – he was in his early forties – but because he was decidedly old-guard Scottish Labour Party. A longtime friend of Smith, obviously protective of his role as gatekeeper, he was also a former high-school classmate and an even closer friend of another undisputed rising star in Scotland's Labour firmament, Labour's shadow chancellor, Gordon Brown. At Magnet, in the JIA and now Jewish Care, I had got used to moving quickly, setting goals and trying to achieve them, getting on with things. Now, I was essentially volunteering to help in modernising what even I could see was a badly creaking system of fundraising for Labour. Elder didn't exactly say no – and part of his reticence was no doubt due to an understandable wish to check out my credentials. But it was months before he finally arranged for me to meet with two – thankfully more welcoming – party fundraising figures: the recently ennobled textile multimillionaire Simon Haskel, and the Salford-born party veteran Lord Gregson. They encouraged me to have a go at increasing support for something they called the Industrial Research Trust. Its name made it sound like some sociology think-tank. In fact, it raised money for the office of the party leader and, to only a slightly lesser extent, that of his heir-presumptive, Gordon Brown.

I often reflect on how differently my, and Labour's – and of course Blair's – future might have turned out if Smith had been the man to lead it back to power. He was warm, charming and broadly reformist, but also instinctively cautious and consensual. I have no doubt that he recognised a pressing need to sort out funding. Yes, even despite Major's victory, the Tories were soon starting to look almost terminally exhausted. But they remained way ahead of Labour in raising money, a gap that Smith must have realised might yet spell trouble at the next election. After all, Kinnock had been leading comfortably in the opinion polls during the run-up to the election, yet had lost. Nevertheless, Smith and those around him appeared to convey no real sense of urgency. I did make a start on raising some money, though not significant sums, for the IRT in the final months of 1993 and early 1994. But I had little sense that things were moving anywhere fast. And I had no expectation at all that another London social event – a small dinner party at the start of March 1994 – would soon make the IRT, and my part in it, utterly irrelevant.

The occasion for the dinner, like my meeting with Smith a year earlier, was connected with Israel. Gilda and I, along with five other couples, were invited on a warm Monday evening to the home of the number-two man at the Israeli embassy, Gideon Meir, with whom I'd become close friends through the JIA. He lived in a large flat, also in St John's Wood, not far from the ambassador's residence. And the guest of honour was one of the many MPs from all parties whom the Israelis routinely invited on fact-finding visits. He was Labour. And while perhaps not yet seen as a Gordon Brown-scale heavyweight, he was on the Opposition front bench – the shadow home-affairs spokesman, Tony Blair.

The atmosphere was pleasantly relaxed and informal, and Blair was very laid-back. I wish I could say he immediately struck me as a future party leader and prime minister. In fact, as the lamb and red wine were served, my first impression of Blair – and of his wife, Cherie, who was then very much in her slightly frumpish, pre-designer period – was that they were bright, articulate, personable. They also struck me as extraordinarily young and unworldly. Tony would later tell me that this was the first time a dinner had been held in his honour. That, I suspect, was a politician's hyperbole. But it was clear he was much more used to beer and sandwiches at the Labour club in his north-east constituency of Sedgefield, or an evening of pizza and political plotting in his Commons office with his close ally Brown, than to sit-down dinners with the kind of guest list Gideon and his wife Amira had assembled. In addition to Gilda and myself, it included the Rubins (as in the Reebok sports-empire founder, Stephen); the Deeches (Ruth was then the head of St Anne's College at Oxford, later chair of the Human Fertilisation and Embryology Authority and a BBC governor); and George and Annabel Weidenfeld (he, already an independent 'crossbencher' in the Lords, was a toweringly successful publisher who had been on first-name terms with every Israeli prime minister since the founding of the state and with more than a few British ones). The final couple was the only one the Blairs knew: Eldred and Jenny Tabachnik. Eldred was then president of the Board of Deputies. He was also a QC who had briefly, and more relevantly, shared chambers with Cherie.

When we withdrew for coffee afterwards, Blair surprised me by making a beeline to the chair next to mine. I smiled, genuinely interested to get a better sense of another prominent Labour politician now that I was finally getting more involved in party affairs. I mentioned to Blair that I had met Smith and had begun raising funds for the IRT. He responded by saying: 'That's great.' He went on to speak briefly about how fascinating he had found his first visit to the Middle East, but was soon enthusing about his determination to see Labour modernise – to reach out to voters who had for too long felt the party was not a serious candidate for government. 'Chemistry' is a word too often used, and abused, in politics. Still, somehow, I felt very early on that he and I spoke the same language: energetic, impassioned, direct. Maybe more importantly, I sensed a broader similarity in outlook, personality and style. He and I were social animals. We liked people. We had an urge to communicate, and the confidence that given the right time and circumstances there was almost no fair-minded person we couldn't sooner or later win to our side. The Americans call it being a 'people person'. But another term – because it so wonderfully conjures up images of the grasp of an elbow, the hand on a shoulder, the broad smile and friendly hug – probably captures it better. The origin is Yiddish, and I first heard it as a child, to describe some of the more gregarious types in my father's Walford Road congregation. But it has become almost universal, and the media seemed to delight in applying it to me once I became known as Tony Blair's, and Labour's, fundraiser-in-chief. I was, they said, a 'schmoozer'. Tony, it seemed to me from that very first meeting, was a schmoozer too. And there was one other thing that struck me very powerfully: the stark difference between the approach of John Smith and his team, their sense that come what may the Tories were somehow bound to defeat *themselves* at the next election, and the passion and urgency with which Blair appeared to feel a need for Labour itself to change.

I went away wondering, however, just how much influence Blair – or the many other young MPs who he assured me shared his impatience – could really bring to bear. And although I felt much more comfortable with him than I had with Smith, or certainly with Murray Elder, I realised that any meaningful input I might have in fundraising would depend much more on them than on Blair. I had every intention of keeping in touch with him, and made a note to myself to phone in a few weeks' time to arrange to meet and talk at greater length. But in the event, by the time I made the call, the entire landscape of Labour – and his place in it – had dramatically changed. On the morning of 12 May, in his flat in London's Barbican, Smith suffered a massive heart attack, and ninety minutes later, he was dead. I remember the moment that I heard the news. I was shocked, of course, and genuinely upset – as, no doubt, was anyone who had met or known Smith, especially those like Brown and Blair who had known him well and worked alongside him. Yet the shock waves that soon reverberated through Labour were not only personal, but political. It soon became clear that Brown, as shadow chancellor, had alienated a lot of his fellow MPs. Blair's populist style, easy media manner and impressive repositioning of the party's image on law and order had quietly yet decisively moved him ahead of Gordon in the succession stakes.

Initially, I watched it all from the sidelines. Blair was in Scotland when he heard the news, but immediately headed back to London. In the days that followed, he was not short of voices urging him to seek the leadership. Nearly all had far greater weight at that point than mine. There was, above all, Cherie – but also Blair's teenage friend, and by now top aide, Anji Hunter, and his hugely self-possessed, if still unofficial, media adviser, the former *Daily Mirror* political editor Alastair Campbell. Also in the mix was the Hartlepool MP Peter Mandelson, Labour's media czar. He had begun his political career as an aide to Brown, and Gordon would always bitterly suspect him of having treacherously 'switched sides' to Blair in the key days after Smith's death. But Peter has always insisted – credibly, to my mind – that precisely because he was so keenly aware of his ties to Gordon, he remained neutral until the leadership die was well and truly cast.

The decisive influence in the early stages was Campbell, who used a *Newsnight* interview on the evening of Smith's death to say that Blair was the obvious successor. The next morning, I phoned Tony, and told him that I had absolutely no doubt he had to go for the job. He was non-committal, and still clearly stunned by Smith's death. But I told Gilda after we'd spoken that I got a strong sense he had made up his mind to stand. By Sunday, when a newspaper poll put Tony at 32 per cent as the popular choice against Gordon's paltry 9 per cent, it was all over bar the argument (an argument that began between Tony and

Gordon at Islington's Granita Restaurant at the end of May, and which I would soon witness at closer quarters as it continued, destructively, throughout the decade which the two men shared as rival powers in government).

Brown did now bow to the inevitable, and withdrew from the leadership contest. Blair enlisted Jack Straw to run his campaign. By then, I had spoken not only to Tony but to Jack, and I agreed I would help raise funds for Tony's leadership run. I didn't head the fundraising efforts, but I was keen to pitch in, and both Tony and Jack encouraged me to do so. I began phoning a handful of friends in the community and in business. I did not make a party-political pitch. This, for me, was not just about Labour, or Tony Blair. It was very much a natural progression from my work at Jewish Care, only on a much wider stage. I was arguing for a cause in which I believed – a fairer and more caring society, in which people who have been fortunate enough to acquire great wealth had a special responsibility, and opportunity, to 'give something back'. Blair, in my mind, was a part of that. He was not yet the finished political article. But he had drive and above all compassion and vision – qualities which Major, it seemed to me, lacked. Blair, I argued with a personal passion that I am sure was evident to all those whom I approached, could give Britain an opportunity to make a fresh start.

I raised all of £10,000 (including the few thousand I put in) towards an eventual campaign kitty of about £75,000. It was a pittance compared to the many millions I would go on to raise for Blair and Labour over the next dozen years. But it did help to kick-start a leadership bid that within a few weeks reinforced Blair's position as odds-on favourite to inherit Smith's mantle, which of course he resoundingly did. And as the vote drew nearer, Tony and I spoke more often, at first by phone, then face-to-face. We talked mostly about the leadership race, or Labour, but also occasionally about music, or football, or what soon emerged as another shared interest: tennis. I felt that a personal bond had begun to form, particularly after we met at another small private dinner, hosted by the Tabachniks, just days after he had been made leader. Over coffee afterwards, I suggested that once things calmed down a bit, he and the family should join us for an afternoon of lunch, swimming and tennis at The Warren.

Later in the summer, Tony, Cherie, their three young children and their nanny, Ros, and Cherie's mum, Gale, drove over from their home in Islington for the first of what would become dozens of visits. By early 1995, they were with us almost every weekend. A pattern emerged, and so did a partnership. It was on the surface an improbable one: Tony, public-school and Oxford-educated, and the ambitious Liverpool-born barrister Cherie on one side; Gilda and I, Hackney Jewish kids made good, but not exactly natural English establishment material, on the other. But it was warm, mutually supportive – probably as close to a genuine friendship as is possible in what I would eventually come to see as the weird, sometimes warped world of national politics. For me, it was undeniably exciting to find myself poised to join the inner circle of the new leader of the Opposition, and very possibly the next prime minister. For Tony, the increasingly frequent afternoons spent swimming, batting tennis balls, and brainstorming came to represent a refuge from his high-octane political team: Brown, with whom there was already an inevitably growing tension, and a private-office team dominated by Campbell, who formally joined as press chief in September 1994, and Anji Hunter.

We soon found that we shared not only interests like tennis, but a broadly similar outlook on the world as well. It was rooted in something that was unfashionable in British politics and still is: a religious faith and tradition from which we each took enormous strength. Cherie, with her strong Catholic upbringing, was the more observant of the Blairs, but the family invariably went to church on Sunday. I began my Saturdays by walking to Mill Hill synagogue – a trek that, in another rashly overlooked disadvantage of our move from Uphill Road, now took the better part of an hour. The Blairs would often visit on Saturday afternoons, after I had walked back from synagogue; or on Sundays after they had been to church. Sometimes, both. Cherie, every bit the get-ahead barrister, would typically sit on the terrace hunched over a brief. The kids, who as the months passed felt comfortable enough to bring along close schoolfriends, would hop in and out of the pool, play on the lawn, and laugh and joke with Gilda.

Tony and I would sometimes take a short swim either before or after tennis. More often, after lunch, we'd stroll directly to the far end of the long rolling lawn and do battle on the court. At first, I won. Tony was almost a decade younger, and clearly had the coordination and natural athleticism to match me stroke for stroke. Yet he was also carrying a few extra pounds. He was out of shape, and often out of breath by the end of the final set. Like all good politicians, however, he was also not short on vanity. Before long, he was dieting, exercising – and taking tennis lessons. It was not much longer before he began winning about as often as I did.

Despite the later media caricatures of Tony and me as 'tennis partners', his visits to The Warren, and our relationship, became something which I think we both valued for reasons that went beyond a few hours on the court. I think what made these early times at our home so special was that they were so totally relaxed – something I value all the more after having seen a decade in Downing Street profoundly change Tony, me, and the relationship between us. Everybody simply fell into doing their own thing and spread themselves around the house and the garden. Tony began to see The Warren almost as a second home, particularly when he was going through preparations for a major speech. I particularly recall the week before his October 1995 party conference speech, in which he drove home his view that a genuinely New Labour could 'not be morally neutral about the family' and added: 'I didn't come into politics to change the Labour Party. I came into politics to change the country.' It was a typically virtuoso performance. But it was preceded by a typically fraught few days during which he agonised about whether he had got the tone and the content just right, scribbling and rejecting draft after draft. He spent much of the week before conference working on the speech in our garden, with Alastair and other aides, including his main speechwriter Peter Hyman, dropping in at unpredictable intervals. I too would come and go, and we occasionally took tennis breaks to clear his mind. But as the week wore on, he worried that all the changes he, Alastair and Peter had made risked losing the core message, the impact, of the speech. On a couple of evenings, he worked straight through dinner and, exhausted, stayed the night so that he could get an early start the next morning.

The 'business end' of Tony's regular weekend visits was equally informal, and took place in the ground-floor room I used as a study. Tony sipped beer. I usually chose shandy. Over the first month or so, our conversations tended to be general: Blair, like Smith if a lot more quickly, wanted to check my bona fides before sharing in full detail his plans for his leadership and for the party. The vetting this time was performed by Anji Hunter, in a series of meetings we had during the autumn. Anji was tall, self-assured, bright – and above all protective, almost proprietorial, about her friend and boss. At first, she was sceptical about me, to put it mildly. Gradually, no doubt urged on by the gathering momentum of my own relationship with Blair, she warmed up. There was no formal signing-off that I was aware of, yet before long my post-game chats with Tony became as long – though nowhere near as competitive – as our on-court encounters.

We talked about how to put his almost evangelical vision of a 'new' Labour Party into practice, and what we both soon identified as a potentially critical role for fundraising. The long-term aim was to secure donations from leading businessmen, not just for the important boost that would give to the party's finances, but because it would imply an extraordinary new credibility for New Labour in a traditionally Tory constituency. At first, Tony urged me to try to ramp up efforts to raise funds for the IRT, and from the autumn of 1994 through the first half of 1995 I managed to raise more than £150,000 from nearly twenty new supporters. When one of the final cheques came in, Haskel scribbled me a note of gratitude mixed with astonishment, saying: 'Congratulations once again – you are one the few people who keep their promises!'

But one of my after-tennis conversations with Tony early in the spring of 1995 (I was still winning, although the margin was beginning to narrow) led to a critically important change of direction. The IRT was by now healthier than Tony could have imagined. But he had two deep concerns. The first was that the scale of government funding to the Opposition leader's office – known as 'Short money' after the name of the minister Edward Short, who had announced the policy in the mid-1970s – was so laughably inadequate that even my IRT fundraising could not really compensate. (Tony vowed that if he did become prime minister, he would significantly increase the scale of funding for opposition parties, and he did.) The other concern was that a fairly major chunk of the IRT money was going not to his office, but to Gordon Brown's. Tony's solution – a strategy which would have dangerously turned up the heat on the simmering tension with Brown had it become public at the time – was for me to take the lead in raising money for a new, separate Labour leader's office fund.

It was out of that conversation that the Blair 'blind trust' – maligned and misunderstood by the media pundits and rival politicians – was born. At the time, *all* party-political funding was shrouded in secrecy. The Conservatives used the system to raise millions, often from benefactors who lived overseas, paid little or no UK taxes and weren't even registered to vote in Britain. Margaret Thatcher, I was told by influential Tories I know, used to bring her key fundraiser along on foreign trips to help top up the kitty. Labour was no more open, but its funding came mostly from the trade unions. What private cash it got was small and UK-based.

Both Tony and I were agreed on the long-term aim to ensure a new openness and probity in all party funding – although I argued strongly that any realistic, long-term changes would have to deal with the Tories as well. In late 1994, a declaration of principles was drawn up, including a pledge that Labour, from the start of the new year, would unilaterally include in its annual financial report 'the name of each donor giving in the aggregate in excess of £5,000 in any one calendar year'. Throwing down a gauntlet to the Tories, who ignored it, we also vowed not to accept donations from anyone ineligible to vote in the UK.

When we started planning the campaign for his new office fund shortly afterwards, Tony was adamant that we get legal advice on how it should be structured. Two top QCs were consulted, and they quickly agreed on the ground rules. Openness might be the ideal, they recognised. But especially since other parties' contributions remained anonymous, they argued it would be not only odd, but would risk the appearance of 'corrupt influence', if Tony were to know the identities of the individuals giving him financial backing. I concurred, even though I have no doubt that I could have raised equal amounts if we had decided to name the donors – so strongly was the political tide beginning to turn in Labour's favour, and Blair's. I accepted the argument that Tony was, politically, best kept in the dark about who was giving the money, and I scrupulously kept to that rule. The trust was established, with me doing the fundraising and three trustees in place to vet all contributions. It was headed by a former Home Secretary, the late Lord Merlyn-Rees – along with the later leader of the Lords, Margaret Jay, and the Salford-born former trade unionist Baroness Brenda Dean.

One reason for the later controversy about the blind trust was a sour-grapes assault, eagerly picked up by the press less than two months before the 1997 election, from a man named Henry Drucker. An American-born, Oxford-based fundraiser, he was asked by the party early in 1996, with my full support, to draw up a report on party fundraising. The expectation was that he would take a role alongside me in helping secure 'high-value' donations in advance of the election. When he was routinely asked for an assurance of confidentiality before coming on board, he replied in writing that he would, of course, oblige. 'We are accustomed to guaranteeing confidentiality to our clients,' his note said, as if the very question were an insult. Later events made it clear he was equally accustomed not to honour such assurances. He claimed to have had a stormy meeting with me at my home in April 1996 in which he warned me about the perils of blind trusts and fruitlessly urged a more open approach in fundraising for the election campaign. The only parts of that fantasy that are true is that we did meet, and that the atmosphere, if not stormy, did turn tense. However, when he raised the issue of funding secrecy, I replied that I favoured openness, too. I explained that the leader's fund donors had been kept confidential on lawyers' advice, but that all of us had agreed that Labour would name all the major donors to the forthcoming election campaign – even if the Tories, as we expected, did not follow suit.

The real reason for his later mischief-making was that the formal funding presentation he prepared for Labour was almost ridiculously thin. When the party decided not to go ahead with giving him an active fundraising role, he was apparently determined to get even. He not only misrepresented my views on the need for transparency in party fundraising, but later related stories of how I supposedly invited potential donors over for tennis with a disingenuous hint Tony might drop in, arranged for him to show up, and then hit them for money. All of which is untrue. The only time in all my work in support of New Labour that tennis, Tony and funding were ever mixed came many months after Drucker was out of the picture. And it was not at all disingenuous. It involved Alan Sugar – who had not only come a long way in business since his days of supplying aerials to Disci, but was also a fellow tennis nut. I did quite openly invite him to join Tony and me on the court, though I don't think any of us had any doubt at that point that he was already minded to back Blair and New Labour.

My concern, unlike Drucker's, was not to write reports but to put in place arrangements that would actually bring in cash. By the time I wound down the leader's office trust campaign in 1995, I had ended up raising nearly £2 million from about fifty contributors, with the top donor putting in £100,000. These were sums previously unimaginable for a Labour leader. In theory, only the trustees and I knew the identities of the donors. In fact, the *Sunday Times* did later uncover some of the names. Among them: my JIA colleague Sir Trevor Chinn; the former Granada TV chairman Alex Bernstein; Sage software's David Goldman; the printing multimillionaire and longtime Labour supporter Bob Gavron; and perhaps most satisfyingly, because he was our first major catch from the Tory ranks, the industrialist Sir Emmanuel Kaye.

But as our personal relationship developed, Tony and I did not talk only about funding. One of the first issues on which I weighed in was politically very close to home: his private office. Once Anji Hunter had finished vetting me, she and I spoke more often and more easily. It was clear to me that for Anji and others on Blair's political first team, I would always be something of an outsider. But along with Anji's determination to protect Tony, she had a strong commitment to support those who were important, politically or personally, to him. Gradually, she came to include me in that circle. The other main figure in his office hierarchy was Campbell, with whom I had less contact. He knew the fundraising was important. It did, after all, help pay his salary. But he was almost ostentatiously hostile – in an oddly Old Labour way – to the very idea of personal wealth and seemed to think that asking people who had made money for support was something best left to the Tories.

Alastair's role in Tony's life – and my own – became clearer when, in the summer of 1995, Blair got an invitation from Rupert Murdoch to fly to Hayman Island off the coast of Australia to address a high-powered conference put on by News International. Tony was naturally tempted by the symbolic turnaround in Labour's standing with Britain's, arguably the world's, most powerful media magnate. Murdoch's *Sun* had famously backed Major three years earlier, with a front-page warning on election day that if Neil Kinnock won, the last person out of Britain should 'turn out the lights'. But Tony was nervous about accepting Murdoch's invitation, openly worried about alienating Labour activists by appearing to cosy up to a man whom many of them distrusted, and some detested. He also wondered whether there might be other, less obvious downsides. He and I spent a long afternoon poolside talking it through, and I strongly urged him to say yes. He did, of course, and he triumphed. But the debate brought home to me how important his dealings with the media, and particularly the Murdoch empire, had become to Blair – and to Alastair. During the years in Downing Street, I would find it increasingly difficult to decide who was winding up whom. But one thing was for sure: the media were becoming all-important. Once Tony was in power, presentation came eventually to trump policy almost every time.

In deciding to offer Tony some strong advice on office personnel, I was not motivated by any desire to undermine Anji or Alastair, though I'm sure that if Alastair had been party to our long, frank discussions, he would have had a few choice, angry words in response. After our Hayman Island discussion, I was later told, he had exclaimed: 'Why the *fuck* is he asking Michael's opinion?' In fact, I could see that Tony relied on both Anji and Alastair, and that both of them were extraordinarily good at what he felt he needed them to provide. My concern was that, in Judy Garland's immortal words, Tony 'wasn't in Kansas any more'. He was no longer just a shadow frontbencher, but a party leader, with realistic hopes of becoming Britain's next prime minister. As the key figures in his team, Anji and Alastair were excellent at what they did, but not sufficient. 'If this were a business,' I remarked to Tony, 'the first thing anyone would tell you is that you need a strong, efficient, experienced figure to provide real structure – to make things run. You need a chief-of-staff.' Tony said he had been thinking on similar lines, and he soon accelerated efforts to find and recruit the right man for the job. By the end of the year, the right man was brought in – from America: the returning first secretary at the British embassy in Washington, Jonathan Powell.

Powell was the perfect choice. With his boyish curls, ready smile, self-deprecating manner and civil servant's sense of order, he was difficult not to like. He wore a public-school and Oxford pedigree lightly. The younger brother of Thatcher's former policy adviser Charles Powell, he had worked briefly for the BBC and Granada before joining the Foreign Office at the end of the 1970s. Tony and Gordon Brown had first met him, and been hugely impressed, when they visited the Clinton White House in

1993. For me, Jonathan soon became the main point of contact in Blair's office – and as the sole member of his initial inner circle to remain by his side until the day he left power, the one with whom Gilda and I would develop the closest personal relationship. Pretty much anything Tony knew, Jonathan also knew. And given that Anji was busy with the pure politics, and Alastair Campbell simply didn't want to know, funding issues now rested squarely with the new chief-of-staff.

He inevitably followed my progress in raising money for the leader's office fund once it began to get up to speed in the middle of 1995, watching with none of Campbell's disdain the emergence of unprecedented business support for Blair. Jonathan recognised early on its political significance in validating Tony's vision that a genuinely *New* Labour could reach new and critically important constituencies. I'm sometimes asked whether Powell was told of the identity of the blind-trust donors. The answer is that neither I nor any of the trustees breathed a word to him. But I am certain he was simply too smart not to have been able to work out the identity of many of them well before the *Sunday Times* unearthed some of the names many months later. The same, I dare say, was probably true of Tony, one reason that none of us was sorry to see the eventual demise of the blind trust and the needless media storm that accompanied it.

Powell, in any case, realised from the start that even if the leader's office trust was blind, it could not long remain secret. Blair would have to declare the money, though not the names of the donors, at the first available update of the so-called Register of Members' Interests in the House of Commons. In early November 1995, Jonathan and I helped draw up a formal summary of the trust's guidelines – essentially echoing the Labour principles of the year before, minus the public reporting of the names of all donors who gave over £5,000. Jonathan circulated additional media-response 'talking points' for the predictable questions that followed Blair's declaration of interests. Essentially, they made public Tony's concern about the pitifully inadequate 'Short money', and the QCs' view that secrecy in this instance was necessary to head off any 'suggestion that the making of donations might be intended, or might in practice operate, so as to exert influence or secure favour' with Blair. The media storm was relatively brief. But it left its mark. I was still angry at the notion that whatever we did, the Tories would continue bagging offshore funds without meaningful disclosure. But along with Tony and Jonathan, I felt Labour must in future take the lead in opening up the system. The blind trust, in any case, began over the next year or so to wind down its operations – not least because of what would prove a genuinely historic shift in the party's fundraising priorities.

It was mapped out over beer and shandy at The Warren in early 1996. Tony was by now enjoying a double-digit lead in the opinion polls. He repeatedly told both the public and the party that this was no reason for complacency. Yet privately, neither of us had much doubt that the election was increasingly becoming his to lose. If he played his cards right, if he fought a relentlessly focused, thoroughly professional – and adequately funded – campaign, Blair had every chance of leading New Labour into power after nearly two decades of bickering, self-indulgent opposition.

'You've raised enough for the office fund, right?' Tony began as we settled down in the ground-floor office after tennis. Given the unprecedented sums he had at his disposal, he knew the answer was yes. But then he raised what was really on his mind: 'Do you think you could start raising money, serious money, for the election campaign?'

'How much?' I asked.

He paused, picking out a figure he knew would dwarf even the record level of support we'd managed so far. 'Five million,' he said. And he added an explanation. His words would have no doubt shocked and horrified the Old Labour left. But they marked the real start of Tony's drive to transform the party into New Labour not only in name, but in practice. 'I am absolutely determined,' he told me, 'that we must not to go into the next election financially dependent on the trade unions.'

I said it would be difficult, but that we would get the five million. In fact, I had serious doubts. I was proud of having helped raise almost £2 million for the leader's fund. I was also encouraged by the extent to which the Major government's growing ineptitude and unpopularity, and Blair's personal and political appeal, were making my job easier. But I feared that to more than double the amount raised for the leader's fund would be hugely difficult. And as affable and attractive as Tony was, the more I got to know him, the more I came to recognise how much work would be required to get him known by the kinds of people who could provide the scale of funds the campaign needed. Having spent nearly all his working life in the closed world of Labour politics, Tony was extraordinarily unaware of what, much less who, made business tick. He had no address book of potential backers, and even if he had, it would have included very few names of much relevance. I soon found that I was not only helping to raise funds; I was helping to widen his world – a process he embraced at times with an almost childlike enthusiasm.

Probably the most engaging example, as it happens, did not involve big business, but private pleasure. On a January Sunday in 1995, I'd invited Chris Rea over for the afternoon and happened to mention it to Tony – who had jokingly told me about his own brief Oxford 'career' as a mop-haired guitarist in a band called the Ugly Rumours. Trying, not that successfully, to sound relaxed about the prospect of meeting one of his pop heroes, Tony said: 'Maybe, I'll drop by.' He did, of course – having rushed back from a speaking engagement in Scotland to make sure he wouldn't miss out. When the doorbell rang, I greeted a sheepishly smiling, suit-and-tie-clad Tony and told him Chris was in the kitchen waiting to meet him. But Tony hesitated. He mumbled something about having to attend to another matter, rushed upstairs, and joined us minutes later – transformed, in jeans and T-shirt, from Tony the New Labour Leader to Tony with street cred. He stayed for hours.

His entry into the world of money and business was even more novel, yet greeted with equal enthusiasm. Beginning in February 1995, Gilda and I began hosting a series of small dinners at which we introduced Tony and Cherie to a range of influential business figures – a world in which they had not been involved, and which Labour had long, damagingly assumed would be for ever Tory. Most were, of course, potential donors. But despite all the later press stories suggesting I'd corral these people for dinner and strong-arm them into taking out their chequebooks when Tony left, that was not at all what happened. These occasions were about talking and listening, with both Tony and the invited guests doing a lot of both. Yes, the dinners would often later lead to contributions to the party election effort, and yes, all involved knew and recognised that prospect existed, and that meeting Tony face-to-face was partly rooted in my and the party's hope that they would be inspired to offer, financially or otherwise, their support for the changes he wanted in both Labour and the country. But the issue of money was never – *never* – raised over dinner. This was about getting an entirely new potential Labour constituency to meet and talk with a very different kind of Labour leader. And the simple fact is that, particularly given the fact that Major's Tories were the alternative, they usually liked what they saw.

One dinner, in March 1996, was organised – as I made clear from the outset to all concerned – with absolutely no fund-raising purpose in mind. But it was a symbolically powerful sign of how we were beginning to change the image and reach of a Blair-led Labour Party. The guest of honour was famously bright and hugely successful. Though he had a home in London, he lived mostly in New York, and when I phoned him there, he listened eagerly to my suggestion that he and the new leader of New Labour might enjoy the opportunity to trade ideas and get to know each other. 'I'd love to,' said George Soros, the currency trader whose bet against the pound on a frantic Wednesday in September 1992 forced John Major out of the European-currency mechanism and in many ways marked the beginning of the end of Tory rule. It was an extraordinary evening. In addition to Tony and Cherie and Soros, we invited Peter Mandelson. Tony and Soros hit it off immediately, and spoke with the ease and intelligence I'd anticipated – helped greatly by Tony's heroic resistance to any mention of 'Black Wednesday'. During the dinner, Peter whispered to me: 'I can't believe Tony is sitting having dinner with George Soros. It's incredible!'

Nevertheless, it wasn't until the summer of 1996 that I came to believe we would not only reach the magic £5 million – but might do much, much better. The breakthrough began with a note to me in February from Jonathan Powell, who reported that Peter had heard that it might be worth approaching a City businessman with a reputation for flamboyance who had taken a major share in Chelsea football club. 'He reportedly has a net worth of £120 million!' Powell wrote.

Matthew Harding, I would soon discover, was a man who lived up to his reputation. Short, a bit overweight, charming, and not infrequently tipsy from lunch onwards, he was wonderful company. He can also justifiably be said to have played a critical role in transforming the ability of the Labour Party to raise really serious money. We met face-to-face in mid-May, along with Jonathan, in Blair's Commons office. Harding was clearly impressed by Tony, and enticed by his vision of a new start and new direction for British politics. When the chat was over, Matthew and I withdrew for a more detailed conversation into Powell's adjacent office. It went very well, but none too quickly, since it was soon apparent that he had had a glass of wine or three over lunch. Our meeting stretched from five minutes, to ten, to thirty, with no sign of an easy exit. Jonathan, by this point, had started hovering, then gesticulating, clearly anxious to reclaim his desk. I repeatedly waved him away, and finally managed to wind things down with an agreement that Harding and I would resume our discussions at his office in June.

We met midway through the month, and it was clear to me that we not only shared a sense of Tony's potential but a genuine enjoyment of each other's company – key in all of the most successful fundraising relationships. Three days later, Matthew phoned me. He wanted, he said, to help. But even in my most optimistic moments, I wouldn't have dared to predict the scale of his pledge – *one million* pounds. Tony was in shock. So was Jonathan. When I phoned the party's general secretary, Tom Sawyer, to pass on the news, Tom was at first silent, and then exclaimed: 'You're taking the piss!' When I assured him I was utterly serious, he said: 'This is simply unbelievable,' a message he repeated in the note that accompanied a celebratory bottle of champagne he sent me the next morning. All of us knew that a watershed had been reached. Within days, I had assured Tony we would not only clear his target of £5 million. We would do better, much better. I suggested a new target of between £12 million and £15 million.

Sadly, Matthew did not live to see the full fruits of the Labour election campaign that his generosity helped make possible. On the night of 22 October 1996, returning from the north after a Chelsea–Bolton match, he and three friends died when their helicopter crashed. Just days earlier, he had transferred the second of the four instalments of his donation. Some months later, the administrators of his estate made it clear they had no intention of advancing the remaining £500,000 – a decision that I am sure would have prompted Matthew to draw on his famously colourful store of swearwords.

More than a decade later, I still can't quite believe the suddenness with which, after throwing his support behind us, he was gone. To this day, Gilda and I cherish one memory, however, that sums up the extraordinary – if sometimes uncomfortable – life he could bring to any party, whether of the political kind or around a dinner table. In mid-July, about a month after Matthew's million-pound pledge, we included him in one of our small dinners with the Blairs. He arrived early and in typically good cheer, and stayed late. Eventually we had to put him in a cab home around one in the morning. But as dessert was being served, he turned to me and said in one of the least silent stage-whispers imaginable: 'Who's the deaf geezer at the other end of the table?' When I tried diplomatically to ignore the comment, he merely repeated the question, more loudly. Finally, I whispered back: 'That's Leo, Tony's dad!' – hoping the 'deaf geezer' was, if not deaf, at least distant enough not to have heard.

Days after the dinner, to my relief, Gilda got a touchingly effusive handwritten note from Leo, a self-made man who had risen from a tenement childhood in Glasgow's Gorbals to become a successful barrister and law lecturer before suffering a stroke when Tony was just eleven years old. 'May I thank you and Michael for inviting me to your lovely home,' it began, going on to say in almost feature-by-feature detail how impressed he had been by The Warren. 'But more than anything, Gilda,' it concluded, 'I appreciated the welcome you and Michael gave me – natural, warm and sincere – which, at once, put me at my ease. For that, alone, was a compliment I shall never forget.' Leo is a truly remarkable, special man. For both Gilda and me, getting to know him was a real privilege.

Another of our dinners, which like the Soros evening was less about raising money than raising Tony's profile, offered a further glimpse of the future prime minister as frustrated pop star. It also provided an entertaining cameo by Peter Mandelson. The guest of honour was George Michael, who I'd been led to believe shared the hope that Blair could lead Labour back to Downing Street and very much wanted to meet him. And as we drew up the guest list, it very soon became clear that Peter also, desperately, wanted to meet George Michael. Peter peppered first Jonathan Powell, and then me, with phone calls to secure a place at the table. In the end, we added him to the guest list. He arrived as usual immaculately dressed, and was in full conversational flow over dinner, clearly delighted to be there. George Michael, to his visible dismay, seemed much more interested in talking to Tony than to Peter – and less interested in making small talk than in politics, a subject on which he proved both well informed and deeply committed.

The dinners were the tip of our fundraising iceberg. They would never have worked, even with Tony's attractiveness and natural gifts as a communicator, without the enormous amount of work that the party devoted from early 1996 to putting a professional structure in place. The first addition to the team turned out to be one of the most important: Amanda Delew, an experienced and utterly unflappable charity fundraiser whom I had met at Jewish Care. In some ways, she fitted in much better than I did with the old-style Labour types at Central Office. Everything about her – her demeanour, her dress, her drive – was frill-less and businesslike. She was very bright and very focused and soon helped bring an organisational rigour to an operation that had, in the past, been frankly amateurish.

Though I didn't recognise it at the time, one of the other moves that I recommended would turn out to have not only fundraising, but potentially political, implications. For several years, Labour had been paying a £10,000 monthly retainer to an up-and-coming PR outfit to put on the occasional fundraising dinner, one of which Gilda and I were invited to attend. It was not a serious occasion for raising money, and made it clear to me that the fees being paid to the organisers were hardly the best use of scant party resources. I had little trouble persuading Tony and others that a change was in order. Amanda, after all, was brought in for a monthly fee of just £2,500. Yet little could I have suspected that one of the founding partners of the PR firm we were sacking – Sarah Macaulay – was also a close friend of Gordon Brown. She is now his wife. Gordon never raised the issue at the time, and I have no reason to feel that he harboured any lasting resentment, but despite the fact that I began to see more of him, it was hard to tell. We got on fairly well, particularly after he accepted my invitation to be the keynote speaker at a Jewish Care fundraising event. Nevertheless, inevitably, our relationship always seemed to be coloured by my closeness to Tony, whom he felt had stolen the Labour crown. I vividly recall an early Labour strategy meeting at which I first grasped the depth of Gordon's anger and resentment towards Blair and those he blamed, rightly or wrongly, for helping make him leader. Tony was in the chair. Peter Mandelson was there, too, as was Alastair. About twenty minutes into the proceedings, a hunched and dishevelled figure walked in unceremoniously, plopped himself down in a chair and, without so much as looking up, took out a pen and a block of A4 notepaper and began scribbling notes. At the end of the meeting, still having spoken not a single word and with only a brief and unfriendly upward glance, he rose, and left. I found the scene astonishing at the time. But it would prove very tame compared with the battles I witnessed once Tony and Gordon were Downing Street neighbours – especially the open attempt by Brown's camp to seize power from Blair in September 2006.

Over the decade that followed, I would also come to understand the complexity of Tony's relationship with Gordon – the mixture of reliance and frustration, of fear and a desire to appease, love and hate, and finally, after the 2006 'coup', a feeling that Brown was, in Tony's words, simply 'a liar'. But from the start, Tony recognised potential trouble ahead. A few weeks after Gordon's strange behaviour at the party strategy meeting, he turned to me as he was towelling down after a swim at The Warren and remarked: 'What am I going to do about Gordon and Peter?' I had by now come to understand that whenever he asked that kind of question, he had a plan in mind – one that almost invariably involved me. 'You're good with people,' he said. 'Why don't you have a talk with them both, see whether you can patch things up?' To which – even though I suspected that raising millions for the election campaign would prove easy by comparison – I agreed to have a go.

I saw Peter first, for lunch in the Commons, and explained how worried Tony was about the friction between two of the people he most relied on to change Labour, and the country. He was sceptical. He'd been at the receiving end of many months of deadly glares from Gordon, who had all but stopped speaking to him. But his loyalty to the New Labour project, and to Tony, was probably deeper than any member of the inner circle. 'It's going to be very, very difficult,' he said. 'But if Tony wants us to have a go at patching things up, of course I'm ready to do anything I can from my end.' Buoyed, if still not confident, I then arranged to have lunch with Gordon.

We met on a Wednesday afternoon in a crowded top-floor restaurant in Millbank, a few minutes' walk from Parliament. Gordon was friendly, at least until I explained my mission. 'Make up with Peter?' he hissed in an angry whisper. Then, his voice gradually rising first to dispatch-box volume and then to a near shout, he exclaimed: 'Peter? He's been going around telling everyone that I'm gay! And I am NOT GAY!' Dozens of MPs looked around in astonishment, no doubt assuming that I had just tried – and thankfully failed – to proposition the shadow chancellor of the exchequer!

Mission, needless to say, *not* accomplished. Yet when a Labour by-election victory in Staffordshire in April 1996 cut the Tories' Commons majority to a mere three, even what Tony delicately called the 'Gordon–Peter problem' could not seriously detract from his focus on ensuring the party was ready for a general election. I played the major fundraising role. In addition to Amanda, Jane Hogarth – or as she was then, Jane Preston – was moved over as the fundraising group's immensely effective research officer from Labour's policy unit. They worked together with Mike Cunnington, who took the lead on direct-mail appeals. And the anchor of the team was an outstanding professional fundraiser, and a Labour man through and through – namely Jeff Shear, with whom I'd been so impressed during my fundraising work for Jewish Care and whose talents I brought to Labour's attention. Jeff was wisely brought in by the party as a consultant and earned the respect and appreciation of everyone who worked with him. Throughout my Labour fundraising years, the team reported to the party's general secretary – a role held before 1997 by Tom Sawyer, and later by Margaret McDonagh, David Triesman, Matthew Carter and Peter Watt.

Our job was clear: to make sure that if we somehow contrived to lose a fifth straight election, it would not be for lack of resources. Harding's gift had provided not only momentum, but indispensable credibility with which to approach other potential donors. Some, like Bob Gavron, had already given to Blair's leadership fund, and now willingly dug deeper. Others had already shown past signs of sympathy, or active involvement, with Labour – like Gordon Brown's friend Geoffrey Robinson, the publisher Paul Hamlyn, or the businessman Sigmund Sternberg. By far the most important in money terms was David Sainsbury. Heir to the supermarket fortune and chair of the Sainsbury's group, he had been a strong backer of the old SDP when it broke off from Old Labour, and thus was a natural convert to Blair's New Labour – similar ideas, he figured, but this time capable of bringing them into government. It was Jonathan Powell who suggested I meet him, and from the start I was impressed by both his personality and his political commitment. He was very shy and, though he would go on to serve as science minister in Blair's government, genuinely not a man who sought the limelight. He was successful and prominent enough already. But he wanted Tony and Labour to win and recognised that he was in a financial position to give valuable support to a cause he believed in. In the end, his pledge for the election campaign – £2 million – dwarfed even Harding's.

We also managed to bring other, newer faces on board – particularly, in a trend that would foreshadow Tony's early 'Cool Britannia' years in Downing Street, from the culture and arts world. The filmmaker David Puttnam and the actor Jeremy Irons both contributed. A letter to the party from the leading, and decidedly non-Labour, theatrical producer Cameron Mackintosh upon agreeing to help the campaign was particularly gratifying. It also helped explain the increasing success we were having in building a sense of optimism and possibility around Tony's vision for the country. 'As you know, I have always voted Tory up till now,' Mackintosh wrote. 'But what I want is the best possible government for this country, irrespective of what it is called, and, to that end, I am happy to contribute £50,000 to your election campaign – whether or not I end up voting Labour or Tory or for an independent Scotland!'

By New Year's Day 1997, with the expectation that the election would finally be called for sometime in May, we were in better shape than I could have hoped when Tony first asked me to try to raise £5 million. Word was inevitably spreading within the party – and through the press – that the Tories' historic monopoly of support from the business community was coming under threat. Ironically, the release of a crowing Labour press release – which I felt should have been spotted and stopped by Jonathan – predicting we would raise 'a record £6.5 million' for 1996 led to a rare bout of friction between us. In an angry note, I reminded Jonathan that we were in fact hoping to do considerably better than that in the coming months. Our fundraising could be undermined if potential donors wrongly thought we no longer really needed their help. 'I find this sort of press release out of order,' I told him. 'I am really unhappy that the historic, for want of a better word, irritants are not being resolved and I do think this needs to be resolved and clarified ASAP.' I later drafted a further detailed memo setting out plans that I hoped would allow us to meet ascending 'target levels', first of £10 million, then £12.5 million and finally £15 million. We weren't close to any of them yet, but with each new meet-and-greet session, each batch of phone calls, each passing week, we were making real progress. In a handwritten note at the beginning of January 1997, thanking Gilda and me for a Christmas present, Jonathan was in an upbeat mood. 'This year we will win,' he wrote. 'And the victory will be in no small part due to you and the unstinting work you have put in over the past two years. Because so much of it is behind the scenes, I worry you do not get the public appreciation you deserve. But you know that Tony and I do know how much you do and are truly grateful.'

We were still, however, careful to take nothing for granted. Early in January, Peter circulated a memo based on press leaks suggesting an astronomical £26 million budget for the Tory election campaign – intensifying pressure on us to reach our more ambitious targets. He argued it was especially important for Labour to be able to match the Conservatives' advertising spending. I worked harder and harder to bring in new money, boosted by a timely commitment from the venture-capital boss Ronald Cohen to contribute £100,000 to the Blair campaign. He also offered to host a dinner with the aim of bringing a number of fellow businessmen on board. Cohen's contribution was substantial, and he followed it up with a series of even larger gifts in later years. But his intermittent offers to bring in major new sources of financial support always proved to be exaggerated. And that would have particularly dire consequences – for Labour, for Blair and for me – nearly a decade later. In the run-up to the 2005 election, Tony turned to Cohen in the misplaced hope of bringing in a rich new vein of support from his venture-capital world. He then fell back on an ill-considered, panic-stricken decision to accept loans, rather than openly declared donations – triggering the 'cash for peerages' controversy.

But the focus before 1997 was on securing a first – not a third – Labour election victory. Gilda and I continued to host our own dinners to widen the party's network of support, and we made steady, strong progress. I was finally able to write

Jonathan a one-and-a-half-page memo that, though heavy on detail and deliberately low-key in tone, conveyed an extraordinary message: we had done it! Specifically, I explained that with just one caveat – about £1 million of the money pledged would actually come in after election day – our 'total election campaign fundraising will achieve the target of £15 million'.

The issue of the 'missing' million, as it happened, would suddenly and unexpectedly resolve itself, with repercussions that would explode in the media six months after the election and confront Blair with his first major Downing Street crisis. It all began with a day out at the races. Tony and the family were invited to attend the British Grand Prix at Silverstone in the summer of 1996, and were introduced to the great and the good in motor racing. A few months later, Jonathan's office forwarded me a briefing note on the Formula One boss Bernie Ecclestone. It had been drawn up by Ecclestone's very capable aide – and onetime adviser to John Smith – David Ward. Ecclestone was coming in to see Blair on the first Monday of October, after which Jonathan had arranged for me to meet Ecclestone and Ward, which I did. I sounded out Ecclestone about the possibility he might want to contribute to the campaign. He was non-committal. But he struck me as shrewd, highly intelligent and highly effective – someone who had fought hard for his success and who would make his own decisions in his own time. He said that he would think it over, and would get back in touch. And though I'd heard nothing at all from him since our brief meeting, Ward suddenly showed up at Tony's office with a cheque for a million pounds from Ecclestone for the election campaign.

By then, it was fairly clear we were heading towards victory.

On 17 March, Major had formally set 1 May as election day, brashly telling reporters that, despite Tony's 25-point lead in the latest polls, 'I think we'll win.' Still, even Major must have realised that was a tall order when the next morning's edition of the *Sun* arrived at Number 10. In the last election, the Murdoch red-top had exhorted readers to turn out the lights if Labour won. Now, its headline read: 'THE SUN BACKS BLAIR'. It was time, the newspaper said, to 'give change a chance'.

Tony and I talked increasingly often as the election drew nearer: about the campaign, the political message, and the prospects for government. In one memorable conversation, we spoke at length about the 'values' that I felt that New Labour had to project and bring into government. Explaining to Tony what had first drawn me to his New Labour vision, I said that my parents' inspiration, my years at Magnet, and my experiences at Jewish Care had all convinced me that societies needed two things to flourish. The first was personal 'ambition', which had for too long been an exclusively 'Tory' cause; the second, a core Labour value, was 'compassion' for the least well-off. Tony replied: 'Yes, that's it. Absolutely.' Increasingly, he championed this combination of values as key to his vision for Britain's future – *ambition with compassion.*

Another conversation also sticks with me – both because it reminds me of how Tony still could not completely bring himself to believe we would win the election; and because it was an extraordinary indication of how close the two of us had become, personally and politically, since our first meeting just three years earlier. 'Michael, I have a few nominations I can make to the Lords as Opposition leader,' he said out of the blue, 'and I'd like to put you forward as a working peer.' I was stunned. Along with the compassion that I proudly brought to Jewish Care, I was still ambitious, too, and honest enough to recognise the extraordinary sense of achievement I'd feel at having made the improbable journey from Alvington Crescent to the Palace of Westminster. Yet somehow I managed to say no – or at least, not yet. 'Obviously, it would be a huge, huge honour, and a chance to make a real contribution,' I replied. 'But it wouldn't be right at this time. Of course, if this is what you want, it would be wonderful *after* you become prime minister.'

'What if I don't *become* prime minister?' Tony replied, smiling. 'That would be hard on you.' To which I said: 'Nowhere near as hard on me as it will be on you, mate!'

It was the last time he mentioned, at least to me, the prospect of defeat at the polls. Nevertheless on election day, a sunny spring Thursday, Gilda and I felt strangely nervous as we walked up the road to Courtland Primary School, our local polling station. It was not that we feared Tony and Labour would somehow lose. The opinion-poll gap with the Tories had become so wide, so consistent, that some form of Blair victory – even if his Commons majority was smaller than was being predicted – seemed certain. I think what unsettled us was a recognition of enormity of the changes in our lives since that first brief dinner chat with Tony in 1994, and a sense that if he really did end up running the country, we – and of course he – were about to embark on an even more dramatic transformation.

Luckily, our election-day nerves were steadied by a social engagement that proved both personally and politically enjoyable. We drove to Graffham to attend the wedding of the daughter of close friends: Lita and David – Conservative Lord – Young. The wedding was lovely, but I must admit the atmosphere was enriched for us by the opportunity to mingle with dozens of dedicated Tories visibly mourning the likely prospect of an end to nearly two decades in power. When we got back home, I had a brief chat by phone with Tony, who was in Sedgefield with Cherie and a clutch of aides, including Jonathan, Alastair, Anji and Peter, who had driven over from his Hartlepool constituency. The team seemed generally upbeat. But Tony, as I'd expected, seemed even more anxious than we were to get on to the main event.

Shortly after eight p.m., we drove into London, through Parliament Square and across to the Royal Festival Hall on the South Bank, which had been rented for the night to allow the campaign team, Labour activists and all the others who had worked for years to make the party electable again to watch as the exit polls, and then the real results, came in. It was already crowded when we arrived, and thousands more people arrived as the evening went on. The atmosphere was electric, almost magical. The TV coverage already made it clear we were winning, and there were soon signs that the margin of victory could be significant. But when both BBC and ITN broadcast exit polls at ten p.m. predicting a landslide, a spontaneous cheer echoed through the hall. Anticipation gave way to celebration, with each new prediction, each new constituency result, making it clearer that we had not only succeeded in booting the Tories out of office, but that we were on our way to a victory of historic proportions. After midnight, a particularly loud cheer greeted the news that Neil Hamilton had lost to the anti-sleaze independent and former BBC war reporter Martin Bell. An even louder roar erupted in the early hours of the morning when the Tory cabinet member and former leadership challenger Michael Portillo lost his Enfield seat to a 31-year-old Labour challenger, Stephen Twigg.

The sun was rising when Tony – along with Cherie, the political entourage, and dozens of reporters and camera crews – finally made their triumphant arrival outside the hall. The open-air setting beside the Thames could not have been more perfect. It was beautifully clear, and just becoming light. Amid applause and yelps of celebration, arms stretching out to touch the new prime minister, and grizzled party veterans in tears, Tony entered the hall, made his way on stage, and exclaimed: 'A new dawn has broken over Britain, has it not?' It was, Gilda remarked as we embraced, almost like the second coming! As we made our way to the car an hour or so later, people were literally dancing in the street, crying and embracing and cheering.

In the three years I'd been involved in helping get Tony and Labour to this point, I had often tried to convey to potential financial backers my conviction that this election was not just about one party, or one leader, replacing another. It was about a rare opportunity for Britain to get a fresh start, under the banner of a truly gifted, and different kind of political leader. I had a strong sense as we set off for home early on Friday morning that the fresh start had now finally, really begun.

Tony phoned around mid-morning. The Blairs were still in Islington amid preparations for their move into Downing Street. Clearly too excited at having actually won to have got any sleep, he asked whether Gilda and I had been at the Festival Hall. When I said that of course we had, he exclaimed: 'Why didn't you come over and hook up with us?' I explained that it would have taken a younger and more agile couple, or possibly a helicopter, to navigate the screaming and teeming crowds, but Tony persisted. It was 'wrong', he said, that he hadn't had the opportunity personally to thank us for our help and friendship over the past few years. This was Tony at his most gracious, heartfelt and engaging. 'Get some sleep!' I told him as we signed off, and we agreed that, particularly since they weren't moving from Islington until Monday, they should come over as usual for a swim and tennis on Saturday afternoon. 'Just like old times,' joked Tony.

But of course, it wasn't. Tony and Cherie did their best to seem matter-of-fact about having finally achieved the prize for which he, and we and many others, had worked and hoped. They tried to act *normal*, or at least as nearly normal as a newly elected prime minister and his wife can reasonably act. Yet when Tony and I finally made our way down to the tennis court, he suddenly stopped dead. He looked around, checking to make sure his security guards were not close enough to overhear him. And then he did something truly astonishing. He literally jumped up and down, like a small kid who had been let out of school for the day, and shouted, laughing out loud: 'I really did it! Can you believe it? I'm prime minister! I'm prime minister! I'm prime minister!'

I remember thinking how wonderfully disarming Tony could sometimes be, and hoping that in whatever other ways Downing Street might test or alter him, something of this childlike, open, vulnerable side would survive. The danger, I knew, was that he – and all of us who had worked alongside him in the relatively low-stakes world of Opposition – would find ourselves dealing with a whole different order of pressures now that Tony was running not just the party, but the country.

What I didn't anticipate is that his first potential problem was already about to come to a head, and that I would be called on to help sort it out. It involved both personal jealousies and political influence, and it risked placing the prime minister in the middle of a test of wills between two people – two women – whom he relied on hugely. I knew there was trouble when our bedside phone rang on Sunday morning. It was Cherie, and she asked me to come over to Islington as soon as I could. 'There's a problem,' she said. 'I need your help.'

CHAPTER 7

Downing Street

'Michael, what are *you* doing here?' Tony said when I arrived at the Blairs' large terraced house in Richmond Crescent, a leafy residential area of Islington a few blocks west of the bustle of Upper Street. When I said I was just there to chat with Cherie – not exactly an everyday occurrence – he arched an eyebrow, and seemed about to probe further when his attention was thankfully deflected by the arrival of a car from Downing Street with the first 'red boxes' of his prime ministership. He looked exhausted, and exhilarated. I eased my way into the living room, where Cherie was clearly eager to talk. And she wasted no time in filling me in on the 'problem' she wanted me to help resolve. It went by the name of Anji Hunter.

I'd been aware – through Jonathan Powell and others around Blair – that the new prime minister's wife didn't get on with the woman who was his longest-serving, and most trusted, aide. But I hadn't been prepared for the strength of her feelings, nor her determination to see they were taken into account. She had, of course, talked to Tony directly. In fact, Cherie was one of the few people who knew at that point that her husband had decided to bring Anji into Downing Street with him as a 'special assistant' – essentially part of the inner sanctum alongside Jonathan and Alastair Campbell. Cherie had tried and failed to argue him out of doing so. And she was clearly resigned to the fact that if she couldn't do so, neither I nor anyone else would be able to help her block Anji's appointment altogether. But because my relationship with her husband was so unlike that of his full-time political circle, she especially wanted my help to achieve her fall-back aim – ensuring that Anji's role was as limited as possible. It was the first taste of an aspect of my role during Blair's Downing Street years that I had frankly never anticipated and which – with the media's focus first on my fundraising, then on my work as Blair's Middle East envoy, and finally on 'cash for peerages' – went essentially unnoticed. It was to act as an occasional envoy of a different sort, to get messages across to Tony that those around him were convinced he had to hear, but which they felt it was difficult for them to raise. As it happened, probably the most delicate of all these problems, besides the Cherie–Anji tension, would come a few years later. It would be directed not *from* Cherie but at her, and Tony. It involved another, quite different, kind of confidante: their 'lifestyle guru', Carole Caplin.

But the first involved Anji Hunter. And its resolution during Blair's heady early months in office – or *near*-resolution, since the issue never really went away until Anji herself left for a public-relations role with BP near the end of 2001 – seemed at times as fraught with long-held enmity as anything I later encountered in shuttling between Israeli and Arab leaders. The core of the 'Anji Hunter problem' was impossible to fix. Anji had got to know Blair when both of them were teenagers in Scotland, years before he met and married Cherie. They had become close, very close, friends – though never boyfriend and girlfriend. While they had fallen out of touch for long periods, she returned to his side in 1987 as an assistant in his parliamentary office. She remained there – with only a brief retreat at the start of the 1990s, to spend more time with her husband and children in Sussex – and became increasingly indispensable to him once he became Labour leader. Anji was, in a sense, everything Cherie was not. Cherie was a Liverpool working-class girl who, with unconcealed ambition and dazzling intelligence, had made good; Anji was a naturally sociable, self-assured middle-class girl from a Tory family who was at ease with herself and, crucially, uniquely capable of putting Tony at ease as well. Cherie had buried her hostility, recognising Anji's importance to her husband during the critical period between his elevation to the party leadership and his election as prime minister. But she genuinely assumed, and certainly hoped, that once he was in Downing Street he would no longer need her. He was running the country now. He would have top-drawer civil servants – and highly competent political aides like Jonathan and Alastair. Anji was surely, she tried to convince her husband, surplus to requirements.

But of course she wasn't. I ended up feeling huge sympathy for all sides in this odd triangle: for Cherie, who had put aside her own feelings about Anji during the push for the premiership; for Anji, who had spent literally every waking hour cultivating Blair's political contacts and giving him the self-confidence necessary to keep on course when things got tough; and perhaps above all for Tony himself. Blair's problem was that he deeply needed both women, and constantly relied on them, in different ways. And he had another problem, too, which I would only later come to recognise fully – not just as an uncomfortable witness but an occasional victim – especially in the months before the 'cash for peerages' crisis erupted. Tony Blair hated personal confrontation. So much so that he would sometimes shirk difficult political decisions in order to avoid it, and end up misleading, even betraying, longtime friends and allies rather than be straight with them.

The Anji saga was also made more difficult in those first few months by another irritant which would repeatedly surface until she finally left her formal role at Downing Street. It involved Alastair Campbell's partner, Fiona Millar – Cherie's personal adviser and the key figure in her office. It seemed to me that Fiona enjoyed playing Cherie and Anji against each other. She would report Cherie's barbs to Anji and then do the same in the other direction with Cherie. The whole mess came to a head in November, when Anji – frustrated at the absence of a finally and properly defined set of duties that would put the dispute to rest – proposed a new job description of her own. Things had got so bad, she hinted, that if they weren't resolved, she would simply quit. Cherie was fuming when she found out. Her anger was deepened by the fact that she discovered that Anji had scouted out the logistic arrangements for a public 'walkabout' with the Queen and Prince Philip without informing, much less consulting, her. She launched a counter-strike, and I was again called in, as part of a process in which Anji's proposed list of duties was literally edited line by line. Cherie icily struck out item five – 'accompanying the prime minister on certain visits to ensure proper presentation' – although, typically for Tony, she did occasionally continue to do so anyway. But the real fire came in a note from Cherie to Anji – after a crisis meeting involving Tony and Cherie, Alastair and Fiona – informing her that both Fiona and another of her senior aides, Roz Preston, would be getting promotions and salary raises to beef up the office of the prime minister's wife. 'The room which is at present partially occupied by you will be turned over to my office,' she wrote. 'Your terms and conditions of employment will remain the same. If anything, your attempt to force a change in your terms by threatening to leave has only hardened my hostility to you. I will not allow either myself or the PM to be held to ransom in this manner.' And for good measure, with all the formal force of a seasoned QC drawing up a legal contract, she concluded: 'In so far as your job brings you into contact with me, that will be kept to a minimum . . . I trust this is clear.'

My own role was, thankfully, less fraught. Yet inevitably it changed now that Blair was not merely running and reshaping Labour, but had been elected on a wave of near euphoria to do the same for Britain. In the first days and weeks, the old ease and sense of intimacy survived. Gilda and I visited Tony and Cherie on the day they moved into Downing Street – not into Number 10, because the living quarters there were too cramped for the Blairs and their children, but into the larger flat above Brown's office at Number 11. We were shocked – or at least Gilda, Cherie and I were – by the state of the place. Tony would gradually develop a taste for creature comforts as he began making the transition from a British to a genuinely international political figure a few years later. And I have no doubt that his decision after leaving office to accept a role as Middle East peace envoy was only partly rooted in a genuine passion for the issue that we both came to share. It was also a way of retaining the sense of status on the world stage he came to enjoy in Downing Street, and the perks that went with it. Back then, however, he was still very much the nomad, with a disarmingly engaging talent for feeling at home in any place that had a spare bed and a kettle. Still, the flat at Number 11 was no White House. It was shabby and dishevelled. It reeked from boxfuls of Havana cigars enjoyed by the previous tenant: Tory chancellor Kenneth Clarke. On the way home, I remarked to Gilda that it was hard to believe that a British prime minister and his family were expected to live, and presumably entertain, in a place like that. To which Gilda replied, 'I'm sure it won't be long before Cherie gets it redone.' And it wasn't.

Tony, in any case, came to view Number 11 as only a home of convenience, a place to sleep and hang his clothes next door to the office. His preference was Chequers, the prime-ministerial country residence in Buckinghamshire. It, too, was a bit worn at the edges. It had something of the feel of a very expensive yet slightly fraying tweed jacket. But with its faded red brick and tall, elegant windows, Tony adored it. It had space, a large and comfortable office with the feel of an old English clubroom, an attentive staff, and beautifully expansive grounds. The only thing his country residence lacked, at least at first, was a tennis court. Yet virtually every Friday morning – Thursday evenings, if he could manage it – Tony would be driven to Chequers, where he would decompress, work on papers, occasionally entertain, and spend time with Cherie and the kids. He would return to London only on Sunday evening, for another week's work in Downing Street.

Almost every Sunday morning during those first few years in power, I would drive up the M1, the M25 and then on to the A41 to Chequers to meet him for our reassuringly familiar encounters on the tennis court. We played on a court at RAF Horton, ten minutes' drive from Chequers. But when I happened to mention this to Sir Emmanuel Kaye – the former Tory supporter who had been sufficiently impressed by Blair to become an early backer of the fund for his Opposition office – he said he would like to do something to help Blair now that he was prime minister, and he volunteered to fund a tennis court for Chequers. Sadly, Emmanuel died before it was installed, about three years into the first term, but his trust followed through on his wishes.

My weekly tennis matches with Tony were not just good exercise, and an enjoyable outlet for the fierce competitive streak in both of us. They were also, much as before, an opportunity for him to talk through the week's political ups and downs in an atmosphere free of the constraints of Downing Street and the formal political roles of his aides or cabinet colleagues. And during his first months of office, there were many more ups than downs. There were, of course, frustrations – occasional bouts of cabinet tension, though none of the nuclear-scale battles with Gordon Brown which would come later. But mostly, he felt very much on top of his game. I particularly remember one Sunday near the end of his first few months in Downing Street, when he turned to me after tennis and said, smiling: 'Michael, I don't know what all the fuss is about. Being prime minister is really pretty easy.'

It would soon, however, turn harder, with his first major crisis – the so-called Bernie Ecclestone Affair. Like his final crisis a decade later, it involved donations to the Labour Party. And in a pattern that would become increasingly familiar to me during Tony's decade in power – but whose lessons I failed to learn until far too late – my own role was limited to the fundraising side. The politics of fundraising was in the hands of others, a potentially combustible problem that I was either too naïve, or simply too focused on bringing in the pounds and pence, to grasp fully. In Ecclestone's £1 million donation before the 1997 election, in fact, even my fundraising role had been peripheral. I'd met briefly with him and his aide David Ward, but had no further meetings or discussions before the surprise delivery of his seven-figure cheque to Tony's office. After the election, I did meet with Ward again. He told me Ecclestone was now considering a series of further contributions, news which I passed on to both Tony and Jonathan Powell. Yet the first I heard of the 'Ecclestone Affair' was when newspaper reports began appearing at the start of November 1997, suggesting that his money had 'bought' a reverse in government policy on banning the tobacco sponsorship on which the sport of motor racing largely relied. In the frantic week that followed, Tony held meeting after meeting – the key players being Alastair, Jonathan, Peter Mandelson and above all Gordon Brown – in the search for a strategy aimed at convincing the media he had done nothing wrong. Day by day, new media revelations made things worse – above all the news that Tony had personally participated in a meeting with Bernie at Number 10 the previous month, during which the issue of the sponsorship ban was discussed. Tony, his ministers and his spokespeople responded either by saying nothing – Jeremy

Paxman on *Newsnight* memorably pointed to an empty chair and said there was 'no ministerial bottom to fill it' – or by obfuscating. Gordon, cornered on the *Today* programme, was flustered enough to lie outright, insisting that he had not been told about Ecclestone's million-pound gift. It was the same 'not me, guv' attitude that he would adopt again during the 'cash for peerages' affair a decade later, when, to my astonishment, the news media swallowed it whole.

In the Ecclestone crisis, it was Tony himself who finally lanced the boil. He accepted the advice of the Commission on Standards in Public Life – who had been consulted by Downing Street a few days earlier mainly as a damage-limitation and delaying tactic – to hand back Ecclestone's donation. And in his first live television interview since taking office, he deployed a combination of qualities on which he would often come to rely during future, deeper crises: a strongly religious man's sincere faith in his own probity, allied with a natural charm and a frustrated actor's instinct for tone and presentation. Insisting he would never do anything improper, and never had, he added: 'I think most people who have dealt with me think I am a pretty straight sort of guy.'

And he was. To my knowledge he never altered any of his policies because of any of the big-money donations I brought in. But I had no doubt that, in this case, he had made mistakes. Personally attending the Ecclestone meeting was one. Dithering and leaving the media with the feeling that he was trying to hide some wrongdoing was another. And putting himself in the position of having to return the £1 million – with the inescapable implication that it was tainted, and the inevitable and understandable fury Ecclestone felt as a result – was a third.

As it happened, I wasn't asked my opinion as the crisis unfolded. Tony called me only afterwards, to say we had to find a way to raise more big money – first and most urgently to pay back Ecclestone's original £1 million, then to replenish the party's bank account. For though I'd helped raise record sums for the 1997 election, we had also spent record amounts, and still had to pay off a substantial debt.

And I obliged, relying largely on a half-dozen or so major gifts to raise several million pounds in the weeks that followed. But one lasting effect of the crisis, and the ham-handed way in which Tony and the government had handled it, would prove deep and damaging. 'Sleaze', a word damningly synonymous with the Tories during their final years in power, had become a Labour issue too. Tony's reputation had been damaged. And questions had been raised in the public and media mind about whether the unprecedented level of contributions I was helping to bring in – until this point seen mainly as an emblem of New Labour change and success – had a darker side as well. From that point on, even had Snow White given a donation to the party, she would have found every bit of her family history emblazoned on the pages of the press – a reality that would have huge implications in the run-up to Tony's second, 2001 election campaign, and even more seriously for the 'cash for peerages' crisis.

Yet with the shift from opposition to government, I was asked by Tony to raise money not only for the party but for policy priorities he felt were central to fulfilling the promises and expectations raised by the end of eighteen years of Tory rule. One of the very first was his literacy and numeracy initiative, an echo of the famous 'education, education, education' speech at the outset of the 1997 campaign. Though Labour had pledged to honour Conservative tax and spending plans for its first term of office, Tony was aware that any nationwide drive to improve the basic skills of primary-school pupils would cost money. And he was determined to move quickly. So was Alastair, who along with Tony knew a good-news story when he saw one and was increasingly impatient to announce the initiative. That created an enjoyably surreal scene, when the three of us met to discuss the details in Downing Street. Among all of New Labour's top team, with the possible exception of Gordon, Alastair was the best example of what I came to think of as financial 'double vision'. He craved the funds necessary for Labour's success, but affected to be not only disinterested but dismissive of the actual business of fundraising. Now, Alastair was itching for his announcement. I had lined up a potential donor, the industrial-electronics entrepreneur and philanthropist Maurice Hatter. I had introduced Tony to him before the election at a fundraising dinner for the Jewish educational charity ORT, in which Hatter was a leading figure and for which Blair had agreed to give a keynote speech. Afterwards, Maurice told me that if there was a specific educational cause for which Tony needed support in Downing Street, he would be happy to help, and I had now asked him to consider contributing the £1 million needed to begin making the literacy and numeracy programmes a reality. He said he was minded to help. But understandably, he wanted a bit of time to think it over, given the sheer size of the sum involved. When I explained this, Alastair insisted we press harder: the launch had to be announced. 'Look,' I replied, 'I am fairly sure Maurice will give the money, but I really don't think it would be right of us to rush him.' To which Alastair shot back: 'Then give me the number and let me speak to him.' I did,

Alastair turned on his trademark combination of charm and muscle, and within twenty-four hours was able to announce the literacy and numeracy drive.

A second fundraising project came at the urging not only of Tony, but the youngest, but by no means least ambitious, member of his Downing Street team, David Miliband. Then in his early thirties but looking even younger, the current foreign secretary sheepishly faxed me his CV shortly after the 1997 election and asked me to help get money to establish a body called the Policy Network. Before joining up with Tony as his policy aide in 1994, David had been working at New Labour's favourite think-tank, the Institute for Public Policy Research. With Tony's encouragement, he now wanted to set up a more explicitly Blairite policy group that could establish links with leading left-of-centre politicians overseas, particularly in Europe. I raised substantial sums – chiefly from donors who either were, or would become, Labour Party backers as well. The Network went on to host a number of high-powered policy seminars, including one weekend event during Tony's second term at which Bill Clinton was the star speaker – and where Clinton and I held a platform discussion on Middle East peace. But essentially it was a vehicle for leading New Labour voices: Miliband, the polling expert Philip Gould, Anthony Giddens – and Peter Mandelson. Though Peter was not involved at the start, in late 2001 he began his bid to rehabilitate himself after his second forced resignation from cabinet – over allegations, eventually disproven, that he fast-tracked the passport application of the Hinduja brothers at a time when they were poised to support the Millennium Dome – by taking on the chairmanship of the Policy Network. I was happy to have made the organisation possible, and I think it has done some genuinely useful work. But it was also an early example of a widening, and time-consuming, fundraising role that I sometimes came to feel was increasingly taken for granted by some of those, like David and Peter, who had reason to be grateful for the results. They were not quite as dismissive as Alastair, or Gordon, of the work required to raise the money required. But nearly. They did politics, they seemed to suggest. The people who secured the resources that made their politics possible – not just me, but the dedicated professional staff in the party – were somehow just a below-stairs means to their lofty ends. 'Michael,' I remember Peter saying to me shortly after I had been made a peer, 'I guess you've got what you want now, so I assume you won't be helping the party any more.' I held my tongue. I didn't quite know what to say. And I had the good grace not to remind him of the remark when the Policy Network came to his rescue a few years later.

Still, Tony's early months in government were an enormously exciting time. I particularly cherished the long talks after tennis. Although I sometimes pretended not to be affected by it all, and tried to play the coolly self-confident man of influence and power who just happened to bat balls with Tony almost every weekend, the fact is that my world had changed beyond recognition. Being friend and fundraiser for Tony Blair, leader of the Opposition, was one thing. Once he had actually moved into Downing Street, it was quite another. Tony was now the most powerful man in Britain. He would soon become one of the most powerful in the world. If influence was measured by access, 'face time', I had far more than most. And Tony understood and appreciated that my commitment to his and the party's success – and the interests and skills I could bring to bear – went well beyond raising money. There was one key, inescapable irritant, however. As I would soon discover, no one – not Cherie or Anji, not cabinet ministers, not even Alastair, or Peter, and certainly not me – had any real political status or influence beyond what was refracted off the prime minister. I remember suddenly putting my finger on what this meant for me personally, why life around Blair was so often difficult no matter how well things were going in my personal relationship with him, during a Friday-night dinner with Gilda a few months after the election. Yes, it was exhilarating to watch Tony rule, to be on such close terms with the man who was running the country. 'But, for the first time since Stanley Prashker, I have a boss.'

My major frustration was in trying to work out what role, beyond answering calls to raise funds, my new boss expected, or wanted, me to play. The only early certainty was that I was heading for the House of Lords. The new prime minister wasted no time in making good on the offer he had extended during his final months in Opposition, placing me on his first peerages list in the summer of 1997. This was Tony at his most sincere, and most generous. I also suspect, however, that in anticipation of possible media sniping, he wanted to get my elevation out of the way while his popularity was at a peak. In any case, as Lord Levy of Mill Hill, I was being nominated as a 'working peer'. When I was formally welcomed into the Lords, I was particularly pleased that my two 'supporters' were dear friends whom I admired and respected: the former Chief Rabbi Lord Jakobovits and Baroness Margaret Jay, who was Labour's spokesperson for health and women's issues in the upper chamber and whom Tony, the following year, would make leader of the Lords. My maiden speech, in December, was an attempt both to convey my sense of awe at the scale of the honour, and to mark out the area in which I hoped to make a real policy contribution. My theme was the huge potential, which I had sensed at Jewish Care, for a fuller partnership among government, business and the voluntary sector to resolve issues of opportunity and inequality in British society. Both of the sentiments in my speech came from the heart. I admit to a feeling of elation when the peerages list was announced. We were in Israel, and I ordered flowers for Friday-night dinner and had them sent to our home – with the same sense of excitement with which I'd asked Gilda on our first date – addressed to 'The Lady Levy'. In my Lords speech, I was more explicit in what the elevation meant to me. 'My lords,' I began, 'it is indeed a great honour and privilege for me . . . also for my family, my wife and children and my dear, late parents.' I didn't say so in the speech, but Gilda and the children knew that I was thinking above all of my mother, wishing inside that somehow it had been possible for her to survive to see this day. It was the exact opposite of the prayer of lonely thanksgiving that I would so often mumble to myself during the darkest hours of the 'cash for peerages' ordeal.

But the policy part of my Lords speech, my call for a new and wider sense of private–public partnership, making use of the special strengths of charities and volunteer organisations, was no less heartfelt. I had witnessed the extraordinary effect at Jewish Care of a new network of 'employment centres' that offered men and women who had lost their jobs a mixture of caring encouragement and practical help in how to equip themselves, and apply, for getting back into work. A sizeable majority of the 3,000 people who had been through these centres – communally focused and communally run – was already back in employment, a result no purely government programme was ever likely to match. I'd also seen our day centres – 'youth centres for the elderly' – transform thousands of lives. It was a model I hoped to explore more widely not only as a peer, but in the expectation of an even more direct input into policy as the head of a new government taskforce. Tony and I saw absolutely eye-to-eye on the issue, or at least I thought we did. It was at a speech to a Jewish Care meeting in 1994, only months after I'd met him, that he had announced a 'Labour Leader's Review of the Relationship between Government and the Voluntary Sector' – which essentially concluded that on social exclusion, work, care and other issues such a partnership was bound to produce far more than the sum of its parts. The aim now, in government, was to see how we could make it happen. Well before my speech in the Lords, with Tony's encouragement, a formal framework had been placed on Jonathan Powell's desk for the creation of 'The Prime Minister's Taskforce on the Active Community'. It was drafted – in his beautiful, ink-pen script – by Alun Michael, the Cardiff MP whom Tony had made deputy home secretary with special responsibility for the voluntary sector. I was earmarked to be the chairman of the group, with Alun as deputy chairman. It was to include leading business and academic figures, as well as another MP, Alan Howarth, who had been given responsibility for coordinating Blair's 'Millennium Volunteers Initiative'. Another key name on the list was Cathy Ashton, who went on to play a key role in the launch of the Sure Start initiative and is now leader of the House of Lords. Jonathan was enthusiastic. Alun's proposal forcefully pointed out that the initiative would make a timely contribution to building both on the government's 'welfare to work' programme and on the fact that, following the death of Princess Diana a few months earlier, 'many people are looking for new ways of expressing positive social and personal beliefs'.

Yet in the end, it was left to gather dust. This was particularly unfortunate given the prominence that the issue of such a three-way partnership has now assumed for Blair's successor in Downing Street, Gordon Brown, and for his Tory challenger David Cameron. I did go on, the following year, to begin enormously satisfying work in helping to raise the profile of Britain's charitable and voluntary sector after I agreed to become the president of Community Service Volunteers (CSV), the country's largest volunteering body. It is a post I still hold, and through which – complementing the vision and dedication of CSV's director, Elisabeth Hoodless, and her staff – I work to promote and expand the work of a truly remarkable organisation. Yet I was genuinely disappointed by the stillbirth of the government taskforce. It was also a lesson to me in Tony's often short attention span, and his and Alastair's tendency to be seized by domestic policy ideas with obvious media potential and then not follow through. Yet I am sure that there was something else at work, too. While Tony could not have failed to recognise my frustration as we tried to define what contribution, beyond fundraising, I might make now that he was in Downing Street, I think he remained genuinely conflicted about precisely what role he intended me to play.

After the 1997 election, he had said to me: 'Michael, I want you to play an important part in what we accomplish,' and then added: 'I see you as my Lord Goodman figure.' The reference was to the Cambridge-educated lawyer Arnold Goodman. Although Goodman was among the most prominent lawyers of his generation, he was better known as the almost legendary behind-the-scenes adviser and political fixer for Harold Wilson. I suppose there were superficial parallels. Goodman was elevated to the Lords soon after Wilson moved into Downing Street, as I was by Blair. We were also both Jewish, and both in different ways prominent in Jewish community life. But I doubt that was in Tony's mind. He was genuinely colour-blind where religion, ethnicity or race were concerned. To the extent he registered my or others' Jewishness at all, it was to value it. Like Margaret Thatcher, he admired the sense of community mixed with ambition of British Jews, and the affinity that Tony felt was deepened by the importance of religion and faith in his own life. Maybe, I wondered as he repeatedly mentioned the 'Lord Goodman' model in describing how he saw our political relationship, he had in mind some broader non-governmental role. Goodman, after all, had also been a hugely influential head of the Arts Council under Wilson. But I think Tony's abandonment of the idea for our community taskforce suggested that a main attraction of the Goodman template was that it was essentially a behind-the-scenes role, without a high public profile.

I still have a brief note he wrote to me a few days after the election – it must have been one of the very first on his 10 Downing Street stationery – in gratitude for my 'extraordinary' help in his victory. 'We did it,' it began, adding: 'You made possible what we thought we could never do.' But the part I cherish above all comes at the end: a 'thank you' to both me and Gilda 'for your friendship, which I value above anything else'. We genuinely were – and, I hope, still are – friends. But I was also beginning to realise that Tony was above all a politician. He could not have failed to have been aware of uneasiness among some in the party over the way he had relied on an outsider to achieve the fundraising aim he had first confided to me when asking me to raise millions for his campaign chest – to free the party from the financial shackles of the trade unions. Particularly among Old Labour holdovers on the backbenches, the resentment rankled. And while Blair could sometimes be immensely brave in defending his vision of New Labour, as in his campaign to repeal the party's obviously outdated but symbolically important Clause Four nationalisation commitment after he became leader, he was reluctant, particularly in the first term, to pick, or even risk, further fights.

Yet perhaps the most important consideration was oddly overlooked throughout his premiership by all except those of us who worked with him closely and knew him best – because the criticism that Alastair faced as his 'spinmaster in chief' acted as a kind of lightning rod. The real spinmaster was Tony himself. Of all the things he loved about being prime minister, and he did love the job with very few exceptions even during its most difficult periods, he most enjoyed the public – and the media – stage. His view was that there was only one person who needed to be in the public eye, conveying how he and his government meant to lead and to change Britain. And that was Tony Blair. He felt that he understood the media, excelled at communication. If others around him tried to share that role they would do it less well, dilute his message – and steal the limelight. It was a feeling he even occasionally conveyed to me in frustrated remarks about Alastair, his only serious competitor as the media face of government – calling him at one point, only half jokingly, the *real* prime minister. His view that he alone should take centre stage seemed to harden into an almost messianic sense of self-confidence after his perfectly pitched tribute to the 'people's princess' after Diana's death. I recognised then, and still do, that this was also understandable. Tony *was* the best stage performer of the entire cast, by far. And he had the advantage of knowing precisely what message he wanted to convey. Still, for the rest of us – particularly for me as I tried to gauge exactly what role he wanted me to play, without as yet any formal title or office – it made any real public profile a recipe for trouble.

It also led to a rare instance of open frustration and anger – in the summer of 2000, when the *Sunday Times* published leaked details of my tax affairs for the previous year, and darkly suggested that my £5,000 bill for 1998–9 meant I'd been hiding income or not paying my full share. I was seething when I got wind of the story, not only because I felt the details could only have been obtained illegally, but because the stain on my character was absolutely unfair. The fact was that I had always made a point of paying my full tax bill. When I'd sold Magnet, I'd paid millions in capital-gains tax. The only reason my 1998 tax was so low was that I was no longer in business. Despite my media caricature as some wildly wealthy tycoon, a large part of my capital was not earning any income, as it was tied up in our homes in London and Israel. Gilda and I were living off capital on which tax had already been paid. What relatively little other income we had was in a separate company that I had set up – and for which I paid the additional required £30,000 in taxes. In the years immediately before and after, I paid much more tax. And I was determined to get that message across. But initially I ran into an unexpected barrier: Alastair above all, but Tony too, wanted me to say nothing at all. 'You can't talk to the papers,' was the unequivocal message. In the end, after I failed to get a court injunction to stop the *Sunday Times* from running the article, I argued that I would simply have to issue a statement setting out my side of the story. And in the end, Tony and Alastair agreed. But so important was the issue to me that, even had they held firm, I would have gone public anyway.

The encounter marked a further stage in what was becoming a difficult personal education in the high-stakes, high-ego, high-exposure world of national politics. And it undeniably reinforced the frustration I was coming to feel over establishing just what role I was expected to play in the constellation of personalities around the prime minister. Our relationship was clearly important to both of us. But it was also difficult to define, and the lack of definition became a growing strain until we finally settled on a role in which both he and I would go on to take enormous, and justifiable, pride. Beginning in the summer of 1999, I formally became the 'Prime Minister's Personal Envoy to the Middle East'.

In political terms, my new role hardly met the 'Lord Goodman' test of avoiding the public eye, and it inevitably led to a round of media criticism and suggestions that I'd somehow bought my way into a diplomatic world in the way top contributors to American presidential campaigns sometimes get foreign ambassadorships. In fact, it was an appointment with a clear logic and a long history. It was the Middle East, after all, that had first brought Tony and me together, at the 1994 Israeli diplomat's dinner after Tony's return from his first visit to the region. And no single issue beyond fundraising, in the years since then, had so often figured in our conversations. Indeed, I was centrally involved in his first real introduction to the promise and perils of peacemaking between Israel and the Palestinians nearly two years before he entered Downing Street. It was 4 November 1995 – a Saturday, just a few hours after he had headed back to Islington from an afternoon of tennis – when the news was announced that the Israeli prime minister Yitzhak Rabin had been shot and wounded at a rally in Tel Aviv's central square. With successive TV bulletins making it increasingly clear that Rabin was unlikely to survive, Tony phoned, shocked and upset, and asked whether I thought it was appropriate for him, as Labour leader, to go to the funeral – something he felt strongly that he should, and wanted to, do. I said yes, absolutely, and added that, having got to know Rabin personally over the previous few years, I was planning to fly out the following morning. We agreed we would travel to Israel together. But a couple of hours later he phoned again, saying that John Major had asked him and the Liberal Democrat leader Paddy Ashdown to join the official delegation. We agreed to link up several hours before the funeral at his hotel in Jerusalem.

When I arrived at Ben-Gurion airport near Tel Aviv, the entire country was in a high-security shutdown. I doubt I would ever have made it to Jerusalem had not my good friend Ephraim Sneh, one of Rabin's closest cabinet colleagues and a key figure in Israeli talks with the Palestinians, arranged to have his car meet me at the airport. The funeral itself was breathtakingly sad – the veteran military man Rabin had always been deeply sceptical about the prospects for a deal with the Palestinians, but he had become openly and passionately more enthusiastic about the peace efforts in the months before his murder. It was hugely moving, too. Among the mourners were not only Western heads of government, including President Clinton, but Egypt's President Hosni Mubarak and Jordan's King Hussein. During the hours beforehand, I had joined Tony in his tiny room at Jerusalem's King David Hotel (a contrast to the whole floor that would be blocked off when he visited Israel as prime minister). He was obviously despondent over the lengths to which opponents of an Israeli–Palestinian peace seemed prepared to go to frustrate those who were brave and visionary enough to pursue it. But typically he was determined to begin preparing himself to do whatever he could if he became prime minister to place Britain actively on the side of the peacemakers. And he was voracious in his appetite for first-hand knowledge. I had arranged to bring a dozen leading figures in Israeli politics to see him – including key figures in the peace talks like Sneh and Yossi Beilin – and also set up a phone conversation with Shimon Peres, the foreign minister, who would now succeed Rabin. It was a whirlwind education in the complexities of finding a way to end decades of hatred and violence. But I also think that Tony, with his deep religious faith, instinctively grasped in those emotionally charged hours just outside the Old City walls of Jerusalem the potentially momentous significance of a lasting peace. It made him even more determined to play whatever part he could in making it a reality.

Back in London, we began talking with increasing frequency about the Middle East. My own outlook, and range of relationships, had broadened greatly since my first days as a local JIA fundraiser. Partly, this was because I had met many more of the senior figures on the Israeli side – not only in Rabin's Labour Party but in Binyamin Netanyahu's right-wing Likud. But more importantly, I had begun building relationships with Arab politicians as well. And just as Gilda had played an important role in my growing interest and involvement in British politics, one key catalyst in my expanding involvement in Middle East affairs was also very close to home: our son Daniel. After he left Cambridge, he had spent two years living in Israel and travelling to Jewish communities worldwide as head of the World Union of Jewish Students. Then, he had stayed on in Israel, joining with a small group of Israeli Labour politicians and academics who had been involved in the 'back channel' talks leading to the breakthrough Oslo Accords and were now trying to work out provisions for a full Israeli–Palestinian peace treaty. In fact, as a startled Gilda found out by accident when an unfamiliar, Arab-accented voice answered the phone there one day, our home in Israel was the site for a number of these secret meetings. On our visits to Israel, I met not only Labour ministers, and Likud figures including future prime ministers Netanyahu and Ehud Olmert; I also began seeing Arab politicians who were involved in the peace process as well. I formed a particularly good relationship with Mohammed Bassiouny, Egypt's articulate and thoughtful ambassador to Israel. I was introduced to him at an American diplomatic reception, and arranged for us to get together and talk – the first of what would be a long series of meetings at his residence on Hanasi Street, not far from us in Herzliya Pituach. Bassiouny in turn introduced me to influential Palestinians, including the current Palestinian President Mahmoud Abbas, or Abu Mazen, whom I also began meeting at the ambassador's home. Blair was always eager to debrief me when I returned from a visit to Israel and, increasingly as the 1997 election approached, to discuss how Britain could play a useful part – alongside, he always recognised, the inevitably central role of the Americans – in making a Middle East peace possible.

When Blair came to power, he had a partner in the White House who was not only a natural political ally but almost a soulmate when it came to the issue of Middle East peace. And though Bill Clinton's presidency would before long be derailed domestically by the Monica Lewinsky scandal and the threat of impeachment, he responded in part by redoubling his efforts to secure a legacy overseas, and especially to broker a stable, lasting Middle East peace. When Blair first moved into Downing Street, he, too, saw this as a central foreign-policy goal, and we spoke frequently about how Britain could best play its part. And with his encouragement, although this went unreported at the time, I also began talking to his foreign secretary, Robin Cook, and others in the Foreign Office about what contribution we could make.

There was every reason to expect at the start, I suppose, that my relationship with Cook – a politically seasoned and ambitious new foreign secretary, anxious to make his mark – would prove difficult. I have no doubt that he was wary at first. But he also recognised that I had experience and expertise on the Middle East, the prime minister's ear, and perhaps crucially that as an outsider to the professional political class I was not interested in a seat at the cabinet table. Over the next few years, until his death from a heart attack in 2005, we would become close not only politically but personally – forging a friendship that, though very different from my relationship with Tony Blair, was in ways less complicated, and closer. In part, this was because we grew to respect each other during our work on the Middle East, but probably more important was the personal bond. I not only respected Robin – his intelligence, his wit, his dedication – but hugely liked him. So did Gilda, who found him not only charming and generous but, like her, much more 'genuinely Labour' than Tony. She particularly admired him for the dignity and principle with which he left government in opposition to the Iraq war.

Ironically, however, it was not Cook's huge strengths but a diplomatic setback that first cemented our partnership. It came in March 1998, on his first official visit to the Middle East, and it was a fully fledged disaster. Since Britain at the time held the rotating chairmanship of the EU, he set off for Israel and the Palestinian territories not only to provide British input into a stalled peace process but to convey new EU ideas on how to unblock it. He was never going to be received with diplomatic garlands in Jerusalem. Peres's brief tenure as prime minister had ended in defeat at the polls to the Likud's tougher-talking Netanyahu. Nor was there ever any doubt that Cook – like any British or European envoy – would have to make a point of reiterating opposition to the expansion of settlements on the West Bank. And he could not realistically have failed to visit the latest, and most controversial, of them all – on a hill the Israelis called Har Homa, on the outskirts of Jerusalem. But in delicate advance work for the visit, it had been agreed that he would limit any public intervention to a visit to an adjacent hilltop accompanied by Netanyahu's cabinet secretary. It all went horribly wrong. In driving rain, with rival left-wing and right-wing protesters shouting abuse at each other, Robin and his British embassy team retreated to another hill, where he spoke to a group of Palestinian legislators, and then, as their car was besieged by demonstrators, drove into predominantly Arab East Jerusalem for a further meeting with Palestinians there. Within hours, the visit was in disarray, with Netanyahu's office claiming that Robin had broken the understanding that he would make only a brief, Israeli-escorted visit to a hill near Har Homa. And it got worse. As Cook arrived for his meeting with Netanyahu, an Israeli spokesman told reporters the prime minister had cancelled the scheduled formal dinner for that evening. Robin bravely tried to emphasise that he'd had not the slightest intention of engaging in political provocation, but had only come 'to advance the peace process' and inevitably to discuss 'big obstacles' including settlement expansion. But the Israelis were adamant. 'The Prime Minister's meeting with the British Foreign Secretary will be shorter than planned,' their statement said, adding: 'The Prime Minister decided not to hold a dinner with the British Foreign Secretary.' Whether Netanyahu was genuinely as enraged by the Har Homa chaos as he publicly signalled – it was as much a result of the weather and the protesters as anything else, and much more cock-up than conspiracy – I was never really sure. The Palestinians, in comments that made the situation with the Israelis only worse, insisted that it was simply a deliberate attempt by Netanyahu to send a message to the White House – that public pressure on Israel over settlements would set back hopes of any early breakthrough. Certainly on the political right in Israel, there was nothing Robin could have done to allay enmity and suspicion. Even before he'd arrived, someone had – appallingly – sprayed graffiti slogans on the British consulate in Jerusalem saying: 'Robin Cook is an anti-Semite' and 'Robin Cook, go home'.

When he did get home, he was shell-shocked. I did all I could to reassure him, greeting him, only half jokingly, by saying:

'Welcome to the wonderful world of the Middle East conflict.' Much more importantly, in the days and weeks afterwards, I made a point of conveying to leading Jewish community figures, and to my Israeli government contacts, a message that I hoped would be reassuring and that I knew to be true – that Robin was an extraordinarily gifted and determined foreign secretary committed to supporting both the absolutely central requirements of any peace, Palestinian rights and Israel's own security. Once the political and media noise around his Israel visit subsided, it was crucial for Israel to build a close working relationship with a man who was certain to emerge as an important player in regional diplomacy. That message, it became clear before too long, was understood, and accepted. Robin did get ever more deeply engaged, alongside Tony, in Middle East diplomacy over the next several years, and my own damage-limitation efforts after his first trial-by-diplomatic-fire were the start of a real bond between us.

Tony and Robin were clearly critical in the political decision to formalise my Middle East role in August 1999, after I'd made an initial series of visits to Egypt, Jordan and Syria, and to redefine the job of Cook's immensely capable special adviser Andrew Hood to support my assignments as well. But the initial push came from a professional diplomat of huge experience in the region who was then head of the Foreign Office's Middle East and North Africa desk, Derek Plumbly. And Derek, who would go on to be ambassador to Saudi Arabia and Egypt, was the prime mover in suggesting I embark on what was probably the most fascinating, delicate, heartening yet finally frustrating of the many dozens of diplomatic missions I went on to fulfil for the prime minister in the Middle East and beyond.

It took place at the end of November 1999. It was my third visit to Syria. The aim – or at least the hope – was to hold detailed talks with President Hafez al-Assad and see whether a way could be found to secure a truly major breakthrough in the stalled Middle East peace process – direct talks between Syria and Israel. My initial visit to Damascus, in the spring, had been my first real experience of the sharp end of Arab–Israeli diplomacy. I had already built up relationships with Palestinians during my visits to the region. I had held the first of what would become many meetings with Egyptian President Hosni Mubarak's veteran foreign-policy adviser, Osama al-Baz, and in mid-1999 travelled to Amman to meet King Abdullah, who several months earlier had succeeded his late father, King Hussein, as ruler of Jordan. But Egypt and Jordan were already formally at peace with Israel, and the Palestinians were at least openly negotiating with the aim of eventually reaching a deal. Syria was a much more reluctant neighbour. And President Assad, during his nearly three decades in power, had built a reputation for ruthlessness against any opposition at home and for *summud*, 'steadfastness', against what his government's client news media routinely called the 'Zionist-imperialist conspiracy' of Israeli and American power. However, he also had a reputation as a pragmatist. Amid huge changes in regional and world politics – the unravelling of his longtime ally the Soviet Union, and the first US-led invasion of Iraq to force Saddam Hussein's army out of Kuwait – there had been glimmers of hope that he might be open at least to considering renewed peace talks. Significantly, he had sent a Syrian delegation to the 1991 Madrid Conference, convened a few months after the first Gulf war, and for a few years there were quiet, steady efforts, largely through the

Americans, to make progress on a Syrian–Israeli peace. Those efforts, however, were finally overshadowed by the Oslo Accords that grew out of the secret talks between Israel and the Palestinians. The Middle East diplomatic and political focus in recent years had been on resolving that conflict.

As I boarded the plane in Cairo to Damascus for the first of my Syria visits earlier in the year, even the knowledge that I was carrying a fulsome personal letter of introduction from Britain's prime minister could not fully quell a sense of apprehension. Assad, whom I hoped but was not sure would see me, was an almost legendary Middle East hard-man. I found myself repeatedly heading for the toilet. By the time we set down at Damascus airport, I doubt I had ever relieved myself so often at 37,000 feet. In the event, my visit was extraordinarily interesting, and encouraging. I met for several hours with Farouq al-Sharaa, Assad's veteran foreign minister. Smooth, articulate and disarmingly frank, he left little doubt about his and the president's deep scepticism regarding Israel's willingness to meet their minimum requirement for any peace – a full withdrawal from the land Israel captured in the 1967 Middle East war. He also delivered further, disappointing news. President Assad was ill – it was known that he had intermittently suffered from heart problems and diabetes for some years – and would not be able to receive me. But he immediately added that Assad would very much like to meet as soon as he recovered, and he invited me to return to Damascus. I did return in June, and had a warm, if slightly formal, meeting with President Assad that I hoped might eventually provide the basis for an ongoing dialogue with one of the most influential, and famously enigmatic, leaders in the Arab world.

Now, on behalf of Tony, I was essentially putting that hope to the test. When I arrived in Damascus for the third time, on Tuesday 30 November, I came with none of the jitters or apprehension of my first visits. The diplomatic atmosphere had also changed, if only slightly, for the better. In Israel, the Labour Party leader Ehud Barak had been elected prime minister in July over Netanyahu's Likud. A tough former commando and army chief-of-staff, Barak was seen as very much in the mould of Rabin, and was pledged to pull Israeli troops out of Lebanon and reinvigorate peace negotiations. Significantly – as he made clear both when I'd met him in Israel, and during official talks with Tony and Robin in London – he was focused not only on negotiations with the Palestinians but also on the prospect of attempting a deal with Syria. Palestinian leaders suspected an ulterior motive – to use the 'Syrian track', and the idea that he might do a separate deal with Assad, as a means of extracting new concessions from them. And they may have been right. But the fact is that peace between Israel and Syria would have transformed the Middle East. And Tony, in particular, felt that even the slightest ray of light on the Israel–Syria front was too important to ignore. More importantly, the Clinton administration had also been in exploratory talks with the Syrians, and Secretary of State Madeleine Albright was due in Damascus only a week after me. Still, no one realistically expected a breakthrough any time soon – as I discovered almost immediately after my arrival. When I arrived at Damascus airport, I was met by the British ambassador, Basil Eastwood, and we drove the fifteen miles into the Syrian capital. We first went to the British embassy, to compare notes with Ryan Crocker, then the American ambassador to Syria and later Washington's envoy to Iraq. After we had retreated to a secure room to avoid the ever-present prospect of bugging, I explained my mission – to convey Britain's views on the importance of a revived peace process and talks with the Israelis. Aware that Albright was also poised to visit, I added that we recognised – and were sure that the Syrians did, too – that any realistic hope for success could come only if the United States led the process. Crocker was supportive, wishing us well and asking us to keep him informed of any developments. But he added that neither he nor Washington thought there was any real hope of an early breakthrough. Even if things went well, we were at the fragile beginning of what would almost certainly be a long, potholed negotiating road.

He was every bit as surprised as we were, therefore, when we were interrupted by a message from al-Sharaa's office. The long-accepted protocol for foreign envoys was to hold talks first with the foreign minister, as I had during my earlier visits, and only then – presumably if those talks passed Syrian muster – to be invited to see Hafez al-Assad. But instead we were told that we would be taken within the hour to the presidential palace, a huge compound on a hill, approached by a long, snaking access road, on the edge of the city.

We were driven into the compound by presidential security guards, since no private cars are allowed to approach, and then entered the building itself. It was presumably designed to present awe-struck visitors with a sense of Assad's all-powerful role, and it did its job. We were taken down a seemingly endless white marble hallway. On each side, rooms opened up, and occasionally faces peeked out, but we carried on to the end of the corridor to a much larger room with a commanding view over the city. Assad greeted us at the door and ushered us inside, where for more than two hours the president and I talked, accompanied only by Eastwood and a Foreign Office specialist on our side, and by al-Sharaa, an official note-taker, and by Assad's longtime interpreter – now herself a cabinet minister – Bouthaina Shaaban. Assad looked somewhat gaunt, but that was the only outward sign of the final illness that would within six months claim his life. His voice was strong, his mind sharp, his command of detail daunting. Determined not to risk misunderstandings, I began by explaining my mission to convey personally from Tony the importance we attached to Syria's role in any progress towards Middle East peace. I was not, I emphasised to Assad's evident relief, here to overshadow or compete with the Americans. And I was not, I think to Assad's dismay, conveying any formal new message or proposal from Barak. But I did speak as someone with first-hand knowledge of Barak and his thinking, and of the current state of Israeli politics, and said that I was absolutely convinced the new Israeli leader was ready for a serious and sincere effort to make peace with Syria. Assad, for his part, said that both the Americans and Israelis were well aware that he had always been open to a peace agreement that ensured the full return of the territory Syria had lost in 1967, but he was cautious about the Americans' stance and very sceptical about Barak's, particularly since the Israeli prime minister's public statements during his visit to London had suggested no new willingness to deal seriously with the core issue of territory. The conversation was business-like but friendly. In terms of substance, however, it fitted the old diplomatic cliché – a full and frank exchange of views. When we left, it seemed to me Crocker had been right. Hopes of any breakthrough would have to wait.

Then, within the space of twenty-four hours, everything changed. The first indication came from the president as we were leaving the palace. He said I should go to see his son, Bashar, who had only recently been formally marked out as his heir-apparent. We were taken in a motorcade with blacked-out windows through a maze of streets to what appeared to be a military base, where Bashar was waiting. Our conversation covered similar ground to my meeting with his father, the main difference being that because Assad's son had studied in London and spoke English, he would occasionally expand on the comments of the interpreter. The meeting went on for almost as long as my talks with the president and ended so late that a formal dinner the Syrians had planned in my honour was called off. When Basil and I left to recap the day's events over a meal at a local restaurant we both agreed that on balance the visit had gone well. In addition to the encouragingly warm atmosphere that developed during the talks with Assad, I had been the first foreign visitor to meet Bashar since he had emerged as his father's designated successor. But barely had we finished our main course, than another – far more significant – development intervened.

No foreigners, indeed very few Syrians, ever disappear off the radar of the government's security services. Farouq al-Sharaa had little difficulty in discovering where we were dining, and the foreign minister's office phoned the restaurant to ask that I call him urgently. He asked me briefly to recount my understanding of the main points the president had made and, when I did, he said with evident relief that my account matched his own. But when I proceeded to thank him for their hospitality, and mentioned I was leaving Damascus on the first flight to Amman the next morning, al-Sharaa said: 'I wouldn't advise you to leave so quickly. The president would like to see you again tomorrow morning.'

It was an extraordinary invitation. Foreign envoys were not always guaranteed even a first meeting with Assad. A second was unheard of, and needless to say we arrived back at the palace on Wednesday morning intensely curious about what additional message Assad might want to convey. The first hour or so did little to clear up the mystery. Like al-Sharaa the evening before, the president – whose own father, I was told later, used to devise memory tests for him to sharpen his intellect – began by asking me in effect to play back my recollection of the previous day's meeting. Privately grateful for the rote learning of my Shacklewell Lane Hebrew classes, and the obsession for detail I'd learned in business, I responded with a precise, in places almost verbatim, account. Assad occasionally broke in, particularly to reiterate our shared understanding that America must play the lead in any renewed peace process, but he finally smiled and complimented me on my grasp of Syria's position. And then, for a further hour, our real talks began – and what I am convinced was the real reason for the second meeting emerged. There was much back-and-forth between us. Assad went through in detail what he thought would be necessary for a peace deal, yet also emphasised the importance of the next stage in contacts with the Americans and cited his reasons for deep scepticism about Barak and the Israelis. For one thing, he said, the Israeli leader was clearly saying 'different things to different audiences'.

But when I answered with my reading of the current Israeli political climate, and of Barak's position – explaining in detail my reasons for believing that while he still had to tread carefully for domestic reasons, the Israeli leader was genuinely serious about pursuing peace with Syria – Assad suddenly went far beyond his previously formulaic insistence on Syria's willingness in principle to make peace. He remarked casually that maybe one solution would be for both sides to 'put together teams to sit and talk until they reach agreement'. When I welcomed the idea, and tried to tease out with him exactly how it could be taken forward, he suggested that the groups should be 'high-level' and added: 'It doesn't need to be the president and the prime minister now, but at the end, yes. We would need to agree the basis of the talks first.' As I pressed the interpreter to confirm the extraordinary message – a readiness to open early, face-to-face talks with Israel with the aim of a peace deal and an eventual summit – she read back his words. Al-Sharaa broke in to go further, saying that by insisting on the 'basis of talks' before any summit the president had not meant that Syria and the Israelis would have to 'first agree what we would agree on'. Only, he said, an 'agenda'. And it was clear as our meeting wound down that only one agenda item – not security arrangements, or water, or any of the other frequently assumed problems – risked truly being a deal-breaker in any peace agreement for Assad: the principle that any deal must be based on 'the June 4 border' with Israel before the war of 1967. Assad had delivered what Ryan Crocker, and Madeleine Albright, least expected: the basis for a breakthrough.

It was a breakthrough, however, that the president and al-Sharaa wanted us to keep to ourselves for a further day. In fact, they insisted we tell no one that we had been called for a second round of talks, out of concern that the media would assume a new British peace initiative was under way, both raising expectations and potentially derailing the prospect of progress during Albright's visit. As it happened, an astonished American embassy did somehow discover that we had had a second meeting with the president – although not what was said. I boarded the first available plane back to London, which went through Vienna, only to find that one of my fellow passengers was none other than Bashar al-Assad, who was on his way for a private visit. We spent an enjoyable hour or so chatting in the VIP lounge and the duty-free shops in Vienna, but the conversation was about his studies in England, not prospects for peace back home. Nevertheless, in the weeks ahead, the relationships I had formed with the three most politically influential figures in Damascus – perhaps most relevantly, with al-Sharaa – were to prove invaluable.

The morning after my return to London, I went into Number 10, which had received a confidential outline of the Assad talks in a cable from the Damascus embassy, to brief Jonathan Powell and frame a summary for the Americans ahead of the Albright mission. While we were scrupulously careful not to go beyond the ground rules I'd agreed with the Syrians, the core of the message was clear, and compelling. Assad had made it clear to us he 'wants peace' and that he was ready for Syria to begin face-to-face talks with Israel to start laying the groundwork. But he clearly saw the Americans' role as crucial, and the Albright mission as a crossroads. He had at one point remarked to me that his proposal for talks was one of 'twenty or more ideas' on both the Syrian and US sides, and in effect was saying it was up to the Americans to use the Albright visit to pick up his overture and build on it. Washington was initially sceptical. But when the US secretary of state and the Americans' chief Middle

East negotiator Dennis Ross arrived for the talks in Syria, Assad proved as good as his word. He surprised the Americans by saying that he was ready for direct talks with the Israelis, initially involving his foreign minister, without preconditions – a turnaround that Ross describes as 'remarkable' in his own diplomatic memoir. 'For eight years, Assad had resisted anything like this,' Ross writes. And when he asked Assad 'off the record' at the end of their meeting why he had suddenly changed his mind, the Syrian president's reply was straightforward: he had concluded that 'Barak is serious'.

Within days, plans were finalised for Barak and al-Sharaa to fly to Washington in mid-December for the 'agenda-setting' talks Assad had suggested during our meeting. With Tony's approval, I flew out to Israel and met the Israeli prime minister at his home in Kochav Yair, near Tel Aviv, to convey the seriousness Assad clearly attached to what, if only in the light of his uncertain health, might well prove the last chance for some years to secure the peace breakthrough Israel had long sought. I outlined, too, my sense that there was willingness on the Syrian side to be flexible on a whole range of issues – *if* ultimately the deal led to a final frontier demarcation based on the border of 4 June 1967. And as I'd told the Syrians, I stressed that while we saw ourselves only as supporting players in an American-led peace process, we were ready to do anything useful to help facilitate it. Barak seemed to grasp the significance of the shift in Damascus, and was in an upbeat mood as he prepared to go to Washington. So was Farouq al-Sharaa, whom I met at the Heathrow Hilton when he stopped over in London en route to the talks. He was, he told me, genuinely optimistic. He felt both sides were serious. Washington was also fully engaged, and had undertaken to hold the negotiations in the US, allaying Assad's concern that otherwise the Americans might send lower-ranking diplomats and the process would founder. Most striking, emphasising that he was making this commitment 'for the first time', he suggested that if Israel accepted the core principle of returning the land it captured from Syria in 1967, Damascus could 'give Israel an honourable peace, and a sense of security in the whole of the Arab world and Middle East – a comprehensive peace'. Moreover, it need not take long, he said: the key issues were 'obvious' to all parties.

For a while, the optimism seemed justified. The talks got under way in earnest at the beginning of January, in a hotel and conference-centre complex in Shepherdstown, West Virginia – some ninety miles outside Washington. Though Albright was in the chair, Clinton himself joined by helicopter at key points in the negotiations. Yet, before long, problems emerged. The first, and less serious, was that while Israel's team was led by the prime minister, Syria was represented by al-Sharaa. He was a particularly powerful foreign minister, in substantive terms not greatly different to having Assad himself on hand. But as the president had told me in Damascus, he felt strongly that the time for summit talks was at the end, not the beginning, of the process. The much more important difficulty was in what was actually agreed, and especially the fact that Barak, having signalled his determination both to us and the Americans before Shepherdstown that he wanted to make rapid progress, suddenly got cold feet because he feared a political backlash at home. When the negotiators divided into working groups on the key issues, Syria was, as Assad had indicated, ready to be considerably more flexible than either Israel or the Americans could have hoped on longstanding roadblocks like security arrangements, the future normalisation of diplomatic relations between the countries, and water resources. But Damascus had assumed a trade-off: an early and explicit recognition that a peace treaty would formally 'demarcate' the Israeli–Syrian border on the basis of the pre-1967 war 'June 4 line'. During the Shepherdstown talks, the Israelis not only held off from giving the Syrians that assurance; they all but ignored the issue, focusing instead on technical aspects of drawing the final border – such as fencing and customs arrangements – rather than presenting the detailed map the Syrians had clearly anticipated. And when President Clinton, Albright and their teams proceeded to produce a draft summary of each side's position, bracketing areas of difficulty or disagreement, the problem was starkly clear. On the issue of a final border, the Syrians insisted that it be based on the 4 June line. The Israelis, although I am sure that Barak did recognise and accept this would inevitably be part of any peace deal, declared formally only that the frontier was to be 'mutually agreed'. Sharaa felt the talks had been a failure, with the Syrians giving ground on a number of issues only to discover that Barak was 'not serious' about what for them was the key: the border question.

He left for home, saying that Syria would resume talks when there was a genuine willingness to engage on the territorial issue. And I have no doubt he fully intended to resume the negotiations. When I spoke to him by phone on the eve of his return from Shepherdstown, he was relaxed, warm. When I asked at what point the talks would get started again, fearing that he might say he and Assad were pulling out for good, he replied that he didn't know, indicating that the Syrians simply wanted time to reflect and to press home their insistence that land was the key to making an overall peace deal possible. It was an impression that was reinforced when I flew back to Damascus at the beginning of February and again met with Assad and al-Sharaa.

In the event, the Shepherdstown talks never reconvened. But there was one last opportunity to rescue the hope for a historic, final peace between Israel and the Syrians. Barak did, I am certain, grasp its significance. Following a brief period of tension after the US talks broke up, serious work was done on all sides to resolve the crucial issue of land. It was a process made no easier for either side when the details of the American 'draft' from Shepherdstown leaked in the Israeli press. Barak, in particular, seemed increasingly worried about potential political backlash at home if he traded peace for a return of the land captured from Syria in 1967. Still, in the end the negotiating gap came down literally to a few hundred metres on the eastern side of the Sea of Galilee. Unlike the great majority of territory captured from Syria in 1967 – the towering, and fairly sparsely developed, Golan Heights – this area is level with the rest of Israel and had become very much a part of the country in most Israelis' eyes since the war. The Syrians ideally wanted it all back – though, since there was never any formal 'map' of the 4 June border, they had made it clear even at Shepherdstown that they would be open to allowing Israel to retain a 'strip' of a few dozen metres so long as the principle of a return to the 1967 line was agreed. Barak would not do that, or at least not unequivocally or publicly – though again, he too had signalled a readiness in private to accept the principle. The crucial, final chance to resolve the dispute and finally to achieve a peace deal came in March 2000, with Clinton himself taking the controls, at a summit with Assad in Geneva.

The Syrian president rarely travelled abroad, and now he was also very seriously ill. I have no doubt that the fact that he flew to Switzerland underscored his determination to deal with the last and most important piece of unfinished business during his years in power. He wanted to be able to say that he had recovered all the territory Syria had lost, and in order to achieve that goal was ready to be flexible on a whole range of other issues that Israeli leaders had pressed for decades. He also no doubt recognised that even if Bashar, when he became president, wanted to secure a land-for-peace deal, it would be some years before he had the power, security and self-confidence to risk reopening such a politically fraught line of diplomacy.

But the summit ended in failure. I was later told that Clinton, who was flying back from a physically taxing trip to India and Pakistan, was feeling ill himself, which cannot have helped. But the real problem was that the delay in getting to grips with the issue of the border at Shepherdstown and afterwards meant that realistic prospects for a deal had now simply run out of time. Clinton made a brave attempt to secure an eleventh-hour breakthrough. By Ross's account, he began the meeting with Assad, after 'initial pleasantries', by putting the best possible face on Barak's latest position. The Israeli leader, Clinton said, was now ready as part of Israel's earlier proposal for a 'commonly agreed border' to accept that part of an eventual peace deal would be a withdrawal to the 'June 4 line'. In fact, the Israelis were still making it clear that they wanted to retain something like 400 metres on the eastern side of the Sea of Galilee, as opposed to the Syrians' apparent readiness to concede only 50 metres. But that wasn't the deal-breaker, I think. It was precisely the kind of issue at which diplomats and draughtsmen excelled in the final stages of producing an agreement. The real problem was that Assad, when we'd met him in Damascus just a few months earlier, had clearly signalled not only his surprising readiness to start negotiations, but an eagerness to achieve an early deal – a point that al-Sharaa had emphasised further to me when he was en route to the talks in Shepherdstown. But Assad, only minutes into his summit with Clinton, must have realised a peace deal with the Israelis, even if it proved possible, was many, many months away. As would very soon become clear, time was a luxury he no longer had. Within two months, he would be dead, of a heart attack. And whatever the explanation for the final failure of the Geneva summit, the result was tragic. A full Israeli–Syrian peace would have changed the political topography of the entire Middle East. At a minimum, it might – as Barak had no doubt anticipated – have held out the promise of renewed progress with the Palestinians in the longer run. It would surely have altered the politics in the region during the later, crucial diplomacy in the run-up to the Iraq war.

Of the many dozens of missions I undertook during my nearly nine years as Tony Blair's envoy, my talks with Assad, al-Sharaa and Barak on a possible peace deal were undeniably a high point, although ultimately a major disappointment because the genuine efforts on all sides to seize a historic opportunity failed in the end. There was also a personal postscript, when I visited Washington and met members of the new Bush administration in April 2001. Inevitably, Syria came up, and we traded impressions on why the negotiations, and particularly the Clinton–Assad summit, had ultimately foundered. The Americans, interestingly, did not blame Barak. Nor even Clinton, except in the sense that they felt he had gone into the Geneva summit not only feeling ill but also ill-prepared on how best to engage with the Syrian president and his concerns. As was made clear in an official summary on my various meetings by the British embassy, a key Bush national-security adviser said, in particular, that he felt 'it had been a mistake not to draw on Lord Levy's experience in the run-up to the Geneva summit'. I mention this not because it was gratifying, though of course it was, but because the note – and its author – are especially relevant to addressing the occasional sniping I got in the media and beyond over Tony's use of me as an envoy. The note was signed: *Meyer.* As in Sir Christopher Meyer, then Britain's ambassador to Washington, who went on to make me one of many targets – along with Tony and others – for criticism in his memoirs after returning to London. Portraying me essentially as a vain diplomatic lightweight, he insisted that members of the Saudi and Jordanian royal families had told him that I was 'not terribly welcome in their countries' and that I had been 'received only out of friendship for Tony Blair'. That my relationship with Blair was crucial to any influence I was able to exert is surely true, and hardly surprising. That is what being a personal envoy of the prime minister was all about, a point I would have thought was obvious to an infallibly modest diplomatic heavyweight like Sir Christopher. As it happens, I never went to Saudi Arabia. But I did build up relationships in Jordan that proved critically helpful during periods of rising tension and violence between Israel and the Palestinians. In addition to talks with a range of senior Jordanian government ministers, during my period as envoy I had six long, detailed, friendly and fruitful meetings with King Abdullah. I came to respect his intelligence, his grasp of issues and his shared passion to serve his own country's best interests and those of an eventually stable, peaceful Middle East – in all these senses, he is very much his remarkable father's son. I do not know whether other members of the Jordanian royal family did indeed make the disparaging remarks that Meyer claims to have heard. If so, it would not upset me – nor detract from the substantive results of the repeated visits I made to Amman. Such remarks – by all players on the complex Middle East chessboard about almost any diplomat, from any country – simply come with the territory.

The crucial point, I think, is that Sir Christopher, and other commentators or Opposition politicians who occasionally engaged in sound-bite criticism of my work as an envoy, tended to have little or no first-hand experience of the Middle East, and certainly no detailed knowledge of my own role. Was I, am I, prone to vanity? The answer is yes, and maybe more than most – the flipside, I think, of the insecurities I still carry with me as the *shammas*'s son from Alvington Crescent. That is why perhaps the far more relevant, and to me reassuring, assessments of my work have come from the seasoned, senior diplomats with whom I worked on my missions as Tony's representative. None more so than our man in Damascus, Basil Eastwood, whose reflections on his years as a British diplomat have been deposited in the 'diplomatic oral history' archive established at Churchill College in Cambridge. Referring to me as Blair's 'special envoy to everywhere' but above all as Tony's fundraiser and friend, he jokes that I used to take every opportunity to let drop that I played tennis with the prime minister. 'Every opportunity' is a bit exaggerated I hope, but occasionally, yes. Guilty as charged. And I am not in the least bit resentful of Basil's portrait of my personal foibles. But as he and I both recognised during our extraordinary role in the unfolding Syrian effort to negotiate a peace deal, I was there in the end to do a job. And of that role, Basil records that the starting point of my visits to Syria was that 'Michael, who had strong connections with the Israeli Labour Party, had concluded, quite independently that there was a deal to be done with the Syrians'. He adds that a key element in our dialogue with the Syrian president was 'briefings about how he, Michael, saw Israeli internal politics in relation to the peace process at the time. It's extraordinary how useful that must have been because I don't think Hafez trusted the intelligence he was getting from his own people – he didn't trust anybody.' The ambassador goes on to recount some of the exchanges between Assad and me on just what was and wasn't necessary, and possible, if peace negotiations with the Israelis were to get under way. And he concludes, after referring to the fortuitous duty-free shopping interlude I shared with Bashar en route back to London from Damascus, by remarking: 'By this time, Michael, who's a very engaging personality, is a friend of the family! A man who was kissed warmly on both cheeks by Hafez al-Assad – a picture I will treasure in my memory!'

There is, of course, a natural, human temptation to overstate my role – a kind of Forrest Gump's-eye view of Middle East and world diplomacy. The fact is I was never a professional diplomat, and in my role as envoy came hugely to respect the career ambassadors and Foreign Office experts without whom I simply could not have operated. But in the same way that my relationship with Tony benefited precisely from my *not* being a professional politician, I think there is little doubt that whatever success I achieved as envoy was partly because I was a personal representative, with Tony's ear and my own idiosyncratic approach. One of the diplomats who accompanied me on a later series of meetings in Latin America – in a memorandum summarising the results of the trip for Robert Culshaw, head of the 'Americas' desk at the Foreign Office back in London – remarked that 'Lord Levy's style is a mix of Jeremy Paxman and Bruce Forsyth, with the direct questioning and sharpness of the former and the warmth, good humour and bonhomie of the latter. He is a shrewd judge of character, summing his interlocutors up quickly and adapting his style to ensure that he gets the best out of everyone he meets.' It was a generous tribute. And no doubt there were times, and missions, in which I did not always live up to it. But I do think it sums up the spirit in which I embarked on each of my trips as Blair's envoy. And I have no doubt that on a range of specific issues, in countries where Tony felt Britain needed a direct voice or firmer friendships, I made a difference. On the Israeli–Palestinian front, I became very much a partner in his increasingly direct and detailed personal involvement in the search for peace. And in my talks in Syria – partly no doubt because Assad chose to use me as a conduit for conveying a potentially enormous shift, but also, as Eastwood suggests, partly because our genuinely open dialogue on Israeli politics helped encourage him in that direction – I had at least some role in a process that very nearly changed history.

The Damascus mission not only reinforced my role as the prime minister's envoy, but drew me into ever closer contact with Robin Cook as well. Since my job description was to represent Tony, with Foreign Office liaison and support, I was not technically working for Robin. But I think particularly because of the scars he carried from his first Middle East visit, and my efforts to calm the waters afterwards, he asked me to join him on subsequent visits to Israel and the Palestinian territories. On a personal level, too, we became closer. I particularly enjoyed his uproariously funny portraits of fellow Labour politicians, and sometimes of world leaders – never venomous, always absolutely to the point, and leavened by the equal wit that he sometimes directed back on himself. He also frequently used me as a line of communication with Tony, particularly in the period before he and Blair began to build a stronger bond through their shared stewardship of Britain's key role in forcing the Serbian dictator Slobodan Milosevic to pull his forces out of Kosovo in June 1999. Tony genuinely rated Cook, respected his intelligence, but I think never really felt the kind of implicit trust and partnership he had with the core of ministers who had been on side since his leadership run, like Straw, or the key 'Blairites', like Alan Milburn, Steven Byers, Tessa Jowell and of course Peter Mandelson. Still, I think this was a disservice to Cook. His history of enmity with Gordon Brown from their early days in the Scottish Labour Party made it highly unlikely he would ever make common cause with the only real internal threat to Blair. Besides, Robin revelled in the job he had, enjoyed every minute and every aspect of being foreign secretary. Having long abandoned any leadership ambitions of his own, he often told me – and I absolutely believed, and believe, this was the truth – that he hoped that his crowning achievement in politics would be as Labour's longest-serving foreign secretary. So much so that when, in 1999, after the Kosovo crisis, Blair offered to nominate Robin as the Secretary General of NATO – an international role, with pay and perks overshadowing even his own as one of the four top ministers in British government – he turned it down. He explained to me that he had a job he loved, that he felt he was good and getting better at, and which he had every hope and expectation of occupying for as long as Tony was in Downing Street.

Robin was not the only person who saw my personal relationship with Tony, and less directly with others in the party hierarchy, as occasionally useful in conveying messages they felt were important but too often unheard. Not long after the Kosovo crisis, Charles Guthrie, the chief of defence staff, invited me to see him and suggested I visit the British troops who were playing a key role in ensuring that Milosevic's climb down could be built upon to establish longer-term stability in the Balkans. I readily accepted the offer. A few days before I was due to go, an aide phoned and asked whether I had my own sleeping bag – to which I delicately replied in the negative. Somehow our Clapton Club excursions to historic sites had never quite stretched to overnights around the campfire. He might just as well have asked me whether I had a rifle, or a polo pony. But I was genuinely excited by the prospect of the Kosovo visit, and was not disappointed. It left me not only hugely impressed, and charmed, by General Guthrie, but in awe of the dedication and professionalism of Britain's troops in the field. The message Charles had clearly wanted me to take away, however, was not so much for Tony's ear as for Gordon Brown's. Charles was convinced, even before Iraq, that in a post-Cold War world Britain's armed forces were likely to face unpredictable challenges. He was deeply concerned by what he saw as the chancellor's lack of interest in, or real understanding of, military matters. He was alarmed that the armed forces, at a time when they were likely to be asked to do more and not less, were being faced with pressure dramatically to cut costs. He warned me that, in years ahead, this would prove to be a false economy that Britain would come to regret. I was persuaded by his impassioned argument, and regretted only that I did not have a sufficiently close relationship with Gordon to press the point with him. I regret that even more now, in the light of the major commitments of our young men and women in uniform in Iraq and Afghanistan. So, of course, does Charles, who along with other senior military figures finally went public with his message after Gordon became prime minister in 2007.

But Tony's own focus, by the beginning of 2000, was increasingly to ensure that his tenancy in Number 10 would last, and that he would break Labour's unhappy history of one-term rule. And my focus, he said, should be on beginning to build up a war chest at least as large as before 1997 to ensure we were ready to fight and win an election in 2001. Thankfully, Gilda and I had now sold The Warren – opulent, but somehow soulless – and moved back a few miles closer to Mill Hill. Our new home was, like The Warren, grand enough to go by a name, not a number. It was called Chase House. It had even larger grounds, with a pond, a huge lawn, both an indoor and outdoor pool, and a tennis court. But the house itself was much more compact, and we refurbished and reworked it around a large, open kitchen and eating area, a comfortable ground-floor office, and upstairs bedrooms that gave it the genuinely family feel we had so loved in Uphill Road. And the location was stunning, tucked at the end of a quiet, narrow back lane yet with a commanding view over London. It also had a large dining room – which was soon the venue for a new round of dinners that Gilda and I hosted with the aim, first, of making sure Labour's general party finances were flush and then, more urgently, building up an election-campaign fund. Though Tony and Cherie were usually the star attractions, both he and I were keen to ensure a clear dividing line between his Labour leader's role and any suggestion of using his office as prime minister to help in our fundraising. From the start, we agreed that fundraising functions would not be held at Downing Street or Chequers, and they never were. But Tony *was* prime minister, and the fact that he headed a government that had every hope of staying in power unquestionably made my job in securing donations easier.

In the end, I helped raise about the same amount as before 1997 – roughly £15 million – for the campaign chest. But significantly, almost all of it was raised well before election day, in the final few months of 2000. And the reason for this foreshadowed a huge change in how we, and other parties, would fund future campaigns – a change that helped create the conditions, just a few years later, for the 'cash for peerages' mess. The catalyst for the change was Tony himself. Having committed Labour to more openness and accountability in political funding before the 1997 election, he had been further hardened in his determination to establish new party-funding rules by his early embarrassment over the Ecclestone affair. With the standards commission recommending major changes, and Jack Straw as home secretary especially convinced that they should go as far as possible, the government drew up the Political Parties, Elections and Referendums Act 2000 – PPERA – which set up an electoral commission to oversee a new set of much tighter rules, including the listing of all party donors and the amounts they gave. Clearly, it was not my place to get involved in the details of the funding laws. In any case, Tony knew that I fully shared his view that the existing rules – or more accurately, the lack of them – had for years given the Conservatives free rein to raise millions, far more than Labour, in utter secrecy, often from overseas. A change was long overdue. But I did make clear both to Tony and Jack two practical concerns. The first was that no matter how tight the rules, political parties would always try to exploit inevitable loopholes. I had deep suspicions that the Tories, in particular, would continue to find a way to get money from sources that were beyond domestic oversight or control. The second was more basic. In an increasingly aggressive 24/7 media age, many potential donors would simply not contribute large sums to a party if and when the system required publication of their names and the exact amount they had given. Jack said that didn't matter, Tony was focused on the principle of necessary reform and didn't see why the details should be a problem, and the change went through. But it did matter. I raised millions from donors before the new law came into effect in early 2001, and many of them explained in similar language why they were giving now, and not later. 'I pride myself in having worked hard to make a success of my business. And I think Blair has done a good job and want to help him get another term,' one of them told me. 'But I'll be damned if I'm going to pay the price of having reporters dig through my life's history or bother my wife and kids in the search for some scandal. It's not worth it.'

As the 2001 election drew nearer – even with internal wrangling over whether to push back the date as a result of an increasingly worrying epidemic of foot-and-mouth disease in British livestock – Tony was in a generally more optimistic frame of mind than before 1997. He still had his nagging politician's paranoia that it could all go wrong, but he fundamentally expected to win – the only concern being by how much, and whether the mandate would be large enough to move beyond the grand policy strokes of the first term and, as he put it, 'really begin to change things'. We spoke, inevitably, less often than in the more relaxed years of Opposition and the early months in Downing Street. But we were still in frequent contact, whether by phone or, if by now much less often, on the tennis court. Interestingly, the focus tended to be less on Labour and domestic government than on the wider world: Kosovo, the Middle East, the US. He still felt that he had much to accomplish domestically, of course, above all a genuine reform of Britain's public services and a shift of power away from Whitehall managers to the ordinary citizen. But he had changed in those first four years, and increasingly saw his role as being not just national, but international. He had tasted the world stage, and particularly after crucially prodding the Americans towards a tough and ultimately successful showdown with Milosevic, enjoyed that role hugely. I, on a much smaller scale, had undergone a similar change – from fundraiser to envoy, from a role limited to my relationship with Tony to an equally invigorating partnership with Robin Cook. And when election day finally came – delayed by foot-and-mouth until June – I looked forward with real excitement to the prospect of Labour winning a second term in government.

So when Tony triumphed, with an only slightly reduced majority of 167, perhaps the last thing I expected was that my first post-election chat with the re-elected prime minister would leave me feeling angry, exposed, manipulated, and misled.

My maternal grandparents, the Reverend Abraham and Bella Birenbaum.

My parents, Annie and Samuel.

(Right to left.) My father and mother, Aunt Cissie and my paternal grandparents, Sarah and Abraham Levy, and me.

Gilda's parents, Mimi and Bruno.

As a young boy.

With my mother at
my barmitzvah.

My best man, Barrie Berns (left) stands with me and Gilda on our wedding day.

With Gilda on our honeymoon.

In my music industry days.

Presenting Alvin Stardust with a Gold Disc.

Presenting Chris Rea with his Gold Disc.

With Yitzhak Rabin, when national campaign chairman of the JIA.

With Shimon Peres discussing the Middle East.

At Babe Ruth's restaurant. With me are Tony Blair (before he was Prime Minister), Catherine Blair, Clive Bourne, Gale (Cherie's mother), Cherie, Joy Bourne and Gilda.

With Chris Smith, Cherie and George Robertson at the Brits dinner.

With Tony Blair.

At a CSV Make a Difference Day, helping to paint a dilapidated centre in London's East End. With me are Oliver Heath and Martin Lewis.

Engaged in charity work with Jewish Care.

With Yasir Arafat, Robin Cook and Nabil Shaath, the former Foreign Minister for the Palestinian National Authority, in Gaza.

With Ehud Olmert and Sir Nigel Sheinwald, British Ambassador to Washington and former Chief Foreign Policy Adviser to Blair, in Jerusalem.

With (right to left) Abu Mazen, Martin Indyk (the former US Ambassador to Israel), Madame Frydman, Mohammed Bassiouny (the former Egyptian Ambassador to Israel) and French businessman Jean Frydman.

With Kofi Annan at the UN Headquarters in New York.

With President Hafez al-Assad of Syria, in Damascus.

With King Abdullah II of Jordan and the British Ambassador, Christopher Battiscombe, in Amman.

With Bill Clinton and Tony Blair at a Policy Network conference.

With Bill Clinton at a Labour party conference dinner.

With Tony Blair lighting Chanucah candles on an official trip to Israel.

With Gordon Brown.

At my introduction into the House of Lords with Gilda.

With Tony Blair.

With Her Majesty the Queen visiting a school on a volunteering day.

Daniel and Juliet.

With the family on safari. From right to left; Vally, my son Daniel, Gilda, my daughter Juliet and Phil.

CHAPTER 8

Storms After the Calm

When the phone rang after the election, and the familiar voice from the Downing Street switchboard said 'the prime minister would like to speak with you', I expected a short, cheerful chat about an extraordinary victory. Tony had become the first Labour prime minister to have won a second successive term in office. But instead, his voice sounded sober and troubled, and he got straight down to business. 'Michael,' he said, 'I need your help – with Robin. I have told him I am moving him from foreign secretary, and he's really pissed off. I've asked him to be leader of the House and president of the Council, but I really don't think he wants to do it.'

I was furious, as Tony must have anticipated I would be.

Twice during the past few years, the second time only weeks before the election, he had told me he was going to keep Cook on as foreign secretary. It was an assurance that he knew (and made it clear he intended) I would pass on to Robin. The first message had been critical in Cook's decision to turn down the top job at NATO, for which Blair proceeded to nominate the defence secretary, George Robertson. Tony also knew how much Robin loved his job, and must have recognised the skill and devotion he had brought to it. What he couldn't have known, but what made me even angrier at Tony as I framed in my mind how I would answer him, was that Robin had been so certain of his reappointment that he had arranged for his son to meet him later that day at Chevening, the lakeside mansion in Kent that is the foreign secretary's official country residence. 'How could you *do* this to him?' I finally said. 'You told me Robin was going to carry on!' He didn't deny that. He couldn't have. But now he said that he had always intended to keep Cook on only for a year or so, and then would have moved him anyway. He had decided it would be far better to make the change at the start. Retaining Robin for just part of the next parliament, he said, would have been messy, and pointless. 'But at least then, you wouldn't have let him down,' I replied, biting my tongue to keep myself from adding the obvious postscript: 'and been *dishonest* with him, and me.' 'You've handled this so badly,' I said. Nevertheless, in the end, as I imagine he knew I would, I agreed to try to talk Robin into taking the new assignment. This was partly because it was not easy to say 'no' to a prime minister, especially a prime minister who was also a friend (as would again prove true, with far heavier personal consequences, in the events leading up to the 'cash for peerages' crisis). It was also because I genuinely felt it would be best for Robin, in some capacity, to stay on.

It was not an easy sell. Robin was crushed, not just by the public embarrassment of his demotion, but by seeing his dream of becoming Labour's longest-serving foreign secretary suddenly taken away. He felt 'absolutely humiliated', he told me. And I remember reflecting that I was not alone in this strange world of politics in sometimes feeling so insecure, no matter how high I had risen, or in having to come to terms with the fact that only one person ultimately mattered – Tony. Still Robin's two new jobs would give him a measure of influence, I argued. They would offer a continued outlet for his energy, intellect and talents. As leader of the House, he would play a front-line role in the party and in Parliament. And as 'Lord President of the Council' – though its one formal duty, Robin well knew, was to preside over meetings of the Privy Council – he would retain a seat at the cabinet table. 'At least,' I quipped, trying without much success to bring him out of his despair, 'they'll call you "Mr President"!' He had every right, I told him, to feel angry and let down. But he had to look beyond the immediate sense of defeat and deflation. His longer-term interests – and that of a British political stage on which there were very few figures of his experience and insight – lay in carrying on. If he walked away now, he would regret having retreated to the bile and bitterness of the backbenches. And upset though he was, I think it was a message he finally accepted because deep down he knew that it was true.

I had got on fairly well with Robin's successor, Jack Straw, ever since I first met him during Blair's Labour leadership campaign. But while we developed an increasingly warm partnership during his five years as a dedicated and effective foreign secretary, I never formed as close a personal relationship as I had with Cook. Blair had decided to promote Straw – Jack expected to be *demoted*, to take charge of Environment and Transport – because he saw him as fundamentally steady, safe and loyal. It was a view not all at Number 10 shared, and one that Blair himself would begin to question in private long before he finally shunted aside Jack, as he had Robin, into the role of leader of the House in 2006. At the time, the media speculated it was because Blair wanted to assuage the Americans' anger – over Jack's tepid response to their insistence on keeping open a 'military option' in order to prevent Iran from getting nuclear weapons. In fact, Straw was sacked because for months he had reverted to what one of Tony's inner circle described as 'student politics' – cosying up to Gordon Brown around the cabinet table in a bid to curry favour with the heir-apparent. The plan had been to move Straw immediately after the 2005 election, not a year later. Tony delayed not because he still believed Jack was loyal. It was because of a familiar tendency – increasingly damaging to all concerned, including Tony himself – to avoid personal confrontation with his cabinet ministers at almost any cost. In Robin's case, I had just witnessed the personal toll of Tony's inability to be straight with his unsuspecting victim at uncomfortably close quarters.

Within days of becoming Cook's successor, Straw invited me to meet him at the Foreign Office. He was already focused on his new job – and well briefed on the work I had been doing as Tony's envoy. He began by saying that he greatly valued my input, and wanted me to carry on with my missions, and we discussed in broad terms the major issues that would demand attention in the Middle East. But surprisingly he went further. Not only did he want me to remain as envoy, he said; he had also decided to make me a privy councillor. It was an idea that had first been raised about a year earlier by Robin. I had assumed Cook would act on it at some point during what we both felt would be a much longer run as foreign secretary. But Jack's decision was obviously gratifying for me, an early vote of confidence. Though it conferred no real political or policy power, a place on the Council – the bulk of whose membership consists of the cabinet and former cabinet ministers – was a huge honour. I left the meeting still feeling immensely sad that Robin had lost a job that he loved, and at which he excelled, but confident that Cook and I would remain personal friends – as we did – and that in my role as envoy I might be able to help build on his record in a steadily closer partnership with Straw.

My relationship with Tony, however, was first hit by another, unanticipated squall. A few days later, he asked me to come and see him in Number 10. I imagined the purpose was to find a way to put the tension over Cook's sacking behind us and focus on Tony's vision for his unprecedented second term as Labour Prime Minister. But instead, it became clear he had another agenda in mind. 'Michael,' he said, 'I'm sorry, but I can't make you a privy councillor.' I expressed surprise, saying: 'But Jack has already told me.' To which he replied: 'I know. He really shouldn't have done that without talking to me. I just feel that I can't do it.' And when I asked why, anticipating that he might cite some compelling reason of protocol or party politics, he replied simply: 'The press would really beat up on you.' I was naturally disappointed by his decision. Yet the main issue was not the honour itself – which although gratifying, was not the kind of thing that even in my most insecure moments I felt was worth getting overly worked up about. I was, above all, frustrated by the way Downing Street appeared to be changing Tony, and particularly by his growing obsession with the press. 'You're going to worry about the *media* when Jack has confirmed this appointment to me?' I said. 'Who's running *who*?' Yet Tony had made up his mind. 'Michael,' he said, 'I'm sorry, but I just feel it would be very bad for you. I'm only doing this for you.'

He was, of course, doing it for himself. His real concern was *his*, not my, image in the media. But to be fair, as I recognised once my initial anger had subsided, it was a call that was entirely his to make. I could hardly argue with the growing importance of the media in British political life. I had felt the effect at first-hand when the *Sunday Times* had run its story on my tax bill, a salvo which prompted me to seek specialist media advice of my own – from the veteran journalist, media specialist and commentator Ivor Gaber, and later from the former *Daily Express* editor Nick Lloyd. I suppose the difference in my mind was that my aim was essentially defensive, to keep my exposure to a minimum and try to ensure that what coverage I would inevitably receive was as positive as possible. Tony, it seemed to me, increasingly viewed the media not just as an important part of his plans and programme in government, but often as the determining factor in a whole range of decisions that he took. I believed that was a mistake, not only frustrating for me but damaging for him and what he hoped to achieve for Britain as prime minister. Yet I also recognised that it was something I would have to get used to if I still enjoyed and felt useful in my role as envoy, friend and fundraiser – and, much more importantly, if I still believed in what Tony wanted to accomplish in Number 10. I realised that I did.

In fact, I think the reason I was so upset by Tony's media-driven veto of the privy councillor's post was that it was not my first taste of his growing tendency to make decisions with an eye towards the next day's media coverage. And his first intervention, just a few months earlier, had placed a much more literal price tag on my role. During my initial series of diplomatic missions in the Middle East, before the exchange of notes between Number 10 and the Foreign Office formally setting out the terms of my position, I had of course made a point of paying for all of my travel costs. But especially after my series of meetings with the Syrians, John Kerr, the senior civil servant at the Foreign Office, and a number of his colleagues suggested that we should review the arrangement in the light of what was becoming a broader and, I suspect, more effective role than they had anticipated. Kerr joked that if I were to keep on footing the entire bill, it would be 'the best deal in the history of British diplomacy'. So I duly raised the question with Tony. Yet his response was that it would be best to leave things as they were. Otherwise, he said, there might be 'trouble in the press'. And I acquiesced – a recognition of 'rule by media' that, by the time I made my final foreign trip as envoy to meet the Israeli foreign minister just months before Blair left office, would end up having cost me a very substantial sum of money.

Not that I was ever seriously tempted to walk away, least of all in those personally difficult early months of Blair's second term. After the later battering of the 'cash for peerages' ordeal, I had forgotten just how badly that first serious period of disillusionment with Tony affected me – until I came across a warm and generous note that Straw sent me while he was on holiday in Italy that August. 'I wanted to write you because I was really quite worried after our last conversation, just before you left for holiday,' he said. 'You sounded so down and depressed. I hope very much that it was just pre-holiday exhaustion, and nothing more. You give so much to other people that it seems to me that you sometimes don't have much for yourself.' And he added: 'I wanted to express my great appreciation of you for all that you have done for the party, for Tony, and for the personal support you have so readily given me.' He now looked forward, he said, to our getting back to work on the major issues facing us in an increasingly worrisome Middle East.

'Worrisome' was an understatement. By the autumn of 2001, the simmering Israeli–Palestinian conflict had exploded into serious and escalating violence, which was one major reason I was particularly determined to carry on in my role as Blair's envoy. After the prospects for the Syrian breakthrough had ended with Hafez al-Assad's death the year before, President Clinton summoned Barak and the Palestinian leader Yasir Arafat for a last-ditch summit at Camp David, in the hopes of securing a peace deal between Israel and the Palestinians. That it failed was bad enough, and perhaps predictable. But the effect was made worse by the fact that Clinton again got so tantalisingly close to success. Barak, in Israeli political terms, was brave. For the first time, he agreed to the idea of a future status for Jerusalem with some measure of shared control with the Palestinians. It was a concession that almost immediately brought cries of betrayal back home from the right-wing Likud, which was now led by a military veteran with an even more daunting battlefield record than his own: Ariel Sharon. But for Arafat, since the Camp David proposals would not have given the Palestinians outright sovereignty over the Arab east of the city, it was never going to be enough to fend off similar charges of betrayal from his own rivals. Sharon soon dramatised his challenge to Barak by marching – along with dozens of Likud politicians, reporters, and Israeli security officers – on to Jerusalem's Temple Mount and into the Al-Aqsa mosque complex, Islam's third-holiest site. The following day, after Friday prayers, rioting erupted. And within weeks the 'second intifada', or Palestinian uprising, was raging. The first intifada, nearly a decade earlier, had pitted stone-throwing Palestinians against Israeli troops. This time there would be gunbattles and firebombs, suicide attacks against Israeli citizens in restaurants, hotels and shopping malls, and Israeli military incursions into Palestinian towns and villages. Sharon, the Palestinians claimed, had provoked the violence. Arafat, the Israelis countered, had been planning a campaign of terror for months, and was waiting only for a convenient excuse. As I would so often discover when shuttling between the two sides for Tony, Robin and Jack, unravelling the truth was almost impossible. And, in the end, irrelevant, too. Our aim, then as now, was somehow to find a way to move beyond the issue of blame – and to get both sides back to the negotiating table. Nevertheless, I must say that the debate over whether Sharon's visit to Al-Aqsa 'started' the intifada always seemed to me particularly fruitless, because the simple fact is that the visit need never have happened. It *could* not have happened if Barak – not just as prime minister, but military man to military man – had called in Sharon and said that on security grounds it must not go ahead. Barak had entered office hailed as a leader in the mould of Yitzhak Rabin, and in many ways he did live up to his billing. He seemed genuinely to want a deal with the Palestinians, and he also came very close, if sadly never close enough, to an agreement with the Syrians. But there is no doubt in my mind that Rabin would have simply and starkly told his old comrade-in-arms Sharon that Al-Aqsa was off limits. End of discussion. Whether this would have avoided, rather than merely delayed, the terrible violence of the years that followed is much more difficult to say.

Sharon defeated Barak at the polls in early February 2001, only months before Tony had won his second election victory, and weeks after George W. Bush had moved into the White House. The Israeli election result was entirely predictable. Despite polls which showed a large majority of Israelis wanted peace with the Palestinians, and were ready for major compromises to achieve it, the escalating violence ensured that they were always going to vote with their fears rather than their hopes. Israel's voters wanted a strong man. And none better met that job description than the soldier-turned-politician known as 'the bulldozer' – Ariel Sharon. He won by a landslide, and Tony felt it was urgent that we should build a relationship with him. Both Tony and I recognised that a new stage in Britain's diplomatic role in the region was beginning. President Bush was almost ostentatiously uninterested in foreign-policy issues. The new administration was determined to avoid the hands-on role to which Clinton had devoted almost all his energy during his final months in office, only to fail and leave the Middle East more violent than he had found it. We both knew that a final peace deal, if and when it came, would not be negotiated by Britain – and certainly not by me. The Americans were the key. But the immediate danger was that in the absence of any negotiating process at all, the violence would get even worse, possibly ending the prospects of a compromise altogether. Our role was to keep talks, contacts, and hope, alive.

I flew out to Israel shortly before Sharon took office. I met briefly with Barak, as protocol demanded, before going on to see his successor. I visited the prime minister-elect at his sprawling ranch in the Negev Desert in southern Israel, and I arrived with some apprehension. I had never met Sharon, and as he and I both knew, I was much better connected with Israel's Labour politicians. But one of his close aides, who went on to head Israel's security organisation Mossad, had agreed to set up the meeting. It began formally, with an hour-or-so of fairly stilted discussion including Sharon's advisers, the British ambassador and the Foreign Office official who was accompanying us. But when I suggested to Sharon that we talk alone, 'one on one', he readily agreed. To the obvious alarm of his policy advisers, not to mention the security guards, we withdrew to the kitchen and talked much more frankly for well over two hours. The new Israeli prime minister was clearly anxious to get to know Blair, a feeling that I assured him Tony fully reciprocated. 'We are determined to work with you to help end the violence and see if together we can restore some hope for peace,' I said. 'We are not going to judge you on the basis of your past positions, or media images. We want to work with you as the prime minister and see how you feel it is best to move forward, and what progress is possible.' It turned out to be an extraordinarily warm meeting, and the start of what I hoped and assumed would be an increasingly fruitful personal dialogue. A measure of that early relationship came the day after our first meeting, when Sharon called me. He had already secured an agreement for Labour to join him in a coalition government, but the party's elder statesman, Shimon

Peres, was wavering over whether to take the role of foreign minister. Sharon asked me to phone Shimon and urge him to accept. With Blair's approval, I did so. And Peres (who I must say needed little persuading, since he was eager for a return to the front line after having been relegated to the regional-development ministry under Barak) did take the job.

But within a year my relationship with Sharon went suddenly, badly wrong, after one of the most difficult – and stormy – meetings I had during my entire period as envoy. Earlier in the day, I had gone to see Yasir Arafat to urge him on Tony's behalf to make a far greater and more visible effort to rein in the violence, in order to help unblock the negotiating process. I had left feeling cautiously optimistic – although, as so often after meetings on both sides as the violence escalated, considerably more cautious than optimistic. By the time I arrived at Sharon's office in Jerusalem, news reports had come through of the latest terror attack. The first hour or so of our meeting was businesslike, if also sombre. I had begun by conveying Tony's heartfelt sympathy for the victims of the latest violence and their families. But amid our detailed discussions about finding a way forward, Sharon abruptly turned angry. 'Anyone who goes to see Arafat – or who *allows* someone to go see Arafat,' he snapped, 'has blood on his hands!'

I anticipated his criticism. I knew his views about Arafat. And though I assumed both he and I understood that any British diplomatic role would be senseless unless we engaged with both sides, I knew that Sharon's frustration and occasional anger over my meetings with Arafat were an inevitable part of the job. Yet to accuse Blair of complicity in murder seemed to me something of a completely different order. 'Prime minister,' I said, 'you're making it very difficult. Are you saying that the prime minister of Britain has "blood on his hands" because he is allowing me – asking me – to go and see Arafat and feed back what my thoughts are?' He shouted: 'That's not what I said!' – although of course he had. I felt, and still feel, I had no alternative but to challenge him. I wanted to make it clear that however angry he might be over *my* dealings with Arafat, there needed to be a recognition that my role was ultimately to represent a British prime minister whose Middle East involvement was rooted in a genuine, honest determination to pursue every avenue in an effort to end the violence. The point was made. But I now said in as calm a voice as I could muster that perhaps 'this is a good time to finish this round of discussions', and Sharon clearly agreed. The British ambassador and the Foreign Office diplomat who was with me were taken aback by the exchange. But I said: 'Let's calm down. I had to say what I said. It was the right and appropriate thing to do' – particularly, I said, if the *really* crucial relationship, between Sharon and Blair, was ever to work. Sharon's aides followed us out, and one of his most senior advisers took me aside. 'Look, it'll be OK,' he said. 'Arik was just tense and upset. He's had a long day, he's very tired, and he's really depressed over the terror attacks.'

Sharon's relationship with Blair did survive, and strengthen. And although for a period of many months after our clash, my own dealings were limited to Sharon's senior ministers, my ties with him eventually recovered. The official seal of peace – between us, if not, sadly, with the Palestinians – came from Sharon himself at a later summit meeting that I attended with Blair. He took Tony and me to one side and, clasping my hand, said: 'Prime Minister' – he was always quite formal, and almost never called him 'Tony' – 'the air is now cleared between Lord Levy and myself. We're back to business as usual.' And we were, although one effect of my period of estrangement from Sharon would prove important after he suffered a debilitating stroke and went into a coma in early 2006. I had built on my very much closer relationship with another Likud minister whom I first met and befriended many years earlier: Ehud Olmert, whom Sharon had named as his deputy prime minister. I made a point of bringing Ehud in to see Blair in London, and the two hit it off instantly. Their relationship would become crucial after Olmert succeeded Sharon (particularly, if not quite as effectively as Tony hoped, during the Lebanon war crisis of 2006). It has clearly been an important asset for *former* Prime Minister Blair in his current role as the international community's Middle East envoy.

But the major turning point in Blair's Middle East thinking came not from events in Jerusalem or Ramallah, but New York City – on 11 September 2001. I was meeting with Jack Straw in his office when the first television bulletins appeared of the terror attack on the Twin Towers. Along with Foreign Office staff, we – like the rest of the country and the world – watched aghast. Tony said to me a few days afterwards that he was convinced the international order had changed for ever. Even at that point, although Iraq was far from his thoughts, he was haunted by the dual threat posed by terror networks like Al Qaeda and 'rogue states'. And from the moment the second plane slammed into the World Trade Center, he was also convinced of something else as well: a new urgency in finding some way of getting the Palestinian–Israeli peace efforts back on track. 'The Palestine issue is *not* the cause of terror,' he said. 'It's an excuse.' But he had no doubt that it helped provide a bogus political 'justification' for terror, and would make it much more difficult for Britain, America and the international community to win the crucial, post-9/11 battle for hearts and minds in the Arab and Islamic world. I absolutely agreed, and his response was a powerful reminder to me – after the period of personal tension between us earlier in the year – of his extraordinary gift for grasping the big issues, seeing the wider picture. Not only Britain, I felt, but the world was fortunate to have Tony as prime minister at this time of obvious and wholly unfamiliar crisis. If there was one difference between us, it was in how he saw the Americans, and especially President Bush. Clearly, their role was paramount – not only in framing the response to the terror attacks, but in any successful effort to inject new momentum into peacemaking efforts between Israel and the Palestinians. But on both fronts I would repeatedly argue that he was much too trusting of Bush. To which Tony replied: 'You've got to understand, Michael. For the Americans, and George, you're either for them or against them.'

In the weeks following 9/11, Blair flew tens of thousands of miles and played the central role in assembling worldwide support for the Americans' initial response to the attacks, their toppling of the Taliban regime in Kabul. I was also asked by Tony to make a series of calls in the aftermath of the Twin Towers attack to senior ministers in the Arab states I had visited. His message to them was that the inevitable US response to 9/11 would be aimed not against the Muslim world, but against the terrorists who had used Islam as an excuse for murder, and those who harboured and supported them. Gilda, meanwhile, took the lead in a much more personal – and typically far-sighted – response to the tragedy. Shortly after the attacks, she phoned

Pinky Lilani, a remarkable Calcutta-born Muslim whom we had met through Robin Cook at his birthday party a few years earlier and with whom she had become close friends. Pinky, a leading expert on Indian cookery, had set up the Asian Women of Achievement awards, and Gilda and she now began work to establish the Women's Interfaith Network. They saw it as one antidote to the danger that 9/11 could lead to a wider rupture along religious lines, particularly isolating the majority of the Muslim community, which was appalled at the carnage in New York. After many months of work to bring in women from across Britain's religious spectrum, the Network was formally launched – with Cherie Blair immediately accepting Gilda's invitation to deliver the keynote address.

Tony's time, attention and energy were increasingly taken up with a political response on a much bigger stage – particularly in his often daily contact with Bush and other senior administration figures amid the ever stronger signals that the Americans were intent on military action against Saddam Hussein. In our discussions, Tony constantly emphasised his certainty that Saddam's WMD programme remained in operation, that it posed a potentially dire threat in a fundamentally changed post-9/11 world, and that – if diplomatic efforts failed – military action would be both necessary and right. But he was equally convinced that revived peace negotiations in the Middle East were essential, and I spent hundreds of hours in talks – above all with the Israelis and Palestinians, but also with leaders and ministers in Egypt, Jordan, North African Arab states, Gulf states, as well as with US, EU, UN and Russian diplomats and officials involved in efforts to bring the violence to an end. I had a particularly strong working relationship with two very gifted European diplomats:

the EU's main foreign-policy representative Javier Solana, and Germany's foreign minister, Joschka Fischer. And my friendship with Fischer would lead to one brief period of tension with Jack Straw – after Joschka stayed with us at Chase House during a visit to London and held his official talks at the Foreign Office only after we had had a long informal meeting over eggs, salmon and bagels.

In the spring of 2003, I held a particularly delicate – and, Tony felt, potentially critical – day of talks with Arafat's senior negotiators in Ramallah. The Iraq war was now only weeks away, and Tony urgently wanted at least some sign of movement towards fresh Israeli–Palestinian talks. Yet instead Sharon – with the fulsome backing of Bush – had declared that the Palestinian leader could no longer be a credible 'partner' for peace. They were refusing to have any contact with Arafat at all. As a way out of the logjam, Britain, our EU partners and the Americans had agreed that we should press him to loosen his grip on power and to appoint a separate Palestinian prime minister. Arafat, to put it mildly, was reluctant. But crucially a number of his top aides, including chief Palestinian negotiator Saeb Erekat and his colleague Yasser Abd Rabbo, shared our determination to find some way of reviving talks. And they recognised that Arafat would have to name a prime minister if there was to be any realistic hope of doing so. They spent hours drawing up a statement formally committing Arafat to appointing a number two, with Saeb and other aides taking the increasingly frayed document back and forth to Arafat for a seemingly interminable series of inserts, deletions and edits. Yet by nightfall they had finally persuaded him to agree. We had our commitment, I told a relieved Tony as I headed back home – and, we both hoped, at least a ray of light in our efforts to end the violence. In fact, as on so many other occasions, it turned out to be a false dawn. Arafat's ultimate refusal to devolve any meaningful authority to his prime minister, and the cold shoulder that Israel and the US continued to show to the Palestinian leader, would end up delaying any real prospect of progress until after his death nearly two years later. Tony did keep pressing Bush on the Middle East issue, particularly after the Iraq invasion. He won a number of isolated victories, including the publication of the 'road map' peace plan and the first formal, public commitment by an American president to the goal of creating a Palestinian state. But the truth is that both Tony and I recognised that the aim of my visits to the region was not to tie up a peace deal – something that would require far more political muscle than he, and certainly I, could bring to bear. Our goal was more modest, but still necessary: to keep the possibility of peace very much on the regional and world agenda.

It was a job I approached with particular passion because it became clear to me during my talks that many Israelis and Palestinians privately shared a quite similar understanding of what a final deal, if ever the political obstacles could be cleared away, would look like. Palestinian leaders would have unequivocally to recognise the State of Israel. They would have to demonstrate not only in words but on the ground a commitment to crack down on violence. And they would have to accept a compromise on the 'right of return', with only a limited number of refugees going back to their former homes in pre-state Palestine, but balanced by a generous, internationally funded, package of financial compensation. The Israelis, for their part, would have to pull out of Gaza and the great majority of the West Bank, and facilitate the establishment of a genuinely viable Palestinian state. They would have to dismantle a large number of West Bank settlements, and agree to a land-swap in southern Israel to compensate for the settlements that remained. And they would have to work out some compromise arrangement on Jerusalem. It was broadly the deal that Clinton had envisaged, with additions negotiated by Barak's and Arafat's representatives in talks that continued during the early months of the intifada – sadly far too late, since not only Clinton but Barak, too, was clearly on his way out. The details were later fleshed out further in a series of meetings involving Israeli and Palestinian peace advocates, in which our son Daniel was a central participant, which culminated in the announcement of an agreed framework in the Swiss city of Geneva. In fact, Daniel's role led to a small bit of United Nations history. I was in New York for one of my periodic Middle East meetings with the Secretary General, Kofi Annan. Next on his schedule was a delegation from the 'Geneva Initiative' – including Daniel. Kofi suggested the two of us join him for a 'father and son' photo to mark the occasion, which we did. I cherish it as a reminder of how each of us, in our own small ways, tried to answer the violence in Israel and Palestine with a determination to see that the possibility for an eventual peace would not be extinguished.

I felt then, and still feel, that there will inevitably come a day when the Israelis and Palestinians, both of whom need a peace deal, will achieve it – with the indispensable, day-to-day involvement of the Americans. Ironically, a politically weakened George W. Bush, like Clinton before him, has embarked on his first really serious effort to help resolve the Israeli–Palestinian conflict in the twilight of his administration. Blair, no longer prime minister but still fired by a conviction that no single foreign-policy issue is more urgent, is well placed to play a role as international envoy. The Bush initiative is likely to prove too little, too late. But it is the best hope for progress in some years. And though at the end of my work as envoy I was deeply frustrated over the lack of major progress towards peace, the relationships that I helped to build among the key players give me additional reasons for optimism in the longer term – with Olmert, his foreign minister Tzipi Livni and other Israeli politicians like Barak, Peres, Yossi Beilin and Chaim Ramon, who became Olmert's deputy prime minister; and with Arafat's successor as Palestinian president, Abu Mazen, his prime minister Salaam Fayyad, and key Palestinian negotiators like Erekat and Abd Rabbo. In fact, Olmert and Fayyad – an enormously impressive, thoughtful and articulate economist – joined us for a small private dinner at Chase House when Olmert was still deputy prime minister. 'Please stay in touch,' I said with an arm around each of them as they were leaving. And they did.

Yet Iraq, by late 2002, was crowding out almost all other issues for Tony – largely without my involvement except for two contributions, both of them at his request. The first had an important, lasting and wholly positive impact. The second ended in abject failure. And neither outcome surprised me. The successful intervention involved filling the post of Tony's top foreign-policy adviser in Downing Street, a job that is always of importance but that had taken on tremendously greater significance as Blair's own role grew on the world stage. Tony had inherited the veteran diplomat John Holmes from the Major years, and grew not only to like him, but to respect, trust and rely on him as he was finding his feet on the international stage.

John Sawers briefly took over until the 2001 election, a period that crucially included the Kosovo crisis. When he left, to become ambassador in Cairo, Tony was keen to make sure he had the top man for the job. A number of names had been mentioned, but he was sceptical for various reasons about each of them, and he asked me whether I had any ideas.

I suggested a diplomat whom I had met during the early stages of my work as Middle East envoy, when he had been ambassador to Israel. David Manning had impressed me from the start. He was extraordinarily bright, encyclopaedic and nuanced in his grasp of the complexities of the Israeli–Palestinian conflict, utterly unflappable, and a thoroughly nice guy on top of it all. We had not only worked together, but became friends. Though he had only recently moved to Brussels, as head of Britain's NATO delegation, I strongly urged Tony to consider him. Although he was non-committal, I knew he was due to visit Brussels shortly, so I phoned David to warn him that I'd put him forward. At the end of the Brussels visit, Tony asked David to join him in his car to the airport. In typical Blair style, after a fairly brief discussion he said straight out that he wanted Manning to come back and work in Number 10. When David asked when, Tony said: 'Now.' Manning, even with my tip-off, was astonished by the suddenness of it all. He and his wife had only just begun to settle in Brussels. But it was clearly an offer he couldn't refuse. In the early weeks, despite a natural sense of excitement over working in Downing Street, I think he wondered whether he had made the right choice. Tony still didn't know him well, and at first David was not really part of the inner circle. Yet after the 11 September attacks, everything changed. He soon became an indispensable adviser, probably the most influential as the Iraq war drew nearer. He was particularly closely involved in Tony's dealings with the Americans and formed a bond of real friendship and trust with Bush's then national-security chief Condoleezza Rice. That was the key reason that Tony, despite a huge reluctance to lose him at Number 10, moved him after the Iraq invasion to succeed Meyer as ambassador in Washington.

My other intervention ended less happily, certainly for Tony. It began very much like his unexpected phone call to me after the 2001 election. As the Iraq war drew closer, domestic opposition was growing. The most dramatic sign was the march by more than a million anti-war protesters through London in February 2003, a month before the invasion. Tony was in fact less unsettled by the march than frustrated and angry – over what he saw as its leaders' refusal to grasp the realities of the post-9/11 world and recognise the scale of the threat posed by Saddam Hussein. His deeper political concern was around the cabinet table. A majority of ministers, although clearly far more worried by the scale of public protest than he was, remained generally supportive. Gordon Brown, though pointedly determined not to get deeply involved in the Iraq discussions, was not stirring up the doubters and sceptics either. Tony assumed that at least one cabinet minister – Clare Short – was going to jump ship sooner or later. And she did, although only after the invasion, with a fairly glancing impact. But his main worry was Robin, no longer foreign secretary but still a cabinet member – and, Tony knew, very much a political heavyweight. In the increasingly fraught weeks before the war, Robin had made it clear that he felt Blair would regret sending British troops to fight alongside the Americans with virtually no international support, at a time when Saddam was militarily weak, and when UN weapons inspections in Iraq had not yet run their full course. Tony gradually came to accept that Robin was likely to resign. But as the war approached, he still hoped to persuade him to hold on at least until after the start of the war. On 16 March – the Sunday before the invasion – he phoned me at home. His voice was heavy with the fatigue and frustration of his long, failed campaign to get a second UN Security Council resolution and tighten the diplomatic pressure on Saddam, and he said: 'Please, Michael, talk to Robin. Try to persuade him to stay.'

I went to see Robin that afternoon in Carlton Gardens, just off Pall Mall, less than a mile from Downing Street. He and his wife Gaynor had continued to live there, because the Straws had chosen to remain in their London home and use the official foreign secretary's residence only for receptions and dinners. Robin told me he was determined to follow through with his decision to resign, as I knew that he would be. I had worked with him for too long, and come to like and respect him too much, to assume he would take such a decision lightly. He was not out to hurt Tony, he stressed, and would resist any attempt by the increasingly vocal anti-war – and anti-Blair – protest movement to use his departure to try to bring even greater pressure on the prime minister. But he insisted, during the many dozens of circuits we made around the small park outside the residence as I ran through the arguments for staying, that this was 'simply a matter of conscience'. Going to war now, in these circumstances, was a mistake. Although Tony knew that I had misgivings of my own about his tight, trusting embrace with Bush, I at that stage genuinely felt Robin was wrong (Gilda agreed with Robin, and feared Britain was hurtling into a dangerously premature invasion to meet an essentially American timetable). I absolutely believed Iraq still had a WMD programme, and so did Robin. But I argued that to pull back now would embolden Saddam, and I shared Tony's view that, in a more dangerous, post-11 September world, that was something that could not be risked. Robin stood firm. Saddam, he said, was militarily hobbled already. He was getting weaker. In practical terms, a continuation of the weapons inspections could be part of that process, and would certainly not undermine it. And, politically, the danger of 'going alone' – in contrast to Kosovo, he said – would do huge and long-term damage. It was a view he had worked through with the qualities of seriousness, self-questioning, and intellect I had so come to respect when he was foreign secretary. I knew there was no changing his mind.

When I got back home, I phoned a disappointed – though I think not really surprised – Tony to tell him the news. Cook did go to the Commons, two days before the invasion. His brief resignation speech carried particular power, as Tony had feared, because it was so reasoned, so strongly argued, so statesmanlike. The effect was all the more devastating because, as he had promised, Robin did not question Blair's sincerity or purpose. He said he had 'no sympathy for, and will give no comfort to, those who want to use this crisis to displace him'. But the invasion to which Britain was about to commit its troops lacked crucial international support, he declared. The weapons inspections must be allowed to run their course. American haste, not a realistic assessment of the scale of the threat from Iraq, was dictating events. For all those reasons, for British troops to join the war that was about to begin, Robin said, was wrong. When he had finished, fellow MPs gave him a rare and spontaneous tribute – next seen when Tony himself made his final Commons speech before resigning four years later. They applauded.

Robin turned out to be right about Iraq. In the light of all that we now know, especially about the absence of Iraqi weapons of mass destruction, the pause for reflection and inspection that he advocated might conceivably have averted the need for military action altogether. Even if it hadn't, it could at least have given Tony time to press Washington much harder on its plans for what came after the invasion. Militarily, it soon became clear, the Americans had committed far too few troops. Logistically, they failed to ensure basic necessities like water, power, and law and order. Politically, despite genuine achievements, including remarkably free national elections, they had no clear vision of how to implement their much-trumpeted commitment to replace Saddam with a stable, representative, democratic government. But all that is easy to say with hindsight, particularly on the issue of WMD. Hindsight was not a gift afforded to a prime minister faced with the decision of whether to send young British men and women into battle.

For Tony, the spring of 2003 – after the first heady military 'victory' and the toppling of Saddam – marked a fateful turning point. During the darkest moments of this second half of his premiership, and they were many and unremitting, I would sometimes think back to his joyous, childlike celebration at The Warren after his 1997 election victory, and to his remark a few months later that being prime minister was actually 'pretty easy'. Those times were now gone. It was not just the constant pressure of Iraq, and the personal pain I could see that Tony felt with the death or terrible maiming of soldiers he had committed to war. He still felt he'd made the right decision, particularly given his genuine belief that Iraq had not abandoned its chemical and biological weapons programmes. And he took heart from the progress, however halting, towards a freely elected post-Saddam government. He was buoyed, too, by a series of statements by President Bush, pledging a stronger commitment to Israeli–Palestinian peace. Yet he knew now that the war in Iraq would not be a quick victory, but a long haul. And as the summer of 2003 approached – normally a time when he began thinking of a luxury holiday in the sun, where he would read and write and gird himself to inject new momentum into his political agenda in the autumn – almost everywhere he looked there was trouble. On Iraq, the BBC journalist Andrew Gilligan claimed that the government had deliberately misrepresented intelligence on Saddam's WMD capability in order to coax the country into war, prompting a furious Alastair Campbell into a war of his own against the BBC. And while Gordon Brown had been quiescent during the run-up to Iraq, he and his allies now began fighting Tony on what he viewed as the centrepiece of his domestic agenda: far-reaching reform of state health and education, as well as a long-term policy to safeguard pensions. Gordon made it inescapably clear to Tony that the real reason for the Treasury pressure was that he felt it was time for Blair to go – and that he, Gordon, should lead a third-term Labour government. Tony was still on balance inclined to stay on. But he was wavering, and Gordon clearly sensed that the top job might finally be his.

Gilda and I had a particularly harrowing experience of our own in the weeks after the Iraq invasion, but it had nothing to do with the war, or with Tony or Gordon. On 29 March, we were spending a quiet Saturday evening at home, reading, chatting and watching television when three hooded men with East European accents blowtorched their way through a living-room window, ordered us not to move, and handcuffed us. One of them wrestled me to the ground and cuffed my hands behind my back, while another of them marched Gilda upstairs. Every time I tried so much as to raise my head to hear what was going on my minder beat me back down. My hair was soon matted with blood. Upstairs, Gilda's minder ordered her to give him 'all your money and jewellery'. But she reacted with her usual breathtaking calm. When he pointed to a wall safe and told her to 'get your husband to open it', she laughed: 'Are you kidding? He doesn't even remember the combination. I'll do it.' And she did, handing him her jewellery and what little money we had in the house. Clearly having no idea who we were, the man added: 'Where's the money from your business?' Gilda calmly explained that we didn't have a business. 'My husband is retired,' she said, which I suppose in a manner of speaking I was. As they came back downstairs, he turned to her and said, 'I hate this. It's a terrible way to have to make a living,' to which Gilda gently suggested that maybe he should try another profession. But it was no laughing matter. When they rejoined us in the kitchen, my head had not only been bloodied, but my wrist had been broken from being handcuffed behind my back. The gang proceeded to herd us downstairs to the cellar, where they tied our handcuffs together with rope, barricaded the door so that we couldn't escape, switched off the lights, and left. It was Gilda who finally worked out a way to call the police. Our alarm system was set automatically to alert the police if our phones were cut. Luckily, the phone lines were in the cellar, and Gilda's hands had been handcuffed in front of her. She manoeuvred her way to a toolkit, found a small knife, cut the lines, and within a few minutes the police arrived. Only days later, once the initial shock of the burglary had passed, did either of us realise how lucky we had been to escape much worse injury – and how frightened both of us had been.

After a particularly difficult political week at the end of June, I spoke at length with Tony, finding him as distracted and depressed as I had seen him as prime minister. He asked me to 'put down some thoughts' on how he could somehow move forward. I did so, in a private memo that I sent him at the start of July. I began by reminding him of 'TB strengths', the qualities that had first inspired me and so many others to support his ideas for a better Britain: 'strategic vision, coalition-building, sense of purpose, leadership/direction'. But on all of these, I said, he now needed seriously to re-engage. As for 'coalition-building', it was surely time to 'isolate those who are really offside and bring back into the fold as many as possible'. And I added a footnote – an issue that had touched me personally in recent months, but that others in Downing Street and the party had been echoing to me privately: 'Knowing how to say "thank you", particularly now, is I think of vital importance.'

I suggested that Tony's main problem, particularly with Iraq acting as a lightning rod for criticism not only in Westminster and the media but nationally, was that for the first time since he had become prime minister damaging questions were being asked about his own role: 'What is TB in it for; what does TB want out of it; is TB just in it for himself?' They were harsh words. But I had agonised over them – I was not alone among those around Tony who feared he was becoming increasingly 'presidential', or even regal, in his tendency to see himself as a one-man show, with even senior colleagues and supporters as mere bit players. But it was a message that I hoped our personal relationship was strong enough to sustain. And I concluded with some specific suggestions of how he might regain control and recapture the sense of purpose and momentum with which he had entered Downing Street. My principal suggestion was that he shift away from 'international issues' and refocus on his key domestic priorities: education and health, crime and pensions. I also urged him to make sure that he was confident he had a team around him in Number 10 who could help make this happen, whom he trusted and could rely on. Anji Hunter had now left. And while she had been replaced by Sally Morgan – whom Tony, with good reason, did very much trust, and rate highly – the close personal bond he had with Anji was simply irreplaceable. Alastair had also made it clear he was going, once his battle with the BBC was over. That was a prospect Tony viewed with decidedly mixed feelings. During his first years in office, he would have felt that Alastair, too, was irreplaceable. He still recognised Campbell's strengths, and valued the no-nonsense advice – and arguments – he provided. But Alastair, as he put it to me, was 'becoming the story', adding to rather than resolving his growing array of problems. I agreed, saying in my memo: 'The attitude towards the media needs to be changed – the continuous headbutting contest is just not going to work.'

And I added the obvious: 'You need to curb the aggravation from Number 11. This to me is the most crucial and complicated issue, and only you know how to deal with it.' In fact, he didn't – as would become clear before long, with the approach of the 2005 election. Tony was increasingly convinced that Gordon would fight him on nearly all of the key planks of his domestic reform agenda, and finally was leaning towards firing him – or, more accurately, moving him from his parallel seat of government in the Treasury to foreign secretary. In the end, however, he dropped the idea. Part of the reason was that he feared he would lose the election without Gordon's open, public participation and support during the campaign. But there was something else as well, something much more personal. It was not just his usual unwillingness to risk confrontation. In Gordon's case, even when Number 11 was engaging in the political equivalent of guerrilla warfare, Tony retained an overriding sense of sadness – and perhaps guilt, too – over how their relationship had foundered. In all his years in politics, Tony told me, 'Gordon is the only friend I have ever lost.'

There was a brief period when I thought I might become the second. The issue was delicate, and deeply personal: Cherie's friend and 'lifestyle' coach Carole Caplin. A former model, she was vivacious, charming but also an advocate of an array of eccentric New Age fads. I had first met her at a private dinner for Tony and Cherie with friends and supporters in an Islington restaurant shortly after the 1997 election victory. She was there, along with her mother. A couple of years later, Cherie phoned me and asked whether I could join her and a friend for lunch in Downing Street. The friend was Carole, the fare was a health salad, and the reason for the invitation was to see whether I could help find Caplin a property in Camden for a new business she hoped to set up. I said I had no real idea about property in the area, but agreed to put her in touch with a friend who did. But nothing came of it. Now, with increasingly worrisome media reports about Caplin's role, a key member of Tony's team at Number 10 asked me to go and see the prime minister and use my personal relationship with him to urge 'distance'. The concern was not just about Cherie, although Alastair and Fiona were increasingly frustrated and angry about their failure to get her to cut Carole loose. The main worry was Tony – specifically, gossip within Number 10 concerning visits Carole was making to Chequers to give an increasingly stressed prime minister long massages. When I went to see Tony, I was deeply uncomfortable about raising the subject. But I told him that there was a real danger Carole could become 'not just an issue for Cherie, but for you'. Tony went bright red. I never raised the issue again, and nor of course did he. But he got the message.

Not only did our friendship survive this bizarre encounter, but our political relationship was broadening, as a result of another appeal from Tony to raise funds. It was for a programme that he increasingly began to see as central to his entire reform agenda: the city academies. Of all the fundraising I did for Labour, this was probably the most personally fulfilling – although it would sadly be soured by the fact that several academy sponsors were later caught up in the media frenzy over 'cash for peerages'. One reason it was so satisfying was that the cause was not one that I ever saw as narrowly partisan. Indeed, a number of the academy sponsors were not Labour backers, but Tories, or simply not interested or involved in party politics at all. My own role had begun during Tony's first term, just as I was getting involved in a quite separate education project very close to my heart. The Jewish community's main state school, JFS, had its roots in the East End of London, where it was established in 1732 as the Jews' Free School. My father had been a student there in the 1920s. Damaged during the Blitz, it had moved after the war to Camden. While it was extremely successful academically, regularly near the top of the tables in exam results, by the 1990s its site was in serious disrepair, a situation made worse for students and their parents by intermittent incidents of vandalism and street violence. I was on the board of governors. Buoyed by its tireless chairman Arnold Wagner and an inspirational headteacher, Ruth Robbins, I took the lead in an ambitious scheme to raise millions of pounds and help build an entirely new campus in the north-west London suburb of Kenton, which was much nearer the area where most of the students lived. Raising the money took several years, but it was a labour of love. All the more so when the new school, a bright, modern architectural joy in expansive grounds, was formally dedicated in October 2002, with Tony as guest of honour. I had already begun raising money for the first city academies – state schools funded with the help of outside benefactors who put in a minimum seed contribution of £2 million. But the experience with JFS brought home to me the truly transforming power on an entire school family – not only students, but parents and teachers and staff – of a 'new' school, even for an institution which had a 270-year record of success behind it.

Tony's commitment to the academies programme was particularly strong because I think he sensed that it was the one aspect of his reform programme that he might get past the Treasury largely unscathed. It was not that Gordon looked the other way. He would regularly raise budgetary and other objections. But the legal structure for the programme was already in place, the Learning and Skills Act of 2000, which had built on the Tories' legislation for their city technology colleges. Tony's confidence also rested on the fact that the academies were being driven forward by an immensely determined and gifted aide in

Number 10, Andrew Adonis. Andrew was a policy wonk, not a politician. But of all the advisers in Downing Street, he was probably the most truly 'Blairite'. In fact, the thinking behind the academies was as much Adonis's as Blair's. Balding, intense and softly spoken, Andrew had the look of an intellectual. But he was unerringly focused on the practical challenge of converting the vision of academies into bricks and mortar – new schools, with not just the funding but the drive and personal commitment of leading businessmen, to replace the most badly failing of Britain's inner-city comprehensives. Andrew was a pleasure to work with. Together we brought in support for a diverse array of successful new schools – ranging from Clive Bourne's academy on the site of my old Hackney Downs school and David Garrard's Business Academy in Bexley to the Bristol Academy, which was backed by the University of the West of England and Bristol City football club. By the time Tony left office, we would put in place well over fifty academies and be on course to open many dozens of others.

For Tony, amid the fallout from Iraq, a series of fundraising dinners that we hosted for academy supporters at Chase House came to represent a respite from his increasingly bitter political struggles. None more so than one evening that included a group of leading hedge-fund bosses who were also deeply committed to supporting educational projects. Tony particularly enjoyed talking to Arpad 'Arki' Busson, founder of the educational charity ARK – 'Absolute Return for Kids'. But Gilda and I couldn't help wondering, after the guests had left, whether the real attraction might have been Arki's partner: the supermodel Elle Macpherson. We didn't have long to wait for the answer. The next morning, Downing Street phoned to ask for contact details for Arki and Elle. Tony wanted to invite them to dinner at Chequers. And he did, sort of. Arki accepted the invitation. But when he mentioned that Elle would be out of town and unfortunately unable to join him, Downing Street delicately suggested that they delay the dinner until both of them could attend.

Tony enjoyed these interludes mostly, I think, because they were becoming so rare. The 'Iraq issue', as his team at Number 10 called it, was a constant and growing problem, sapping not only the government's morale but its poll ratings. Every time it appeared to subside, it would resurface even more threateningly. Still, nothing prepared me for the tone of depression and despondency in Tony's voice when he phoned me a few weeks after I'd sent him my private memo. The call itself was not a surprise: the news had already broken that the government WMD expert David Kelly – named as the source of the Andrew Gilligan radio reports amid Alastair's escalating fight with the BBC – had been found dead. Although initial indications, ultimately borne out, suggested suicide, the political impact would obviously be serious. Tony phoned from the Far East, where he'd flown for an official visit after talks in the US. He sounded utterly devastated. 'When will all this *end*?' he said. 'What am I going to *do*?' He had already decided to set up an inquiry, but kept saying how horrible it was that someone had lost his life because of a battle over politics. I tried to calm him down, to get him to focus on the reality of the situation. Kelly's death *was* horrible, and tragic. 'But you have to ask yourself whether anything you did, or could have done, was responsible. You've done the right thing by setting up an inquiry. I *know* you'll want to blame yourself. That's only human. But you can't help anyone by beating up on yourself. You have to try to put it in perspective. I know it sounds hard, but you have to.'

For a while, he succeeded – although one question at his joint news conference with the Japanese prime minister suggesting, in an echo of Ariel Sharon, that he had Kelly's 'blood on his hands' badly hurt and shocked him. But during the final months of 2003, and particularly the spring of 2004, he seemed to be gradually worn down by the twin weight of Iraq and by Gordon's pressure for an announcement that he, not Tony, would lead a third-term Labour government. Even the report of the Hutton Inquiry into David Kelly's death, which cleared Blair of any blame, only briefly revived him. By early May, he seemed to have finally lost the will to fight on. He would see out his second term. But he felt that the repeated media assaults over Iraq, and Gordon's fixation on replacing him, were making his job as prime minister – obviously difficult, but until now also challenging, fulfilling, and redeemed by a real sense that he was making a positive contribution in Britain and abroad – virtually impossible. His Downing Street aides were alarmed over his mood. Cherie was even more so. Leaving now, in her view, would mean 'surrender to Gordon'.

On Tuesday evening 11 May, Gilda and I arranged to have dinner with the Blairs. We met at Wiltons, the restaurant in Jermyn Street known as a favourite lunchtime meeting place for Tory grandees, and made our way to the small private dining room at the back. The setting was very much olde England, with a painting of a red-coated man on horseback over the fireplace and equine sculptures on the mantelpiece. But the topic of conversation was the country's future, and that of its prime minister. As in my Magnet days, I'd prepared by making a list in my cramped longhand of the pros and cons of Tony staying on. There were, I tried to persuade him, many more pros. Yes, he should call it quits if he genuinely felt there was nothing more he wanted to, or could, accomplish. But he had come to power on a remarkable wave of popular enthusiasm for change. He had made a start: the minimum wage, unparalleled investment in the NHS, but above all a transformation in the country's political tone and temperature. Britain was more open now, more tolerant, less selfish, better equipped to play its part in the modern world. The central question he had to ask himself was if the job was done or – whether on Iraq or domestic reform – he would regret leaving in midstream, risking the reversal of the changes he had begun to make and in effect admitting that all the critics were right. We spoke for more than two hours, not only Tony and me, but Cherie and Gilda, and I could almost see Tony starting to recover his will to carry on. He *did* have real work left to do, and was convinced that, despite inevitable mistakes and setbacks, he had been right on the big issues. Being prime minister was no longer easy, he accepted. But it was more than just a job. It was a responsibility, a privilege, and he had to get back to the business of proving that he was equal to both. In the end, this was not just about him, but about the country he had been elected to lead. The next morning, Jonathan Powell called from Downing Street. 'I don't know what you said to him last night,' he said, 'but it had its effect. He's a different man.'

Cherie, too, called to say how grateful she was. And I do think our dinner was one reason Tony carried on. But only one. There were many other voices too, Cherie's above all, urging him to pull out of his increasing frustration and despair and re-engage with the challenges he still believed were central to making Britain safer, fairer, more confident, more vibrant, more successful. And the fact is that even Cherie's voice was not the crucial factor. Gilda and I used to laugh at occasional suggestions by the Blairs' media critics that she sometimes 'bullied' him into decisions of one sort or another. Tony did value Cherie's opinion. Yet in every political decision that mattered, even her voice was always less important than his own. It had been true, in the early days in Downing Street, with the decision to make Anji Hunter part of the team. And it was true now. Yes, Cherie's input – and mine – did no doubt make a difference in persuading Tony not to walk away from the job. But none of our words would have mattered had not Tony himself, in the end, genuinely wanted to carry on.

Still, the Wiltons dinner was for me a reminder that despite our occasional difficulties and disagreements, the closeness and openness that Tony and I had so enjoyed as he led Labour back into power still survived. And not long afterwards at a much larger and quite different kind of dinner – in the Banqueting House, across from Downing Street – our friendship would be on very public show. The occasion was my sixtieth birthday. Gilda had banded together with the organisations to which I had devoted my many years of fundraising – Jewish Care, the JIA, JFS, CSV and Labour – to stage a surprise party. I began to suspect something in the days before the dinner, but nothing even remotely on this scale. The hundreds of guests included our closest friends, and of course Gilda's and my extended family. There were also friends and colleagues from the Jewish community, my Magnet days, the charities I'd supported, politics and peacemaking. Pete Waterman was there. So was Alvin Stardust, who teamed up with a group organised by Pete and performed a beautiful rendition of Magnet's old Guys 'n' Dolls hit: 'There's a Whole Lot of Loving.' Ehud Olmert sent a message, as did Shimon Peres, and the chief Palestinian negotiator Saeb Erekat. Yasser Abd Rabbo flew in with his wife to attend, and so did Yossi Beilin and Chaim Ramon. Virtually the whole of the cabinet was there – and Robin, too. And of course Tony. Striding on stage to open proceedings, he began lightheartedly. 'The first thing to say is that whenever anyone criticises Michael, and just *occasionally* they do, I say: "Remember Gilda" – who, he said when the laughter and applause had died down, was 'simply the tops'. And he was right. Though this was meant to be my night, it above all reminded me of how fortunate I was to have Gilda at my side, a feeling that would only deepen in the unimaginably difficult years of my life with Labour that still lay ahead.

Then Tony went on to speak about me. 'The first thing to say about Michael is that he has absolutely no ego at all!' he began, to a building crescendo of laughter in the hall. When it was quiet again, he added: 'You can't say either that he's not intensely competitive, not utterly persistent, not someone who doesn't much care whether he achieves his goal or not – who is pretty indifferent . . . No, none of that is Michael.' He was right about all of that as well. The ego, the drive, had always been part of me, and I imagine they always will be. The insecurities, too. But Tony also went on to say that what he most valued in me, and in our relationship, was the desire to help people that I had shown through my charity work – and, as his envoy, an equal passion to do all that I could to help both Israel and the Palestinians achieve security, stability and peace.

It was an incredibly generous tribute. And I think it reflected a closeness and mutual respect that we both felt. But while I could not have imagined this at the time, it would also prove to be the high-water mark in a relationship that had begun almost exactly a decade earlier but, within months, would turn much, much more difficult. My work as Tony's envoy did continue to make a contribution to his increasingly international role as prime minister, and not just in our stubborn but frustrating attempts to unblock Israeli–Palestinian diplomacy. I made a particularly timely visit to Brazil, to see the recently inaugurated president, Luiz Inácio Lula da Silva. Lula had been strangely cool towards British diplomats since his victory. And when I arrived and had a preliminary meeting with his aides, the reason became clear. It was, as I was often finding in my work as envoy, the result of a misunderstanding. Peter Mandelson had paid a private visit to Brazil during the election campaign, and made comments that President Lula viewed as an endorsement of the rival candidate. At the outset of a long meeting with the president, I tried to clear the air. Whatever remarks Peter may have made, I assured him, the prime minister wanted me to convey his sincere desire for a close relationship in all areas. It was a desire that, it became evident as the meeting went on, the new Brazilian leader shared. Lula respected Blair, and wanted to work closely with him. And they did go on to do so, on issues ranging from world trade to global warming. More practically, as our ambassador, Peter Collecott, wrote me in a note on my return home, 'many doors' were now suddenly opened to our diplomats in Brazil. 'The Brazilians, from Lula downwards, got the substance they wanted from us, and felt the intensity and warmth that you ably transmit on behalf of the Prime Minister.'

Closer to home, too, a series of missions as Tony's envoy would turn out to be important in forging a more effective, and assertive, role on the European stage. It is a role I feel he is now minded to resume, if possible, as Europe's first 'president' under the EU's new constitutional treaty. Indeed, Tony has let it be known privately that one reason he has been keen to accept lucrative board appointments and speaking engagements since leaving Number 10 is in anticipation of that 'window' closing should he seek the top EU job. But in the wake of the Iraq war, his ties with a number of European leaders were badly strained. The most obvious point of tension was, of course, with France's President Jacques Chirac. But relations were also especially delicate with Spain. Prime Minister José María Aznar, a supporter of the war with whom Tony also had become personally close, announced that he would not seek re-election in 2004. And with the terrible Madrid train bombing just days before the election adding power to the opposition Socialists' anti-war message, Aznar's party was defeated at the polls by José Luis Rodríguez Zapatero, who soon proceeded to pull Spain's small troop contingent out of Iraq. When it was suggested that I go and see the new Spanish leader, Tony was at first strongly opposed. He was angry over Zapatero's policy shift on Iraq, not least because he feared it would be seen as a triumph for the terror bombers, and he also felt that any attempt by me to build bridges with Aznar's successor would simply be a waste of time. Eventually, however, he agreed I should go to Madrid. During the first of two visits I made to the Spanish capital, the atmosphere was, as Tony had suspected, fairly strained. Zapatero was keen to put on record his continuing opposition to the Iraq war. But during my second visit, it became clear that he also wanted to build a strong working relationship with Tony. And that process began in earnest the following month at a luncheon

Tony hosted for Zapatero at Downing Street, where it was clear to me that both men were intent on putting the disagreement over Iraq behind them and cooperating on a range of other issues in Europe and beyond.

I also played an unexpected role in a rare diplomatic success in Tony's – and the Americans' – campaign against the WMD threat from 'rogue states'. A few months before the Iraq war, several of my Middle East contacts asked me whether I would be willing to meet the son of the Libyan leader Mu'ammar Gaddafi, Saif al-Islam Gaddafi, who divided his time between Tripoli and London. I went to see Tony, who had restored diplomatic relations with Libya during his first term, and asked whether I should take up the suggestion. At first, he said no. But amid reports from both US and British intelligence suggesting that Libya seemed genuinely serious about a rapprochement, he changed his mind. 'Go and see him,' he said. 'But be bloody careful!' Saif and I met at the Dorchester Hotel less than two months before the war, the first of several long discussions on issues ranging from the continuing repercussions of the 1988 Lockerbie attack to the broader outlines of how Libya could rejoin the international mainstream. Saif was open, articulate and very well informed on the issues that would have to be resolved. Some months later, detailed talks were under way between the Libyans and the British government to work out a pledge by Gaddafi to abandon his WMD programme. I arranged for David Manning's successor at Number 10 – the enormously impressive, focused and intelligent diplomat Nigel Sheinwald, who has now also succeeded him as ambassador to Washington – to join Saif and me for lunch at the House of Lords to discuss plans for a possible visit by Blair to Tripoli. And Tony did seal the extraordinary turnaround in relations with a summit meeting in Libya in 2004. Like so much else of my work as envoy, I was by no means the lead player in this historic shift. Yet the fact that I was able to act as Tony's representative without fully and formally committing the prime minister at an early and delicate stage in the process did allow me to play a supporting role.

Yet by the final months of 2004, Tony's central preoccupation in our meetings and discussions was not diplomatic. It was domestic. He had by now firmly decided to fight a third term, but was seized by the fear that Labour would find itself fatally outgunned financially during the election campaign. He was especially worried by reports that since their 2001 defeat, the Conservatives had begun raising many millions of pounds in loans – which, unlike donations, did not have to be publicly declared. We, by contrast, were still paying off debts from the 2001 election. And while I was continuing to raise money, the fact is that I was finding it increasingly heavy going, particularly after Iraq. A mixture of the effects of the war, the fact that Tony was no longer a fresh face but a two-term prime minister, and a growing reluctance of many would-be donors to invite the media exposure involved in giving large-scale contributions was making my task much harder. I had managed to raise nearly £6 million since the weeks before the war in 2003. But almost all of it was from a small number of established supporters – and £2.5 million of it came from Lord Sainsbury, a minister in Tony's government. It was clear to all of us that it was going to be very difficult to raise anything like the £15-million campaign chest we had amassed for each of the first two elections. Still, I assured Tony, we were stepping up our efforts with an eye towards the likely May 2005 election date, and were on course to bring in a total of about £1 million in two large donations for December.

He and I travelled to Israel at the end of the month for summit talks with Sharon and Abu Mazen. When we were leaving for home, one of the Downing Street party pulled me aside and said: 'Tony wants you to ride with him to the airport. He has something he wants to talk to you about.' Though generally I travelled in one of the other cars, I figured that he wanted to talk in greater detail about the way forward in the Middle East. But after a fairly general chat about the summit results, he suddenly changed gear as we were approaching Ben-Gurion airport. 'Oh by the way, Michael,' he said, 'don't worry on the Ronnie Cohen thing.' I said I didn't know what he meant. '*What* Ronnie Cohen thing?' I asked. But he replied: 'Oh. Just don't worry about it.'

Baffled, I phoned Jonathan Powell the following morning. 'You mean he didn't *tell* you?' he said. 'Typical Tony.' And he proceeded to inform me that, obviously due to concern over the level of donations I was bringing in, Ronald Cohen had been enlisted to seek out new sources of support for the election campaign. I was upset and angry with Tony. It was not the fact that Cohen had been approached. I did recognise Cohen's drive, his single-mindedness, his business success, and the series of very substantial sums he had personally donated to the party. But I found the decision to give him a wider fundraising role puzzling. It is true that Cohen had given generously – a total of some £2 million beginning with the £100,000 he pledged when I went to see him before the 1997 campaign and found that, despite having stood unsuccessfully as a parliamentary candidate for the Liberals, he was now enthusiastically supportive of Blair and New Labour. But in the years since then, although clearly very keen to cultivate a good relationship with Blair, Cohen had built much closer ties with Gordon Brown. Moreover, his earlier offer, before the 1997 election, to bring in other Labour donors had produced limited results – as, indeed, would prove the case this time around as well, despite two dinners that Tony attended at the Cohens' London home early in 2005.

Yet the main reason I was so furious was that Tony had gone behind my back, despite the role I had played over many years in helping Labour attract the funds to fight and win elections and to put his programme into practice. In effect, he was saying that he believed I could no longer do the job, or at least that I needed help if it was to be done well. It was a judgement that he had every right to make, of course, even though in my view it was unfair. But what I found so difficult to accept, or forgive, was that he hadn't been straight with me. After the 2001 election, I had been shocked, and angry, over his betrayal of Robin Cook's trust. Now I felt he had betrayed mine. And though I told Jonathan I would take time to 'think things over', I told him that my strong inclination was to end my fundraising role and leave the pre-election efforts in the hands of others.

A few days later, Tony called me into Downing Street. He never exactly apologised, but said that it would be terrible if a 'misunderstanding' led to losing the 'absolutely crucial' contribution I had made to his and Labour's successes. Again citing media pressures, he said it had never been his intention to show anything but appreciation for my efforts. He had only meant to 'spread' the fundraising network more widely, in the light of the press's constant focus on my role. I replied that the only issue for me was openness and honesty, and I felt badly let down by him on both counts. But he was at his most persistent, and persuasive: 'Please, Michael,' he said. 'Let's go away and think more coolly. You really must carry on. No one else can be as effective in raising money as you have always been – we both know that. We can't run a successful campaign, and we can't win a third term, without you.'

Over dinner that night, Gilda was furious and forthright. 'Do *not* go back!' she urged me. 'After the way they treated you, there has to come a point when you just say no. Why not just let them rely on Ronnie Cohen? You've *done* your bit – *more* than your bit,' she insisted. 'It's not your fault that people have gone off Tony after Iraq. And he has got to realise that loyalty is something that goes both ways. She was as single-minded as Tony had been a few hours earlier. Yet, for one of the very few times in my life, I did not take her advice. Partly, it was a genuine and continuing commitment to helping Labour win the next election. But, as Tony himself had said only half jokingly at my birthday dinner, there was no doubt ego involved, too. Just as it was partly a sense of bruised ego that had ignited my anger over Tony's back-door approach to Ronald Cohen, I am sure that I now wanted to demonstrate that I *could* still do the job. And I also felt an inescapable satisfaction at having been implored by the prime minister not to walk away. It would prove to be the biggest mistake of my life.

I was no less angry by the time I finally talked with Jonathan face-to-face in Downing Street late in January 2005 – a tense and difficult meeting in which I confirmed that I would continue to raise funds, but only until the election in May. 'I was lied to!' I fumed – prompting Jonathan, exactly as I had with Ariel Sharon, to leap to Blair's defence. 'No one lied,' he said. And technically at least, I suppose he was right. I followed up our discussion with two handwritten letters to Jonathan, one a personal note, and the second a more formal one outlining my position. 'You got very upset when I said I felt I had been lied to,' I said in the first note. 'There is a nuance – I had *not* been told the truth. But at least you were the *only one* who actually told me what was going on.' I said that I had always valued my work with him and hoped and trusted that we would remain friends. And I added: 'What a sad state of affairs that after all these years – I really feel giving my life and energy on so many issues for now nearly 11 years has been taken for granted.' In the second, more formal letter I stressed my 'paramount' desire '*not* to create any worries or negativity before the election'. I reiterated my intention to step down from my fundraising role after the election. But I said I would do my very best to bring in as many donations as possible in the meantime. I was determined, I added, that until I left it would be 'business as usual'. I would ensure that no one outside Downing Street, least of all the media, would get wind of what had happened and risk undermining the election campaign. And no one did.

Tony was obviously relieved, but he also recognised that fundraising had become more and more difficult. And there was a further surprise when I met at party headquarters in Victoria Street with his designated election chief, Alan Milburn, and the party's general secretary, Matthew Carter. Matt informed me of a dramatic change in party policy – a change that, on a number of occasions since the 2001 election, I had strongly opposed. Tony, he said, was alarmed at the obvious difficulty we were likely to have in finding anywhere near the scale of donations we had raised for the past two elections. We would have to widen our net. In a shift that would prove to be a fateful step towards the 'cash for peerages' debacle, Tony had decided that Labour would now adopt the Tories' strategy. For the first time, we would look not only for donations. We would also take loans.

Tony, I think, recognised as much as I did that this was potentially difficult territory. He stipulated that there must be legal advice, and firm conditions, on how any loans were taken. They would have to be at a commercial rate of interest and could not be 'open-ended'. For my part, I was still hoping to avoid taking loans altogether. The suggestion in the press by one major lender, after the 'cash for peerages' furore erupted, that I had turned down donations in favour of loans was, I can only imagine, the product of impaired memory. The notion that I would have preferred a loan to a gift was nonsense. There were many reasons that I had long been against Labour taking loans. But one of them was both obvious and straightforward: loans, unlike donations, had to be paid back.

In the months before the election, we did bring in nearly £3 million in donations, but the lion's share was again from Lord Sainsbury, who donated £2 million just before election day. But as the campaign got under way, both Tony and Matt were very close to a state of panic. All the indications were that the Tories were far better funded, in large part as a result of a series of major loans. Michael Howard had also brought in Lynton Crosby, the hard-hitting architect of John Howard's election victories in Australia, to coordinate his assault on Labour's bid for a third term. And particularly with the debt burden from 2001, we were badly in need of funds. The situation was not helped by a state of nearly open war between Gordon and Blair's handpicked campaign chief, Alan Milburn. That potentially fatal battle was resolved at the very end of March, when Gordon agreed to fight the campaign at Tony's side – in return for the effective sidelining of Alan. But even that, without the funds with which to fight the campaign, might not have salvaged things. I was left in no doubt by Tony that money, serious money, was needed. And urgently.

The result was a series of what amounted to emergency loans during the month of April. One of the first, for £500,000, was from the dotcom multimillionaire Gordon Crawford, whom the party had suggested might be willing to help. Another existing Labour donor, the curry-meal magnate Gulam Noon, agreed to lend the party a further £250,000. David Sainsbury, having donated £2 million in March, now also agreed to lend the party a further £2 million. And I secured a further £4.3 million in loans before the election from three others whom I had earlier helped enlist as sponsors for city academies: David Garrard, Barry Townsley and Andrew Rosenfeld. It was enough, just barely, to see Labour through to election day. It was nowhere near sufficient, however, to balance the books after what proved to be a bruising, and expensive, election campaign. Again rashly ignoring the advice of Gilda, I agreed to help raise more funds in the months after polling day to try to clear the party's large election debt: a donation of £2 million from the industrialist and longtime Labour supporter Lakshmi Mittal and several smaller donations, but also a further several million pounds in loans.

Labour did win the election, if with a greatly reduced Commons majority of sixty-six. Tony, who had for the first time genuinely feared losing, was hugely relieved. He was also, as he made a point of telling me, grateful. So was Matt Carter, who wrote me a note saying: 'Everything we achieved was built on the foundations established through your hard efforts.' Yet for my part, I found that I felt nothing resembling the elation I'd experienced after the earlier election victories. Part of this may have been down to my resentment of Tony's approach to Ronnie Cohen. But only a part. My initial anger had by now subsided. The main reason that this election victory seemed so different, so hollow, went deeper. The more that I had struggled to raise donations, and then loans, the more I began to feel a sense of confusion and frustration that was strangely reminiscent of my final months in Magnet. My falling-out with Tony was not remotely as important as my mother's amputation, final agony, and death. But I think that in its own way, it was also something of a wake-up call. It prodded me to take a step back, and to take a more serious and reflective look at the years I had spent by his side.

It was a sobering exercise. I did still admire many of Tony's qualities as a politician, and as prime minister. Certainly during the campaign, any fleeting doubts had been outweighed by my sense of real anger over the bleak, alternative vision for Britain that the Tories were offering. As the grandchild of East European Jewish immigrants, always keenly aware that I could never have achieved any of my success without the haven and new life that Britain had offered them, I was particularly outraged by the cynically subliminal message that Howard, a fellow Jew, was peddling on immigration. Alongside a message that it wasn't 'racist' to cut back on the number of immigrants, Tory posters asked the voters: 'Are you thinking what we're thinking?' 'My God, I *hope* not,' I remarked to Gilda the evening after they appeared – and thankfully, as the election result showed, they were not. Particularly when Blair's achievements were measured against the alternative, I found that I still broadly believed – as I had told him a year earlier, when he was so near to quitting, at our dinner in Jermyn Street – that Tony had changed Britain for the better. And I still believed much the same could be said of his work, in which I had been privileged to participate, to salvage hopes for peace in the Middle East. Yet I had also come to recognise that for all his attractive qualities – his talent for friendship, his acts of personal generosity, his genuine religious faith – Tony was at the end of the day a politician. There had also been a real element of truth in the challenge I had put to him in my private memo in July 2003: on some level, it seemed to me, TB really *was* sometimes just 'in it for himself'. I liked to think that was less true of me. At least I hoped it was. But I also had to accept that along with the nobler reasons that I had supported Tony, worked as his envoy, and raised money for Labour, I, too, had at times become a 'politician'. I had sometimes revelled in the public attention. I had enjoyed my media image as Tony's 'friend and tennis partner' – even, in an odd way, the references to 'Lord Cashpoint'. In the same way that I had come to realise when finally forced to look back on my dizzying years of success at Magnet, I saw that in politics, too, I had sometimes been blinded by the light.

This new sense of perspective, literally of disillusionment, became increasingly powerful and unsettling during my final months of fundraising for Labour. When I first began raising money for Tony and for Labour, I had had a genuine sense of mission – a feeling I was drumming up support not just for a politician or a party, but a cause. I saw in Tony and New Labour a message of hope, and change, for a country that I felt had been led astray. The passion with which I believed in the brighter future that Tony offered was one reason I was able to attract unprecedented levels of donations. It also helped, of course, that many of the people whom I approached – indeed, millions of people throughout Britain – shared that vision. Now, as I had discovered when struggling to raise money for the 2005 campaign, that was no longer true. And I think it was no longer true for me either. I remember remarking to Gilda as election day drew nearer that I still had a sense of real idealism and purpose when I approached people to ask them to help CSV, or Jewish Care – or Tony's academies programme. But I had come to feel differently about raising millions for this election campaign. The academies were *above* politics. The campaign was *nothing but* politics.

And it was just the latest in a series of projects great and small for which Tony had intermittently called on me during his first two terms to 'please, see if you can raise the money'. Sometimes, they would be genuinely part of his political programme, as with his urgent call to raise funds to fight a referendum on the EU constitution – a battle, of course, that he never had to fight after 'no' votes in France and The Netherlands. Sometimes, they were more trivial, an issue that would be brought home to me with particular force by a phone call from Cherie just after the 2005 election. In the glow of Labour's third election victory, Tony had arranged to purchase 150 'thank you' umbrellas as keepsakes for the dozens of key staff, supporters and volunteers who had helped deliver the triumph – only to be told by Labour's head office that because this wasn't technically a party expense, it would be more appropriate for the prime minister to foot the bill. Cherie, no doubt in part because she, unlike Tony, had known periods of financial deprivation as a child, was from the start much more concerned about the financial details of their life in Downing Street – and afterwards. It was a concern that sometimes seemed almost an obsession, even when small sums were involved, and this proved no exception. She wanted me to see whether I could persuade one of the party's donors to foot the bill for the umbrellas. It would only, she added, be 'a few hundred pounds'. In fact, the bill came to slightly over £2,000, and Gilda and I decided that in the end it would be much easier to pay it ourselves.

The fact is that despite the enormous fulfilment I had drawn from my various roles alongside Tony over the past decade – despite my belief that I, too, had made at least some small contribution to helping Labour change Britain – I found increasingly that I no longer retained the sense of idealism that I had at the beginning. I also came to feel an uncomfortable disjunction between my fundraising for charity and for Tony – made more acute by a growing feeling that while Labour's tax and other policies since 1997 had redeemed the 'ambition' part of his agenda, Tony had missed the opportunity to insist that the wealthiest in an increasingly well-off Britain respond with an equal measure of 'compassion'. In America, the most successful business leaders almost without exception gave huge amounts to charity, not least because of a tax system explicitly designed to encourage them to do so. Britain, and particularly London, now had a growing number of millionaires and even billionaires. But with few exceptions, they contributed a proportionately much, much smaller share of their wealth to help others. It was an issue that I had raised personally with Tony. But, perhaps because he always felt that taxation was 'Gordon's territory', he never acted on it.

More immediately, my scramble to raise campaign money in

2005 had left me wondering whether all parties – Labour most definitely included – were now so obsessed with winning elections and with raising the increasingly large sums needed to do so that they were losing sight of the real purpose of politics: the issues, the policies, the vision. Four months after the election, in September 2005 – well before 'cash for peerages' was an issue – I publicly called for a fundamental change in the way British politics was financed. It was time, I said, to look at a system of state funding of political parties. Maybe that would help them return to the part of politics that ultimately mattered: a national argument over the ideas and vision by which Britain should be governed. My proposal provoked a series of responses in the letters columns of *The Times*, though perhaps predictably the stir was brief and fleeting. The media soon moved on to other issues. Nevertheless, alongside my continuing work for the academies programme and as Tony's Middle East envoy, I still hoped I might somehow play a part in provoking a genuine national debate over the way Britain's political parties, and politics, were funded. The system was broken, I had come to feel. And it needed fixing.

I suppose I should have been careful what I wished for. Within a few months, an initial scattering of newspaper reports – on Tony's latest peers list, on Labour's 'secret loans', and the Des Smith 'exposé' suggesting that academy sponsors were being promised honours in return – built into a media tidal wave over so-called 'cash for honours'. I watched at first with bemusement, mixed with private anger over inaccuracies great and small in many of the stories; then with growing concern over the scale and ferocity of the allegations being hurled at Labour, at Tony and at me. Yet I fully expected that when a fuller and more accurate picture of events emerged, the more outlandish of the allegations would fall away. Perhaps even some good would emerge from it all: the very kind of national debate over reforms in party financing that I had advocated.

Yet all that soon proved to be an illusion. It was shattered, in two brief sentences that I will never forget, on a sunny Oxford afternoon: 'Michael,' my lawyer, Neil O'May, said when I had phoned him in response to his persistent voicemail messages, 'the police have told us that we are to report to Colindale police station at ten o'clock tomorrow morning. You are going to be arrested.'

CHAPTER 9

A Year in Hell

I was still feeling shattered, shamed and afraid when we got home from Oxford. Only minutes later, my lawyer Neil O'May arrived. Over the next twelve, terrible – and sometimes terrifying – months I would spend almost as much time with Neil as I did with Gilda. Without both of them, I doubt I would have been able to cope. Certainly on that first night, they were both crucial in helping me to recover a sense of focus without which I could not have faced the initial impending ordeal: the ten-minute drive to the police station the next morning to be arrested, booked and interrogated. Neil provided much else as well. Balding, slightly built, gap-toothed, he looked on first sight more like some absent-minded professor than a high-flier in the legal world. Rarely can appearances have been so misleading. From that very first evening, when we worked well past midnight, Neil had the steadying presence of a lawyer whose unerring expertise, sharply analytical mind, command of the facts, no-nonsense approach, and utter unflappability I came to rely upon – and to trust absolutely. He also had a wonderful lightness, warmth and sense of humour. Yet those were qualities neither of us had much occasion to enjoy until many, many months later. Not on the long night of 11 July 2006.

Neil had been blowing up balloons at his son's birthday party when Scotland Yard's assistant commissioner John Yates phoned to tell him they planned to arrest me. He was as surprised as I was. He suggested to Yates that since we had already offered him our full cooperation with whatever information or documents they might require, surely there was no need to arrest me. But Yates made it clear that if we didn't want to report to the police station, I would be arrested at my home. With the exception of another meeting with Neil before my second round of questioning in September, it was the only contact we had with the man in charge of the investigation. When the Crown Prosecution Service finally decided a year later that it was all over, it was not Yates who contacted us, but his number two, Graham McNulty, with a brief, formal, faxed note that concluded: 'The requirement for Lord Levy to return to Colindale Police Station on 24 July 2007 is cancelled.'

Yet with the horror of my first trip to Colindale station only hours away, Neil and I worked meticulously to draft a 'witness statement'. Eventually typed up on four sheets of A4 paper, it would remain the centrepiece of our defence against what sometimes seemed an ever-expanding array of accusations in the months ahead. Neil and I had spoken before in general terms about the allegations and innuendo surrounding 'cash for peerages' that had been building in the media. In what we both still assumed would prove only a precaution, he had drafted a broad summary of my position in the event we were ever called on to provide one. But now we clearly needed much more than a 'broad summary'. As we sat at the kitchen table with Gilda alternately reassuring me, prodding my memory and making steaming cups of tea, Neil proceeded to ask me hours of much tougher and more detailed questions. How, *exactly*, were Labour funds raised, and processed? When, and by whom, was the decision made to accept loans? Who decided the terms, drew up the agreements, talked and handled paperwork with the lenders? And how and by whom were nominations for peerages made? What meetings or conversations had I had with each of the 'secret' lenders who had helped fund the 2005 campaign, and especially with those whom Tony later nominated for peerages? In an odd way, Neil's constant cross-questioning helped drag me out of my initial sense of shock and helplessness. But it was also gruelling. And frustrating, too. Because neither of us had any idea why – beyond the 'case' being assembled in the media – the police had decided to arrest me.

An increasingly ominous media narrative had been building for many weeks. It began with a first 'cash for peerages' headline, in the *Independent on Sunday* at the end of October 2005. The paper had got hold of a 'leaked list of forthcoming honours' that it said included four men who had donated many thousands of pounds to Labour: the Priory healthcare founder Chai Patel; Gulam Noon, the 'curry king' of Britain's Indian-food industry; the property developer David Garrard and the stockbroker Barry

Townsley, both of whom were also prominent academy sponsors. Some of the sting in the story was briefly drawn when Gulam gave an interview to the *Daily Telegraph* in mid-November. He rejected any suggestion that he had asked for, or been promised, a peerage. When asked outright whether the £220,000 he had donated to Labour since 2001 had helped get him nominated for a seat in the Lords, he joked: 'If a peerage was so cheap, all sorts would buy one.' But then, barely a week later, the *Independent* reported that the House of Lords Appointment Commission – HoLAC – had rejected Blair's peerage list. And the paper suggested that this was because it had included 'several Labour Party donors'. Early in the new year came the *Sunday Times* sting, with Des Smith lured into his claim that academy sponsors could expect 'knighthoods and even peerages'. Finally, in March, the first newspaper reports emerged of the 'secret lenders' to Labour – a list that also included Patel, Noon, Garrard and Townsley. The circle, or so it seemed to conspiracy theorists in the media and the opposition benches, was complete. Or nearly so. When Jack Dromey came forward with his claim that, as party treasurer, he'd been unaware of the loans, it remained only for an SNP politician to cry 'foul' and the police investigation was off and running.

Des Smith's arrest in April left little doubt that it was serious, and that it would run and run (though long before it was over, the police reached the obvious conclusion that, whatever 'conspiracy' they were determined to find, a now-shattered sixty-year-old model headteacher was not a part of it). Yet there were other early victims, too, particularly after Tony moved to regain political control of the crisis by publicly naming all of the twelve supporters who had given Labour a total of nearly

£14 million in loans. Rod Aldridge was one early casualty. He was the multimillionaire head of the Capita outsourcing group – and also a generous supporter of the NSPCC and other children's charities, as well as the chairman of a new government-backed initiative to encourage volunteering among young people. He confirmed to reporters that he had indeed loaned Labour £1 million, but stressed that this was in a 'personal capacity', on commercial interest terms and with the expectation of repayment. And when asked whether this was all part of some 'cash for peerages' deal, he replied: 'I was absolutely not offered anything in return, nor did I request anything.' All of which was absolutely true. But it did not save him from feeling he had to resign as founding chairman of Capita to safeguard 'the reputation of the group'. In May, Sir David Garrard, amongst other lenders, was interviewed under caution. One of Britain's leading charitable donors, he remained obviously and understandably shaken by the time he told a reporter a few weeks afterwards: 'I bailed the Labour Party out and now I am in the worst position I have ever been in my life.' He said he had given his £2.3 million loan because he wanted to help a party leader he respected and an academies programme of which he had become a passionate sponsor. 'At no time was it said to me either expressly or by implication that by making a loan to the Labour Party I would obtain any honour.' Again, absolutely true – but again, no protection against a rising tide of media accusation and innuendo. And two further twists in the increasingly worrisome media coverage would clearly have implications for me: a reported claim by Chai Patel that he would have been delighted to give a donation but that I had asked for a loan instead, in order, he presumed to ensure 'anonymity'; and a similar claim by Gulam Noon, along with reports that I had advised him not to declare his loan on the peerage candidacy form for HoLAC.

Neil and I agonised, as we drafted my initial statement, over whether to answer those claims, and in the end decided not to. It was not that I had no answer to give: the suggestion that I had preferred Chai to give a loan rather than a donation was simply wrong. And the media accounts of my conversation with Gulam about his HoLAC form were seriously, and damagingly, misleading. In fact, he did phone me after filling in the form and sending it back to Number 10. He said he had included mention of the loan. I said that was fine, and that he should provide whatever information HoLAC wanted. But I had never seen one of the forms: HoLAC had been set up in 2000, well after I entered the Lords, as part of Tony's pledge to begin reforming the upper house. So I asked Gulam where and how he had listed the loan on the form. When he said he had included it under donations, I replied that while he should by all means include the loan if he wanted, he should check with the Labour Party for guidance on how to complete the form. And I simply added what I'd said to him when he had first agreed to make the loan: that it was my understanding from the party's legal and compliance officers that, under electoral law, a loan on commercial interest terms did not fall into the category of a donation. Gulam thanked me and, quite on his own, decided to retrieve the application and amend it. Our decision to leave the issue out of my declaration for the police was because we assumed they would unravel the true details of our conversation from questioning Gulam. The last thing we wanted to do was to get into answering allegations in the media – at least some of them, no doubt, an inadvertent result of honest confusion, and others the result of the traditional competitive hyperbole of the newspapers – rather than focus on the simple facts of the 'case' that the police appeared to be building against me.

The facts were straightforward, and the most crucial of them were laid out starkly in my prepared statement. 'Ever since my involvement with fundraising, no donation could be accepted without the approval of the party,' I said. 'Compliance with the Electoral Commission rules was the responsibility of the Labour Party General Secretary, its officials and compliance officers.' Whenever I 'secured a pledge', I would 'immediately report this to the Labour Party, allowing the General Secretary and the fundraising department to take the matter forward'. And I added, crucially: 'I advised the Prime Minister, as leader of the Labour Party, and others at No. 10 of any significant gift secured.' The same, I said, went for all of the loans and the lenders. 'As leader of the party, the Prime Minister took an interest in the party's financial situation and knew all the major benefactors.' I also reiterated a point that Tony himself had made publicly, in defending his peerage nominations, when the crisis had first erupted. 'I do take the view that, whilst a large donation or loan demonstrates a person's commitment to the party and its ideals, the fact of the donation or loan should be neither a qualification nor a disqualification for a peerage or, indeed, an honour.'

I saw no point in revealing that I had opposed the idea of taking loans during discussions with Tony and others, but I did make it clear that the decision to do so had not been mine. 'The decision to take loans was made by the Prime Minister in his capacity as Leader of the Labour Party in February 2005,' my statement said. I suggested it had been the result of the party's 'poor financial state', a knowledge that 'other parties had been taking loans for some time', the unwillingness of many Labour supporters to 'make large donations'; and the fact that 'large donors sometimes felt deterred from making donations because of the threat of unfair publicity'. Donations would 'always be preferable' to loans, I was keen to emphasise, particularly in the light of the inaccurate reports that I had turned down a donation from Chai Patel and insisted he make a loan instead. But I explained that 'since the party was not as popular as it had been, and donors were disinclined to part permanently with the substantial sums that the Labour Party needed, loans were sometimes the only way that a supporter would help'.

Finally, turning to the other part of the 'cash for peerages' equation, I made what seemed both to me and Neil the critical point: that Tony and his Downing Street aides, not I, drew up his peerages lists. 'Appointments to the House of Lords are not in my gift,' I said. 'They lie solely with the Prime Minister.' I did not play a part 'in the process at Number 10 by which candidates for peerages are considered and decided upon'. I did acknowledge that I had 'recommended or supported recommendations' for peerages or other honours in the past – as many people do, sometimes successfully and sometimes not. But I also made a point of including as examples candidates whom I supported but who had never given a penny to the party. Most importantly, I added: 'I have never accepted a gift or loan for the Labour Party as an inducement or reward for procuring or attempting to procure the grant of a peerage or any honour.' As for Tony's controversial 2005 peerages list, I said that 'if I was asked my view of a particular individual, I would give it'. (And that proved to be a statement that would suddenly take on huge importance during the most frightening single period of the police investigation, after inaccurate media reports appeared that Tony's chief political aide, Ruth Turner, had claimed that I asked her to 'lie' for me.) But while I had indeed raised all the loans for Labour's 2005 campaign, never, as the peerages list was being drawn up, did I 'urge that any lender should be considered for a peerage or any honour on the strength of their financial support for the party'. And in bringing in the loans, 'in no case did I offer a peerage or any honour. Nor did I suggest that such a position would be available.'

When we'd finally agreed the statement, I felt oddly relieved. But the stark reality of the seriousness of my situation was brought home to me when I formally signed the completed document. Its opening paragraph could not have been more clear: 'This statement, consisting of four pages each signed by me, is true to the best of my knowledge and belief and I make it knowing that, if it is tendered in evidence, I shall be liable to prosecution if I have wilfully stated in it anything which I know to be false or do not believe to be true.' Now, said an exhausted Neil as he headed home for a few hours before the brief drive to Colindale that would for ever change my life, 'You get some sleep!'

That proved impossible. However drained I felt from the nearly twelve hours since Neil's call in Oxford to tell me I was to be arrested – and however much Gilda urged me to 'please, *try* to sleep, for your own good' – I couldn't escape the horrible, humiliating sense that all I had worked for and achieved in my life was suddenly in jeopardy. It was only when Neil returned in the morning that I began to regain some sense of perspective, and control. I had signed and sworn that the statement I was about to hand to the police was entirely true. And I knew that it was. But more than that, I was galvanised by a mixture of adrenalin and anger, and a genuine pride in the commitment to a life of 'ambition with compassion' that had begun in a one-room flat suffused with the love, support and moral guidance of two remarkable parents. I was absolutely determined that however long the battle to clear any stain from my name, and from theirs, it was a battle I would win. The news of my arrest had been a terrible and frightening blow. I had trembled. I had shouted. I had cried. But as I got behind the wheel to drive with Neil to Colindale police station, I resolved that I would face my interrogators in a very different spirit: unfailingly courteous, calm, and unafraid. For the police and the media, my sudden centre-stage role in the most serious political crisis of Tony Blair's career was a question of cash and of honours. For me, it had become a question of honour.

We arrived at five minutes before ten. Detective Superintendent McNulty met us in the car park. He led us through the custody area and down a hall to a tiny interview room, with a table and four plain chairs, and read out a two-page document laying out my 'grounds for arrest'. This was not, he stressed, a 'fishing' expedition. But as he listed the reasons for arresting me it became clear that – at least at this stage – that is exactly what it was. The thrust of his case was that there were 'reasonable grounds to suspect' that I had 'conspired with others, on behalf of the Labour Party, to obtain financial loans' – which, except for the notion that this was a conspiracy – was, of course, true. But he also suspected I had 'offered as an inducement the reward of an honour or peerage', which was not. And he said he had grounds to suspect that I had 'conspired with others' illegally to hide donations to Labour from the Electoral Commission. I could only assume that this meant the police assumed that the terms on which we'd accepted the loans were not really commercial, meaning that they were actually donations. I thought to myself: what about the *Tories*, and the many millions of pounds of loans they were bringing in long before Labour had followed suit? But that, of course, was not the point. As for our own loans, my clear understanding – or more accurately, the understanding of the party's legal and compliance officers who were wholly in charge of resolving such issues and drafting the loan agreements – was that, at 2 per cent above the Bank of England interest rates, they were, in fact, commercial loans. In any case, as McNulty read out the arrest sheet, it was clear that, if not on a 'fishing expedition', the police were at least in the process of trying to fit a jumble of puzzle pieces into a picture that would look like a crime. McNulty said that police enquiries had revealed that seven of the twelve people who had given loans to Labour 'were subsequently put forward for consideration for nomination for the 2005 Working Peers list'. He added that he had grounds to suspect that I had 'played a role in influencing the formation' of the peers list by 'proposing the names of lenders to the Labour Party'. Yet the only two specific items of 'evidence' he offered of such a conspiracy – drawn, as we had expected, from the statements we had seen in the media by Chai Patel and Gulam Noon – were that 'at least one of the lenders offered the party a donation, which was then turned into a loan at Lord Levy's instigation', and that I had 'advised at least two lenders in relation to the completion of their House of Lords Appointments Commission nomination forms'.

By 10.30, I had been formally arrested and booked. I was told that after my questioning I would be fingerprinted and a DNA sample taken. In one welcome concession, the police did agree to Neil's request not to take a mug-shot – signalling their 'acceptance', enormously ironic in the light of the media's later reporting of virtually all the key details of the investigation, 'that this could be leaked and might be highly sensitive'. We then worked out arrangements for the police, over the next several hours, to take away my computer, e-mails, correspondence, other files and diaries, and Neil and I were driven away in a police car to accompany officers to my mews, near Marylebone High Street in central London. I still, briefly, harboured the hope that I was living through a nightmare that would soon be over. Just after we arrived at the mews, a courier was making a delivery upstairs and I breezily assured him that all the commotion was because 'the computers are being repaired' – only to see my PA frantically pointing at a brightly labelled police evidence bag that promptly ended that fiction. It also brought home to me the fact that this 'nightmare' had become very much part of my, and Gilda's, waking life. It was not until 3.30 in the afternoon that we were back at the police station. In the morning session, I had kept without much difficulty to my self-imposed rules of courtesy and calm. And at the mews, too, Neil and I had made a point of producing as promptly as possible any and all material the police felt they might want for their enquiries. However, now I assumed the greater test would come: the battery of questions I'd be asked to answer in the small, spare interrogation room at the end of the hallway.

In fact, the questioning never got started. The police began by handing Neil a lever-arch file with some of the documents on which they had based their 'reasonable suspicion' that I had broken the law – a list of all the loans, the detailed loan agreements, and several typewritten lists of names from the Number 10 honours unit. Neil accepted the file, but wanted further clarification on the arrest document that had been read out to us in the morning. Who were the 'others', he asked, with whom I was supposed to have conspired? And on what basis were the police alleging that I had 'conspired with relation to the peerage list'? We were told that I was being accused of conspiring with 'the lenders, and other individuals involved in compiling the 2005 list'. This was partly on the basis of 'the relationship of Michael Levy with individuals who prepared the list for approval by the Prime Minister' – Ruth Turner, the Downing Street political adviser John McTernan and Jonathan Powell. And 'so far as HoLAC is concerned', they said, 'one of the lenders, Chai Patel, says that he was advised that it was not necessary to show his loan on the HoLAC form. The other lender is Gulam Noon, who says the same.' Patel, he told us, had also said that he had 'offered the money as a donation'. Feeling increasingly worried at the picture the police seemed to be drawing about my role – and frustrated by Neil's and my agreement that I would not reply to any of the police accusations, however unfair I felt they were – I was at least slightly reassured by their final reply to his enquiries. The 'grounds of arrest' had been drawn up, it was clear, not on the basis of a coherent picture, much less any evidence, of wrongdoing. They had 'come from the inference from the fact that a significant number of people who made loans found themselves recommended for a peerage'. And the main reason they were focusing on me was that I was 'sufficiently well-placed to bring influence to bear'. I knew that my 'influence', as our formal witness statement would make clear, simply meant that

I was just one of a considerable number of people who were asked for recommendations at the preliminary stage of a peerages process that was decided entirely by a small group at Number 10, which did not include me – and ultimately by Tony. I knew that deciding on who got a peerage was something well beyond my influence. But most importantly, I knew I had never made any such promises.

But Neil's immediate focus was more narrow, on the specific allegations from Chai Patel. And he was reading through a transcript we had been given of Chai's statement to the police when wisps of greyish-black smoke began seeping from the air grille at the top of the room. My first, bizarre thought was that we were in some made-for-TV police drama and that a nefarious gas was being piped into the interrogation chamber – when an officer suddenly rushed in to tell us there was in fact a fire in an adjacent building. We were hurriedly evacuated, and I was bailed to return at ten the next morning for the questioning to begin. After leaving, Neil and I drafted a press statement – which upset some in the police by its inadvertent suggestion that we had not known I was to be arrested when we arrived at the station. But the main point Neil wanted to make was that the arrest had been unnecessary, a piece of grandstanding that did not bode well if the investigation was genuinely intended to produce not political heat, but light. 'Lord Levy has made it clear that he is ready at all times to co-operate with the police investigation,' the statement said. 'He therefore complied with a request to attend today at a police station where the police used their arrest powers, totally unnecessarily, apparently in order to gain access to documents that he would quite willingly have provided.' And it added: 'He has not been charged and does not expect to be, as he has committed no offence.' I had no doubt at all that the second part of that sentence was true. And I still assumed, and hoped, the first part would be, too. But the outward look of confidence that I wore when we returned to Colindale the next morning hid a growing worry that it might take weeks, perhaps even months, before I – and I presumed others – could convince Yates's team that their search for conspiracy and crime was misplaced.

We were greeted on the morning of 13 July in the interview room by Detective Sergeant Paul Kelsey, who, though always accompanied by a fellow officer, would be my main interrogator as the weeks of the inquiry became months, and finally a year. Over six feet tall and massively built, he looked like an investigating officer right out of Central Casting. But he was correct and businesslike, making it not at all difficult for me to be polite, and as helpful as possible, in return. 'As helpful as possible' was the operative term, because Neil had advised me that I was not to go beyond the statement we had provided. For roughly two hours, Kelsey asked me a total of more than 170 questions, to which I answered: 'You have my statement. I do not wish to make any further comment at this time.' In fact, there were times that it strained every fibre of my self-control *not* to answer. The great majority of his questions were covered by my witness statement. But some of them seemed to me to reflect important, and potentially damning, misunderstandings or misrepresentations that were being used to create a picture of conspiracy and crime where none existed. Particularly when Kelsey repeatedly pressed me on whether I'd 'put forward' a range of lenders or donors who later appeared on the various drafts that he showed us of Tony's 2005 peerages list, it was especially hard to keep quiet. For the fact is that this was the first time I'd seen in black and white how the process worked from the inside. I had indeed contributed my views, when asked by Downing Street, on a variety of the names being considered for peerages. But I had never attended any of the crucial meetings at which the inner circle – and Tony – ticked people on and off their list and discussed the merits of each candidate.

And there were other specific assumptions on which it seemed to me Kelsey was relying to create a picture of conspiracy from puzzle pieces that simply didn't fit. 'Is it the case that the rationale for secrecy was that the lender was to be recommended for a peerage without scrutiny?' he asked me. To which I very much wanted to reply: 'Since the lenders were already on public record as having given *donations* to the party, *what* lack of scrutiny? HoLAC already *knew* they were donors.' And when he asked: 'The loans were always donations, weren't they?' I very much wanted to answer that they were not. They were at a commercial interest rate, vetted and drawn up by Labour's legal and compliance advisers and intended for repayment, and as such they didn't have to be declared as the electoral law now stood. It was true that when repayment of the loans came due, the lenders could, if they wished, donate the money to the party instead – with a full and open declaration of the gift to the Electoral Commission. And what I had really wanted to add is that yes, the entire system was complicated by what Kelsey rightly called this 'loophole' – a loophole that had been exploited for much longer, and for hugely greater sums, by the Tories. What was really required – as I had said publicly before the issue had burst into the media, and before the police investigation had begun – was a radical reform of what I had become convinced was an inherently untenable marriage of fundraising and party politics. Britain needed finally to consider state funding for the political parties. The current system *was* open to abuse, or at least a corrosive appearance of abuse. The reality was that very few of the businessmen who gave large-scale donations to any of the parties did so without at least the vague hope that they might get some honour in return. That was by no means the only reason that they supported the party. At least in my long experience with Labour, there was *always* also a genuine, core political commitment – often a passionately personal commitment when Tony was at the peak of his powers. But history, and a mere cursory glance at the number of major Conservative donors sitting in the Lords, would suffice to inform anyone who had been smart and ambitious enough to make millions in business that an honour might – *might* – come with the territory. None of which meant that I had ever offered a peerage to any of the lenders who had bailed Labour out before the election. I had not. Ever. But it did mean that if the inevitable suspicion of deal-making was ever to be removed, it was time for a radical re-landscaping of the territory.

Yet at no point during the hours of Kelsey's and my frustratingly stilted dialogue was it more difficult not to answer back than when he declared: 'Jack Dromey says he did not know about the loans. Surely you would involve the treasurer in the process. Why was he not informed? Was it because he could not be trusted not to criticise the loans?' As the sharp, cautionary glance from Neil must have made clear to Kelsey, I ached to answer him – in the same way I had answered Dromey himself when he phoned me at home to apologise a few days after his public declaration that he had been in the dark about Labour's loans. He hadn't *meant* to suggest we had deliberately kept the information from him, he said. It was all a 'misunderstanding'. I listened in astonishment. In fact, the day-to-day responsibilities of treasurer rested with Labour's general secretary, at that time Matt Carter. But Dromey, in his elected role, did have the responsibility of reporting on financial matters to the NEC, the National Executive Committee of the Labour Party. And if he hadn't, that was not because the details had been somehow hidden. The loans were not in some separate, secret cache. They had without exception been paid into Labour's bank account. They were included in the party's regular cashflow reports and other financial documents – all of it material to which Dromey, like his predecessors as party treasurers, would have had access. How he could have taken even a cursory glance at the regular financial reports and failed to have been aware of the loans was extraordinary. 'If you didn't know, it's because you didn't look!' I fumed at him. 'If this was a charity or a business, you'd have been replaced! And now you go off all holier-than-thou and try to blame everyone else.' The truth is that Dromey *should* have been replaced. And he *would* have been, I am convinced, were it not for the fact that 'cash for peerages' seemed increasingly to be about something well beyond 'crimes' or 'conspiracies'. It was about politics. And I never assumed – Tony certainly never did – that it was about Jack Dromey. It was about Gordon Brown.

It may have been sheer coincidence that Dromey's statement came just hours before a second crucial Commons vote on Tony's education reforms, and hours after he had won the first vote only with Conservative support. Maybe reports reaching Number 10 that Dromey had paid a visit to the Treasury earlier in the day were wrong. Maybe Gordon's later protestations that he had nothing to do with Dromey's remarks were absolutely true. But what most upset Tony, I think, was a further, irrefutable coincidence: that the treasurer's assault had come at a time when one of New Labour's flagship reform policies was balanced on a knife-edge and when Gordon was seething over Tony's decision to fight a third election rather than turn over the reins of the party, and the country, to him.

But to Detective Sergeant Kelsey, I said simply: 'You have my statement. I do not wish to make any further comment at this time.' I realised Neil had been right to insist that I keep to our prepared statement. It was not that I had anything to hide. But from the tenor of Kelsey's questions, it seemed to both Neil and me that the police were trying to make a jumble of information and allegations somehow fit into a picture of conspiracy with me in the centre of the canvas. Innocent, irrelevant and misleading details were already being marshalled to make a case against me. I had no idea how or whether an ill-phrased reply to one of Kelsey's dozens of questions might be used as further 'evidence' of a crime that I – and Tony, and others – had simply not committed. I agreed with Neil that it was not a risk worth taking, particularly when we were told as the questioning finally wound down that I was being bailed to return for another round – in late September.

I was determined in the intervening months to do all I could to put my worries about the police inquiry to one side. It was a task made easier by the fact that as Tony's envoy I would soon be asked to help him respond to a Middle East crisis with political implications every bit as serious as 'cash for peerages'. Only hours before McNulty read out my 'grounds for arrest' at Colindale police station, the Iranian-backed Lebanese Muslim group Hizbollah had seized two Israeli soldiers on the border. And as Kelsey was questioning me on the following day, Ehud Olmert, who had succeeded Ariel Sharon as prime minister, ordered the first cross-border raids in what would become a fully fledged campaign of air and infantry attacks in Lebanon. Tony phoned Ehud and left him in little doubt that he understood and supported the reasons for the Israeli reprisal. For Tony, Hizbollah's abduction of the two Israelis was no coincidence. He was convinced that it had been done with the encouragement, perhaps at the urging, of the Iranians, who were for the first time facing a concerted international effort to stop them from acquiring a nuclear-weapons capability. He genuinely felt that it was important that Hizbollah's action not go unanswered. But although most of the news media, and his increasingly worried and critical cabinet colleagues, were apparently unaware of this, Tony also used his conversation with Olmert – a leader with whom he had built a strong relationship – to urge the Israelis to show 'restraint' in their reprisal. He said Israel must to do all it possibly could to avoid civilian casualties, especially since Lebanon was finally regaining its economic strength and political stability under a broadly pro-Western government. Olmert listened, but his reply was far from encouraging: Israel's national security was at stake, he insisted, and a strong reply to Hizbollah's 'provocation' was needed, not least as a signal to the Iranians. The increasingly intensive Israeli attacks, including air strikes as far north as Beirut, prompted not only international outrage that left Blair in familiar isolation alongside President Bush, but also something very near to a cabinet rebellion. As the violence escalated, Tony, who was on a visit to America, changed tack, and began to take a prominent role in getting a

UN-brokered ceasefire. He also decided that after the Lebanon crisis, there was an urgent need for Britain and others to make new efforts on the Israeli–Palestinian issue, particularly since there had been a change of Palestinian leadership as well. After Arafat's death, Mahmoud Abbas – Abu Mazen – had become Palestinian president.

At the beginning of August, I travelled to Israel and met at length with Olmert and Abu Mazen, as well as with their senior ministers and negotiators, in preparation for a summit visit by Tony in September, during which I joined him for his meetings in Jerusalem and Ramallah on the West Bank. The visit did produce at least one sign of hope: a commitment by both Olmert and Abu Mazen to begin talks 'without preconditions'. But when I joined Tony and his advisers for a late-night snack in his King David Hotel suite at the end of the visit, his mind was clearly as much on domestic politics as diplomacy. The cabinet revolt over Lebanon had by now subsided. But he had only just seen off an open campaign by backbench Labour MPs, including allies and protégés of Gordon Brown, to force him out of Downing Street. In order to stave off the 'coup', he had finally had to declare publicly that he would retire sometime before the 2007 party conference. And his habitual tone of forbearance and forgiveness towards Gordon seemed finally to have gone. Brown, typically, had assured him during the MPs' rebellion that it had been nothing to do with him. But Tony, it was clear as he ended his Jerusalem visit, simply no longer believed him. With his aides coming in with reports that the Sunday papers were poised to run stories alleging that Gordon or his acolytes had met personally with at least some of the plotters, Tony got angrier and angrier. More furious than I had seen him in all the years I had known him, he kept saying that he had never realised how *duplicitous* Gordon was – and what a 'liar'. In the months ahead, Tony would gradually steel himself to hide any public animosity towards his successor, convinced that he had to do so for the good of the party. And the media speculation that he *hoped* Gordon would lose to the new Tory leader, David Cameron, at the next general election was untrue. But he did tell me on a number of occasions during his final period in Downing Street that he was convinced that Gordon 'could never beat Cameron'. Even with Iraq and all his growing political problems, Tony still felt that if he stayed on, he could lead Labour to a fourth victory. Yet he recognised that was impossible, having publicly declared his decision to serve only three terms before the 2005 election. 'But Gordon? He can't defeat Cameron,' Tony told me. He did not buy the suggestion that the new Tory leader was an 'heir to Blair' in terms of policy or vision. And politically, Tony felt, he was not yet the 'finished article'. But he did believe that Cameron had major strengths – a sense of political 'timing', a winning personality, and a natural ability to communicate and connect with people outside the closed world of politics, particularly in the 'middle England' constituencies crucial to a general-election victory, that Gordon would simply be unable ever to match.

He was also increasingly angry at Gordon's behaviour as the 'cash for peerages' crisis erupted and escalated. I know he was convinced that Gordon saw the issue as a further weapon in getting him out of Downing Street. And though Tony never said this to me directly, I got the strong impression that he also resented Gordon's public posture of being somehow above the slightly dirty business of raising money for the party. To be fair, the decision to accept loans was Tony's. But I certainly never had any doubt during the 2005 campaign that Gordon – despite his spokesmen's denials whenever the issue came up in the media – was absolutely aware that loans were being taken. Particularly in the home stretch of the election campaign, Gordon was the leading figure. Tony's chosen campaign coordinator, Alan Milburn, had been relegated to the junior role. And it simply defies belief that, with money so critical an issue in the cash-strapped campaign, that a chancellor as interested in detail as Gordon would not have known where the money was coming from. In addition, an e-mail went out early in the campaign telling the leading figures *not* to attack the Conservatives for taking loans – because now *we* were taking loans too. I do not know whether Gordon himself was on the list of recipients. But his key representative on campaign issues, Spencer Livermore, certainly was.

During his Middle East visit, Tony tried to avoid commenting on 'cash for peerages' altogether – although when asked about my envoy role at a news conference, I was pleased that he did make a point of saying that I was doing valuable work and would continue to do so. But during our private conversations, it became obvious that there was – inevitably perhaps – a further new distance between us. Clearly, neither he nor I could discuss details of the police investigation, and we didn't. But we both knew that my arrest had made the situation far more serious than either of us had assumed when the 'cash for peerages' stories had first appeared in the media. It was clear to me that Tony still genuinely felt the police would soon conclude that no one had done anything wrong. In his mind, the entire furore rested on a misunderstanding of the 'political' peerage lists – names each of the party leaders put forward for 'working peers' not because of public service but openly and explicitly because they supported the party cause. Obviously, as he had said publicly, financial backers were among those whom he and other party leaders considered when drawing up their lists of working peers. Tony didn't think that a gift or a loan should guarantee an honour. But he felt it was ridiculous to suggest that financial support should disqualify someone from consideration. And he genuinely rated donors whose contributions reflected a passionate commitment to particular policies and projects central to his vision of a New Labour Britain. Long before the *Sunday Times* sting prompted accusations that academy sponsors were being promised honours, I recall his joking to me after an aide had remarked that one sponsor seemed to be hankering for an honour, 'I don't know what the fuss is about. As far as I'm concerned, anyone who sponsors a city academy *deserves* a "K"!' But both of us, I think, knew that the time for levity had long since passed. And despite his view that the 'cash for peerages' investigation would soon be over, and his expressions of sympathy for the ordeal that Gilda and I were facing, I flew back to London to prepare for my next round of questioning with a renewed sense of apprehension.

For a few hours at least, it receded, as Neil and I prepared a second, much shorter statement on the night before returning to Colindale – to put on record my denial that I had taken the initiative in urging Chai Patel to make a loan rather than a donation. When we arrived at the police station the next morning, I hoped that however unpleasant the experience of a further round of questioning, it might finally help bring the inquiries to an early end. Yet within minutes there were signs that the police had different ideas. As soon as we had taken our seats in the interrogation room, Kelsey declared: 'One of the persons who gave a loan to Labour has been arrested this morning under the Honours (Prevention of Abuses) Act of 1925.' I tried to hide my sense of shock, though less successfully than I would have hoped, and much less successfully than Neil, who responded calmly by asking who had been arrested, and whether the arrest had been by 'arrangement' or 'surprise'? Kelsey said he would not give us further details. And when Neil asked whether, as in my earlier questioning, we would be given relevant documents on the arrest and other issues that Kelsey planned to raise with us, he replied that this time there would only be 'staged disclosure' as he opened new avenues of the inquiry. Barely twenty minutes later, after ominously suggesting that Neil and I might want to break for a 'private consultation', Kelsey did suddenly lift the lid of mystery. The latest police target was obviously one of the Labour lenders who had barely been mentioned in the media, and who hadn't even been on Tony's 2005 peerage list. Kelsey told us: 'I am going to provide diary entries for Mr Christopher Evans.'

'Mr' Evans was in fact Sir Christopher Evans, a leading light in Britain's biotechnology sector who had been made an OBE under the Conservatives and knighted in 2001. Like many of the donors I dealt with after my initial years of fundraising for the party, he had got to know Tony, Gordon and a range of top Labour figures long before the party suggested that I approach him for a donation a number of years earlier. He was bright, highly intelligent and almost flamboyantly self-confident. I particularly remember attending a dinner in Scotland at the home of the businessman and philanthropist Tom Hunter at which Evans held the audience literally spellbound as he rhapsodised about the future prospects for biotech. He had also long been openly ambitious to carve out not only a role in business, but a national political profile too. Still, as Neil and I withdrew and began reading the photocopied pages we had been given from Evans's handwritten personal diary, I became increasingly astonished – and apprehensive. On the face of it, Christopher's often rambling references to money and honours might provide the 'smoking gun' that the police, and the media, were clearly hunting.

As the BBC would report nearly two months later, one entry – for 30 October 2000 – claimed that at a meeting for tea in the Lords he had agreed to give Labour £100,000, and that I had asked if he wanted a 'K' or 'Big P'. Increasingly upset, I told Neil that we'd have to put the record straight to Kelsey: Christopher had long hoped for a place in the Lords. So did lots of other people, the only difference being that Evans was so frank about his ambitions. He had made a point of mentioning to me on various occasions that he had been told by senior people in Labour that he would make a worthy addition to the upper house. But for my part, I had never, ever, offered or promised him a peerage. I had always made it absolutely clear to him, as I did to other party donors or lenders, that such matters were in any case not in my gift. Evans was indeed knighted in the 2001 New Year's honours. But not only did I have no role at all in the process, I also wasn't even aware of it until the honours list was published in the press.

As I pointed out to Neil, there was in fact a clear indication in one of the diary entries that Evans himself recognised that I neither could nor would promise him an honour in return for a donation. 'Levy fleeced me for £200k and now I'll really have to get my finger out,' he wrote. 'And what will I get for it?' Still Neil would not budge as I implored him to let me put the 'real picture' to Kelsey. 'You can *not* go beyond our witness statement,' he said. He tried to reassure me by adding that the diary would almost certainly not be admissible in the event the case ever got that far. Beyond any legal arguments, he argued, the contents were peppered with rhetorical flourishes, expressions of frustration and wishful thinking, and even the occasional hint of an extra glass or two of wine over a nice dinner. One entry recorded – with Chris's typical forthrightness and flair – that he had been 'pissed' the night before. The diary would inevitably be read as one man's highly subjective, after-the-fact creation of a narrative from assorted conversations or experiences that he had had. But the crucial thing, Neil kept telling me, was that I knew that to read the diary as suggesting a 'cash for peerages' deal would be untrue – something Evans himself would later confirm in a letter to his shareholders, saying that I had 'never' promised him 'anything in return for my donations or my loan'. By the time we emerged to face Kelsey again, I had managed – only just – to regain some sense of calm. As he reeled off question after question, I referred him to our written statement. It was, and remained, a true account of what I had done and, more importantly, what I *hadn't* done as Labour's chief fundraiser. Yet as we left, bailed to return yet again at the beginning of December, I felt increasingly trapped in some Kafkaesque drama where events were simply spinning out of my control.

It marked the start of a period of many months that were particularly tough on Gilda, Daniel and Juliet. In public, I somehow managed to keep up a front of self-confidence, with a series of meetings with visiting Israeli and UN diplomats in London and at various community events. At home, I sunk into depression, frustration and anger. Even occasional games of tennis with friends – my days as 'Tony's tennis partner' were now over – offered no relief. On a number of occasions, helicopters circled overhead taking television pictures, presumably to illustrate what the media were increasingly presenting as a web of conspiracy that seemed to be drawing nearer and nearer to the prime minister himself. There was a brief respite when the police pushed back our next round of questioning until January. But with Tony himself interrogated, as a witness, in mid-December, there seemed every prospect the investigation would push ahead well into the new year and perhaps to the very end of his period in power – with me still very much on centre stage. There were times when I wondered how long I could cope with the rising pressure. With Neil's and my family's support, however, I tried to tell myself that, after the Evans diary, things were hardly likely to get any worse.

But then, as my return for a third round of questioning in January drew nearer, they did. At 6.30 a.m. on 19 January, police knocked on the door of Ruth Turner's London home, instructed her to get dressed in front of a female officer, and arrested her. She had already been questioned twice before, first as a witness, then under caution, and clearly the police had been building up to her arrest – with me, it would soon become clear, again very much in their sights. Tony, Jonathan and others in Downing Street were furious at the way Ruth had been set upon. So was I – particularly since I knew at first-hand how gut-wrenching it was to be placed under arrest and confronted with accusations I knew were unfounded, even with the few hours of warning I had been given before my first trip to Colindale police station.

And I was genuinely heartened to see Tony personally come to Ruth's defence, declaring that he still had 'complete confidence' in her. Yet at the same time I could not help but feel let down by his failure to provide similar backing for me as the police pressure steadily mounted. To Neil's dismay, for the first time in many months I broke our self-imposed restraint in joining in the off-record briefings that were so poisoning the police investigation, and let it be known that I did indeed fear being 'hung out to dry' by Downing Street. I instantly regretted doing so, above all because I felt Neil's judgement was right. I was particularly keen to prevent friends in the Jewish community from suggesting that I was somehow being made a victim of anti-Semitism. I even had rare harsh words for my own rabbi at Mill Hill, Yitzchak Schochet, a dear personal friend, when he did so – although I was, and remain, deeply grateful for the support, guidance and understanding he showed me throughout the 'cash for peerages' ordeal. And never during the long months of the investigation did I disclose any details about my own questioning or the case the police seemed intent on building, much less try to use the media to rebut it – even after my third round of questioning on 30 January set off a chain of events that tested that statute of self-denial almost to breaking point.

At 10.02, as soon as we had made our way to the interview room, Kelsey's colleague, Detective Sergeant Tony Blake read out the now-familiar refrain of 'suspicion' that I had conspired to trade loans for peerages and had helped hide the loans from the Electoral Commission. But he added that I was now being arrested on a further count: 'reasonable grounds to suspect' that I had 'sought to pervert the course of justice – by asking Ruth Turner, the director of Government Communications at No. 10

Downing Street, to lie about your involvement in committing the offences I have described, and conspiracy to mislead police investigations'. I was dumbfounded, and despondent – feeling, I imagine, very much the way Tony did when he had phoned me from the Far East in his cry of despair. I had, over a period of months, slowly come to terms with the pace and parameters of the police investigation. I was buoyed, even after the jolt of the 'Evans diaries' by a confidence that once the 'evidence' had been thoroughly and dispassionately evaluated it would show what I knew to be true: that there had been no trade in 'cash for peerages' by anyone, least of all by me. But now, like Tony in the Far East, I began to wonder when it would all *end*. Every time the investigation seemed to show signs of reaching its inevitable conclusion, a new avenue – a new allegation – appeared. Now it was not just the suggestion that I had promised peerages, but that I had got someone else to 'lie' for me to hide my 'crime'. It was, I knew, untrue. But as Neil and I awaited Kelsey's 'staged disclosure' of the basis for this latest accusation, I began to wonder whether, for the police and the media, that had simply ceased to matter.

It was more than three and a half hours later – after dozens of further, familiar questions about my alleged role in recommending some of the names on the peerages list – when the 'disclosure' finally arrived, and the damning new scenario the police were suggesting became clear. 'I wish to read over a note,' Kelsey declared, looking directly at me. 'This note represents a meeting between Ruth Turner and you on Wednesday 24 May 2006. We are led to believe it was typed up on 25 May 2006. She has told us she typed it as a recollection of the meeting between the two of you.' He then handed us a three-page document. By the time it became the focus of the latest and most damaging of the many media leaks in early March, it seemed finally to create an inescapable public picture of what was being branded a 'Watergate-style' conspiracy.

Yet as I began reading Ruth's memo, my anguish and apprehension began to subside. I did fear – rightly, as it turned out – that by the time an inevitably skewed version made its way into the newspapers and TV bulletins it risked adding further damaging momentum to the police's determination to charge someone, anyone, at the end of their long and costly probe. And I had no doubt at all by this point, of course, who the 'anyone' of choice would be. But Ruth's note to Jonathan Powell, which was apparently never sent, in fact broadly confirmed what I and others had been telling the police from the beginning: that whatever views I had expressed, along with those of many others during the preliminary stage of the 2005 peerages list, it was Downing Street – and ultimately Tony – who decided who was nominated.

Ruth began by saying that she was having a further meeting with her lawyers and wanted to speak by telephone with Jonathan, and 'maybe with Tony', about a 'conversation I had with Michael'. Our conversation did happen, in Downing Street. I had gone to Number 10 for a meeting on Middle East issues and I had a chat with Ruth afterwards. It was only weeks after the police investigation had been announced, and two months before I would first be arrested. But Des Smith had been arrested, and both Ruth and I were clearly puzzled – and vaguely worried – about where it was all heading. It was probably a mistake, I now saw, to have talked with her about the case at all – although it seemed perfectly natural at the time, since neither of us had any inkling the police would actually arrest us or be suspicious that either of us had done anything wrong. But it was not, of course, illegal, much less 'conspiratorial'. I simply outlined my own honest view of my role and what had happened. It was essentially that I had been asked to put in my views on a number of the names during the preliminary stage of drawing up the peerages list – and that Tony and his Downing Street team, who of course knew about all of the loans and donations, then discussed and decided the nominations on their own.

Ruth wrote that she was worried this would 'almost entirely' remove me from everything and place the focus of any police inquiries on her and McTernan instead – an echo, I suppose, of my own concern over media coverage that was hugely overstating my own role. However, as the memo made clear, the only substantive difference between her recollection of events and my own was the degree of Ruth's and John's specific knowledge of several of the lenders who were later put forward for peerages. That was an honest difference of opinion. And it was in any event far from crucial, since Tony himself had by now publicly confirmed that he had personally known the details of all the loans and the lenders before he decided to nominate any of them for a peerage. Ruth's note added that she had explicitly reminded me during our Downing Street conversation that 'as far as I'm concerned there is a crucial separation in all this – money is his [Levy's] business; the list is my business'. She confirmed that she had been 'vaguely aware of their [the lenders] status as significant financial contributors' but that frankly she 'didn't think it mattered. I will say it wasn't a significant factor in my mind and wasn't part of any discussions of suitability or otherwise of possible names.' And she added that while I had made 'suggestions that several people would make good Labour peers', I 'didn't put pressure, push or follow up on these suggestions. I will confirm what Michael says: that I didn't tell him who was on the list until after the decision was taken by TB.' Her note concluded: 'I took responsibility, with others within No. 10 and after wide consultation, for recommending all of the people on this list. In each case, we had good reasons other than money for doing so.'

Yet even those clear confirmations of my own account of how the list was drawn up were not the most significant omission or distortion in the later rash of news reports about the so-called 'Turner e-mail' as the investigation was building to its crescendo. A number of the reports said outright that her note had accused me of trying to get her to 'lie'. That single, damning word was in fact never used by Ruth at any time – although, according to a brief extract from her police interrogation that Kelsey read to us, it *was* used by the officer who questioned her. The 'lie' allegation got into the media through inaccurate comments from the judge at one of the hearings during which the Attorney General's office was seeking an injunction against media reporting of the note. Unfortunately, the judge – and the government barrister – had not actually read Ruth's words.

But, by far most importantly, what was utterly missing from all the news reports was the very first sentence of Ruth's account of her conversation with me. It began: 'He says he isn't going to lie about anything.'

And I hadn't. Still, as the media storm surrounding Ruth's memo erupted in early March, I think I reached the lowest point during the entire long investigation. I began to despair of the possibility of ever getting the police, much less the public, to see the true picture of what had actually happened. As I tried somehow to get on with my life as the weeks went by after the Turner memo, the almost daily chats with Neil and the constant drip of ominous speculation in the press left me more and more despondent. Gilda had ceased being able to sleep through the night. It was not because any of us ever thought that a jury of fair-thinking Britons could conceivably find me guilty of any of the widening allegations suggested by the police or the press – but because the investigation seemed to have gathered a force of its own. And when, finally, the police declared their work was over and handed the last of their files to the Crown Prosecution Service in late April, the dramatic front page of the *Daily Mail* confirmed all my worst fears. With photos of me, Ruth and Chris Evans, its big, bold headline screamed: 'Charge them!'

There were few, very few, shafts of light during the dark months of spring and early summer 2007. Friends provided the ones I cherished most. Feeling at times so alone and cornered, I felt a gratitude I will never forget and can never repay for their attention, support and encouragement. And I remember above all two excursions I made that literally moved me to tears, and helped me to put my own predicament – however difficult – in context. The first was to visit one of Britain's most gifted *chazanim*, or Jewish cantors, Simon Hass, at his daughter's home in St John's Wood. The Reverend Hass had been ill, and I had been meaning to go and see him for many weeks, but had been so distracted by 'cash for peerages' that I had failed to do so. But when I arrived, he gave me no time to apologise for not having visited. Instead, he wanted me to know he had been thinking about *my* plight. He said that the important thing was not to lose sight of the fact that even the most difficult times eventually pass, and that one way or another justice always prevails. Speaking movingly of his own childhood and of his family's suffering under the Nazis, he made his way to the piano and began to sing an almost spine-tinglingly beautiful rendition of *Kol Nidrei*, the prayer said in synagogue during Yom Kippur. For the first time in many weeks, I was suddenly aware of how relatively small my own burden was. Only days afterwards, I visited a CSV centre in north-west London to meet with a group of seriously disabled young men and women who had benefited from a programme we ran to help them to rebuild their lives. One woman's story, in particular, moved me profoundly. She was in her early twenties, and had been about to marry when a back operation went terribly wrong, leaving her disabled. But she had now begun running a phone and computer service from her flat to help other disabled people get back into part-time employment. These were young heroes, I realised, who had problems much, much greater than my own – but who had shown courage, resilience and faith, and they were winning through.

I was also struck by a gesture from the JLGB, or Jewish Lads' and Girls' Brigade. It was set up in the 1890s as the Jewish community's equivalent of the Scouts. And despite the growing media frenzy surrounding the 'cash for peerages' probe, the charity approached me and asked me to become its president. It was an offer that I of course accepted and, especially given the timing, one that deeply touched me.

There were two much more public figures who also provided extraordinary support, all the more important and gratifying because it was the exception to the rule. David Blunkett, alone among leading figures in the party, had gone on record the day of my initial arrest to criticise the police's action and express full confidence in me. And in the many months afterwards, he frequently phoned me at home simply to say he was thinking of me and Gilda, and to wish us well. And there was another show of support that particularly pleased, and frankly surprised, me. I had, of course, known Alan Sugar from our Disci Records days, as well as through his generous contributions to Jewish Care and other charities, and to Labour. I liked him enormously. But I also knew he was very much his own man, increasingly disillusioned with British politics – and, I figured, about the least likely person I knew to weigh in on 'cash for peerages'. Yet just days after the media reports on Ruth Turner began appearing, he did so, on the BBC's *Today* programme. He was speaking out, he said, 'from the periphery' because he felt I was being made 'the scapegoat' and being 'set up as the bad guy'. But he said: 'You have to ask yourself: "What's in it for Levy?" This is not a man who has lined his own pocket. This is not a man who has done some insider-trading dealing or something like that in the stock market and has stolen from shareholders. This is a man who has blind devotion – I don't know why – to Tony Blair, blind loyalty for Tony Blair and has gone out and blagged people for money for the party. That, to me, is his worst crime.' When I phoned to thank him, his response was typically Alan. He was, he said, just saying what he believed.

Few others, however, seemed to be listening as the weeks dragged on – through May, June and into July – without any hint of what, and when, the CPS would decide. I gave up counting the number of newspaper stories claiming an announcement was imminent. And I don't think either Gilda or I would have been able to cope without one huge – and hugely happy – distraction. Our son Daniel had proposed to his fiancée a few months earlier and they had decided they wanted the wedding to be in the garden at Chase House. We were obviously overjoyed, and back in January had confidently set the date – for 29 July. We had figured the investigation would be over long before then and, as I'd told the rabbi performing the ceremony, 'we will be in happier times'. Now, of course, I could not be so sure. But if there was one thing on which both Gilda and I were resolutely agreed, it was that we were not about to let the police, or now the CPS, overshadow one of the most important and joyous days in Daniel's life – and ours. We sent out the invitations late in April, only days before the CPS began its deliberations, and were soon busy arranging for everything from the catering and marquee to transport and table settings for what we prayed would be, for all the right reasons, a day to remember. As the wedding date drew nearer, it thankfully crowded out almost every other aspect of our lives. Even Tony's final departure from Downing Street at the end of June barely registered with us – although I did write a brief personal note both to Tony and Jonathan Powell in mid-May, on his tenth anniversary in power, wishing them well – to which they each replied thanking me for what I'd done for them, the government and the country. Jonathan added: 'When all this current nonsense recedes, that is what will stand out.' And he wished me 'strength for the final weeks'.

But the 'final weeks' kept receding further, well into July. The CPS had had the police files for nearly two months. I was still 'bailed to return' to Colindale police station on 24 July, and we had heard nothing from the CPS or the police to suggest otherwise. By mid-month, however, we and others began receiving increasingly strong indications that a decision was in fact finally near. On Thursday 19 July, I left home about noon for the

Cinnamon Club, the Indian restaurant a few blocks from the Commons best known as a lunchtime haunt for politicians and journalists – having been invited to a 'thank you' meal by the BBC's director-general, Mark Thompson, for my work with Abu Mazen and other leading Palestinians to help secure the release of the kidnapped BBC reporter Alan Johnston in Gaza.

On the way, I phoned Neil, and when he came on the line I could tell he was worried. 'What's wrong?' I asked. He said he had just made a call to Carmen Dowd, the head of the Special Crime Division at the CPS, who was handling the 'cash for peerages' decision. Since Neil had been hoping to be away for part of the following week, and with signs that an announcement might in fact be near, he had asked her as a matter of professional courtesy whether she could give him any more specific signal on the timing. 'She told me: "You will hear early next week,"' he said. 'But she was very cool, and curt. And when I asked how we will be informed, she just said: "You will be hearing from the police." I don't want to alarm you,' he said, 'but I have to be honest. My talk with Carmen makes me feel worried.' The lunch with Thompson, although he was enormously engaging and warm, went by in a blur. I headed immediately to the House of Lords, where I phoned Neil again – but then, thinking better of discussing the case from there, walked to the small park beside Parliament and called him on my mobile. Neil remained deeply worried. And when I phoned the two truly outstanding barristers with whom we'd been working for many months, Roy Amlot and Mark Dennis, they said they also felt the signs were not encouraging. I phoned Neil again, and said: 'Shouldn't we tell Gilda about this? There is no way I want to speak with Daniel about it, or Juliet, but I think we've got to tell Gilda.' Neil agreed.

When I got her on the phone – she was shopping in Waitrose – she was badly shaken. 'How is this *possible*?' she said. 'I can't understand it!' I told her that we would just have to find a way through if Neil's fears proved right. 'Look, just drive home very carefully, and I'll tell Neil to call you there.' He did, explaining in detail his concern but also doing his best to reassure her. I phoned her again, too – because I was going into a meeting of Jewish community leaders at the Lords that I had helped set up and would be out of mobile contact for the next few hours. Gilda and I had already arranged to meet at a London restaurant at eight o'clock for a small birthday dinner for close friends, Tricia and Michael Levin, along with another couple with whom we were close, Victor and Sylvia Blank. I said we would talk then, but that we would just both somehow have to 'find a way to keep strong'.

Yet when I phoned Neil again on the way to the restaurant, he had some further news. Dowd had called him back and, in a much friendlier tone, said that we would be told the final decision not next week, but the next day. 'She still said we would hear it from the police,' Neil said. 'Honestly, I don't know what to draw from any of this any more. I've never experienced anything quite like it, but I think it might still be good news. We'll just have to wait.'

The waiting was agony. Neil had phoned to update Gilda by the time we met at the restaurant, and neither of us could really focus on the dinner. By this time, I later found out, several reporters had called Nick Lloyd's office to say they were hearing that the CPS had decided it was all over, and that no charges would be brought. But when Nick and his son Ollie had phoned Neil, he told them to delay passing on the 'media gossip' to me and Gilda. It wasn't official, and we were more than confused enough already. But then Gilda's mobile rang. The call was from Lisbon, where former prime minister Blair had arrived for his first formal engagement as international Middle East representative. It was one of his aides, who asked: 'Is Michael with you? Tell him that Tony's in a meeting but he wants to speak to him and he'll call you in twenty minutes.' Almost exactly on schedule, he did. 'Look, I think it's all going to be OK,' Tony said. Increasingly tense and confused, I asked how he knew: was it 'media people'? He replied that he couldn't tell me anything else at this stage, but repeated: 'I think it's going to be fine.' When I phoned Neil again, he was relieved, but also cautious. We had been through too many twists and turns since our first trip to Colindale a year earlier to assume anything until it was absolutely definite and official. Then, twenty minutes later – by now it was about 9.45 – Tony's aide called back, with a one-sentence message: 'What Tony said to you before, he wants you to know now that it's definite.'

I felt, as I had twelve months earlier after a very different phone call in Oxford, the tears welling up in my eyes. Gilda was crying, too, as we embraced, trembling with relief that the long nightmare was finally ending. When I phoned Juliet, she shrieked in delight, and said that she and Phil were immediately driving down from Oxford and would meet us at home. Then I called Daniel, who was by now the head of a Middle East policy think-tank in Washington. Having for months tried to buttress Gilda and me by being outwardly strong, relentlessly confident and reassuring, he shouted and laughed and cried – letting out all the emotions he had been bottling up as the investigation had turned more and more ominous. 'It's over! It is *finally* over!' he said.

As we left the restaurant to drive home at ten o'clock, the first television reports appeared saying that the CPS would indeed announce there would be no 'cash for peerages' charges. Within seconds, my mobile, and Gilda's, began ringing – with calls first from our nephew, Steve Kutner, then from dozens of other family members and friends. When Steve asked Gilda whether the news was true – 'is it *definite*?'– she told him we thought so, but that we still hadn't heard anything officially. Tony called again, too, and said how happy he was for everyone – but above all for me and for Gilda – that the ordeal had finally ended. By the time we got home, there was a small army of reporters, photographers and cameramen outside. But on Neil's advice, I told them I could say nothing yet – not, Neil had insisted, until we had heard officially.

We still hadn't received word by the time Neil joined us for breakfast the next morning and we set off for his office on Gray's Inn Road, near King's Cross. I had forgotten the scale of the sheer relief and elation I felt, on emerging for the first time in months to find a media horde that did not look threatening or unfriendly, until I looked back at a *Times* diary piece by Anne Treneman that I kept as a reminder. 'Lord Levy had been told to say nothing, but he just could not stop himself,' she wrote. My 'face cracking with happiness', she said, I was asked by the waiting press whether I'd had a glass of champagne with breakfast. I jokingly replied: 'Did you say *one*?' Then, I 'shook hands with every photographer, reporter and cameraman there'. In a generous further note, Treneman's account added that after months in which 'we [in the media] have been his very own vultures, endlessly circling', it was 'an extraordinary gesture'. But it also genuinely reflected how I felt.

We finally heard from the police at Neil's office, a four-paragraph letter faxed from Graham McNulty. It began by listing the major allegations the police had put to me during the long sessions of questioning in Colindale over the past year, and ended by saying we would no longer have to report back to answer bail the following week. In between was the news that, particularly over the past few weeks, I had begun to fear we might never hear – delivered, I couldn't help sensing, with a sense of disappointment and distance. 'The Crown Prosecution Service has, at noon today, informed me that they consider there to be "insufficient evidence to provide a realistic prospect of conviction in relation to Lord Levy". I am therefore writing to formally inform you that the Metropolitan Police intend taking no further action in respect of these allegations.'

Though there would be reports in the days that followed suggesting that the police felt let down by the CPS's decision not to press ahead, the detailed public statement Carmen Dowd made only minutes later went considerably beyond McNulty's letter. 'For the avoidance of doubt,' she said, 'we wish to emphasise that today's decision indicates unequivocally that there is insufficient evidence to support proceedings against any individual' – whether on 'cash-for-honours', or 'any offence of perverting, or attempting or conspiring to pervert, the course of justice'. She added that Tony's list of 'working peers', as he had for months been trying to emphasise, was always explicitly intended to include party supporters, and was drawn up on a 'party political basis'. Not only was there 'no direct evidence' that anyone had bought or sold peerages, Dowd said; but there was in fact 'substantial and reliable evidence that there were proper reasons for the inclusion of all those whose names appeared on the

2005 working peers list, or drafts of that list: that each was a credible candidate, irrespective of any financial assistance that they had given'.

Dowd ended by tackling head-on what to me had seemed from the start the most difficult, frustrating, and at times anguishing aspect of the entire 'cash for peerages' saga: that ultimately it was not about legal argument, and 'crime' or 'conspiracy', but about politics. The CPS's ruling was an assertion of one of Britain's longest, proudest traditions: the simple rule of law. 'The investigation has been primarily concerned with the conduct of individuals working within Downing Street and who were, therefore, closely connected to the former prime minister,' Dowd declared. 'Owing to the political context of the matters investigated, it is inevitable that the issues raised by the inquiry have become the subject of political debate, often conducted in partisan terms.' But, she concluded: 'The CPS makes it clear that political questions have played no part in its analysis of the case. The criminal law in England and Wales applies to every citizen alike, regardless of his or her political affiliation or official status. Equally, the criminal law cannot be used to single out a citizen for adverse treatment because he or she has such an affiliation or enjoys such status.' I found her words enormously moving, even if they made it into very few of the hundreds of news reports on the CPS ruling in the days that followed. But I couldn't help also reflecting that if the decision had somehow gone the other way, if the damaging police and media narrative of crime and conspiracy and cover-up had somehow been allowed to overshadow the simple facts, politics *would* inescapably have come very much to the fore. For the fact is that even if I *had* done the things which Detective Sergeant Kelsey, in question after question and hour after hour, seemed intent on proving that I did, there was always one crucial piece missing in the narrative. There was only one person in the picture the police seemed intent on painting who knew who every last one of Labour's lenders and donors were, and who also ultimately decided whom to nominate as a peer. In the event that I had in the end been charged and brought to trial, the very first name on the witness list for the defence would – inevitably – have been the man I had helped, supported, believed in and still considered a friend: Anthony Charles Lynton Blair.

But thankfully, the rule of law prevailed over the pressures of politics. And there was one further, final statement to be made that day. Neil and I had agreed with the media that I would read out brief remarks to them in a basement conference room once the official announcement had been made. There was – Anne Treneman's account says, I hope rightly – not even a 'trace of triumphalism'. I began with what mattered to me most: my 'delight' that the ordeal was finally at an end, and a recognition that I could not possibly have coped alone. 'I would like to start by thanking my family, particularly my wife Gilda, our children, my friends and colleagues for the unwavering support,' I said, 'and of course my legal team for their guidance throughout the duration of this police inquiry, which has been incredibly long and really stressful. For the past sixteen months, the people closest to me have had to endure the intensity and pressure of this long investigation. We are all relieved it is over.' From the outset, I said, I had had 'every confidence that no charges would be brought against me' – though I did not confide just how sorely that had been tested, particularly over the past few weeks and days. 'Nevertheless,' I did say, 'it comes as a great relief that after a complete and thorough investigation which has been assessed by the country's leading legal experts, I have been exonerated as expected.' I added that I had been 'disappointed' by the 'constant leaks to the media which have been misleading, factually inaccurate and personally damaging'. But I was careful to steer clear of direct criticism of the media, or of the police. I said only that I still believed in 'the importance of public service and in the duty of individuals to be willing to serve their country' – and that I hoped that 'the way that this inquiry has been played out' would not 'deter people from feeling that politics and political debate is an area where they can play their full part'.

Back home that evening, able for the first time in more than a year to enjoy a family dinner without worrying about the next day's newspapers or the next round of allegations, I couldn't help feeling along with my real sense of joy some regret at my own experience of 'politics and political debate'. I thought back to that first meeting with Tony thirteen years earlier, both of us burning with the idea that a 'new' Labour Party could not only reinvigorate and elevate itself, but Britain as well. Politics, and above all his move from opposition to power, had changed both of us. Certainly for me, the longer I stayed and the higher I rose alongside Tony, the more difficult I often found it to recapture the idealism with which our relationship had begun. I had almost walked away before Tony made his fateful decision to take loans, and of course I now wished that I had. But I think one of the things that had most angered and depressed me during the long police investigation – as the headlines progressed from 'Lord Cashpoint' to 'cash for peerages' and finally 'Charge them!' – was the absence of any understanding that whatever I had done in my years of working with Tony had ultimately been about helping a politician, a political party and above all a vision for Britain that had truly inspired my support. Of course, I had personal ambitions. I always will. And vanity sometimes, too. I enjoyed the honour of being made a peer, felt fulfilled by my work as diplomatic envoy, and a sense of accomplishment over the tens of millions of pounds I helped to raise. But at the core of it all, until the very end, I can honestly say that my fundamental drive remained unchanged: to help a political leader, a party, and a vision for Britain's future in which I deeply believed. I am still proud of my role in bringing in the funds that made it possible for Tony to win his three elections; to make at least a start on the political changes necessary to ensure a caring, tolerant, fair and modern country; and perhaps particularly, in the light of the many hundreds of hours I spent helping him against sometimes extraordinary odds, to keep the hope of an eventual Middle East peace alive. If I still felt a tinge of real sadness even on that first joyous night of rebuilding my life after the terrible months of the police investigation, it was because amid the endless allegations about a role I never played in a 'conspiracy' that never existed, the part that I *had* played in the positive things that Tony sought to accomplish seemed utterly forgotten.

Still, there was only joy when, eight days later, we welcomed Daniel, our new daughter-in-law Vally, and hundreds of their friends and ours to celebrate a wedding that we had feared might be held under the shadow of the CPS's deliberations. The sun shone. Daniel and Vally looked radiant. The ceremony was enormously moving. Indeed, the only real reminder of the months of tension and occasional terror that had just ended was among the invited guests: Tony and Cherie, of course, joined us to honour Daniel's marriage. It must have been one of the very few times since becoming Labour leader that he had been in such a large crowd but had no speaking part. But now he and Cherie were there, despite all we had been through, simply as friends.

That friendship, too, had been fundamentally changed by politics – by Tony's move into Downing Street and by all that happened since, particularly over the last year. He did make a point of attending a farewell reception for me at Lancaster House in June, shortly before he stepped down. It was hosted by Margaret Beckett – who, as Straw's successor as foreign secretary, had endured unfairly negative coverage in the media despite the keen intelligence, professionalism and effectiveness with which she had steered Britain's foreign policy. And Tony used the occasion to praise me in generous terms for the work I'd done in the Middle East. Yet when I attended his farewell Labour gala dinner, I could not help noting – and feeling saddened by – the fact that a sense of political calculation seemed to outweigh our long personal relationship. 'Cash for peerages' was not yet over. And although Tony publicly praised and thanked a number of the people who had helped him become prime minister and govern Britain, he made no mention of me. I said nothing, though I am sure I was not alone in noticing the omission. Gordon Brown certainly had. 'Michael,' he said to me, 'I want to tell you that I will find the right time and occasion to thank you for everything you have done.' I was touched by the sentiment. But I couldn't help wondering whether, as I had so often found the longer I was involved in Labour, there was more than a little political calculation on Gordon's part as well. He had developed a fail-safe instinct for taking the opposite side of any issue from Tony – even, no doubt, this one.

Gordon, not Tony, is now the custodian of the vision that

first inspired me to raise money not only for charities, but for a political party and, during Tony's time in government, for the dozens of schools I hoped would offer new hope for children who are too often trapped in a cycle of underachievement in our inner cities. I do not know whether, as Tony told me, Gordon lacks the political qualities to lead the party to a fourth victory, over David Cameron. I certainly have no reason to believe Tony's view has changed. In fact, in the weeks after Gordon's politically disastrous handling of the 'general election that wasn't' in the autumn of 2007, Tony said to me: 'You know, it's one thing to spend years fighting *me* when I was prime minister. But it's not the same as running the government and the country.' Personally, I do hope that Gordon somehow recovers and wins the next election. I continue to believe that Labour has much to offer in making Britain a better and fairer place.

But the main lesson, I suppose, that I have drawn from the unhappy ending to my own part in Labour's return to government is that not only for the good of Labour, but for all parties and for British politics, a fundamental reform of funding has become more urgent. The fact that I helped to transform Labour by raising private support on a scale it had never imagined was, at the beginning I think, something wholly positive. It was not only critical in helping New Labour to succeed. It was a central part of redefining the image, identity and constituency of a party that might otherwise still be in Opposition. Some of the supporters whom I brought in may well have hoped for some form of honour. Yet I cannot think of a single one who would have contributed without the genuine belief they had in Tony, New Labour and their hopes for Britain. The fact is, however, that I am convinced that it is no longer possible to keep the growing importance of political donations to all the parties – and the increasingly larger sums each of them spends on general-election campaigns – from adding to the public and media cynicism about the political process as a whole. That is by far the greatest danger, for Labour, the other parties and the country.

On the face of it, Gordon is particularly well placed to begin tackling the problem. After all, his initial honeymoon period as prime minister was rooted in projecting an image of change – a sense that while he was 'New Labour' he would define himself above all as 'not Blair'. But in fact, it has always seemed to me that Gordon was deeply conflicted about the 'high-value' donations I helped to secure for Tony and the party. Every autumn at the party's annual conference, we would hold a dinner for Labour donors, preceded by a drinks reception for the party's high-value supporters. Gordon would inevitably attend the reception, where he would make a point of meeting, greeting, and wooing all the most important Labour contributors. Then he would leave before the dinner, allowing his spokesmen to tell reporters that 'Gordon doesn't get involved in party funding'. The irony struck me particularly at the conference following the 2005 election. Gordon had only just arrived with his wife for the reception when I overheard him say to Sarah: 'There's a new major donor. Spend some time with him and get to know him.' And there was an even more significant, and potentially embarrassing, signal of the importance Gordon attached to fundraising shortly after he became prime minister. One by one, he invited virtually all of Labour's 'secret lenders' – who Jack Dromey, and it appeared Gordon too, felt had so tarnished the party under Blair – for long, private chats at Number 10 Downing Street. The new prime minister was, one of them remarked to me afterwards, 'absolutely charming'. His message was that he valued them, and their financial backing for Labour. And his hope, it became clear as the charm offensive progressed into the early months of 2008, was that they could be persuaded to extend the term of the loans. Not just for a month or two, or even a year or two, but on a generous schedule of repayments that would not start immediately and could stretch on for nearly a decade.

I guess that like Tony before him, Gordon knew that Labour – like all the parties – needed the money.

CHAPTER 10

Postscript

Raising money for Labour is no longer my job. That is not only because, as Gilda put it when she tried and failed to encourage me into the political equivalent of early retirement, I've 'done my bit'. It is not even the trauma of 'cash for peerages', although the writing of this book has brought home to me how disturbingly fresh the bruises and the battering remain. But in the words of the Bible, and then the Byrds – voices from two different chapters in the varied life that I have been so privileged to lead – there is a time for everything under heaven. Now is the time for me to move on: to new projects and new horizons after the turbulence of my very public years in politics.

When I began work on a book I had never expected to write,

I told myself that it would be a story without bitterness or regret. It turned out that I was only half right. The pain and pressures of the year between the shock of Neil O'May's phone call in Oxford and the terse, liberating fax from Graham McNulty were just too recent and too disturbing to avoid stabs of bitterness in the retelling. Sometimes, when working on the 'cash for peerages' chapter, I would find myself reliving them all over again, unable to concentrate, sometimes even to sleep. I still remain particularly upset, I think, by the 'process' of the 'cash for peerages' investigation – the fact that an ostensibly legal question was provoked and powered by politics; and that it was further polluted by persistent and often inaccurate leaks in the media. As Assistant Commissioner Yates would no doubt put it, I have 'reasonable grounds to suspect' who was responsible for many of them. And I have no doubt at all that Carmen Dowd was right to conclude that one effect of taking legal action against me and the other 'suspects' would have been to allow 'the criminal law [to] be used to single out a citizen for adverse treatment' for political ends.

Thankfully, that didn't happen. And while I do remain more bitter than I'd realised about some aspects of 'cash for peerages', I would like to think that the passage of time and the writing of this book have begun to give me what the Americans like to call a sense of 'closure' – a new distance, and a wider perspective. Most importantly, I have been able to separate the issues of 'process' and personality. With very few exceptions – Jack Dromey will not be on my Chanucah card list – I have come to see that most of the individuals caught up in the 'cash for peerages' drama acted honourably. Once the investigation was unleashed, the police obviously had a job to do and by and large they got on with doing it. I certainly harbour no resentment towards my principal interrogator, Paul Kelsey, who acted correctly throughout. The same goes broadly for the news media. With few exceptions – and there were some shocking instances of truly incendiary and inaccurate coverage – most in the media were simply doing what reporters should and must do in any free society: putting the information they possessed in the public domain as accurately and honestly as they could. As for the problems of 'process', as I said in my statement when it was all finally over, the job of untangling what went wrong and learning the lessons must now be for others to pursue. So, too, is what I hope will emerge as an equally important bit of unfinished business from the entire affair: the need fundamentally to reform the way Britain's politics are financed and to consider state funding for all political parties.

Yet in looking back on my life so far, there are genuinely no regrets. I have been extraordinarily fortunate. With the selfless support of parents who struggled financially but never lost sight of the things that really mattered, I have been able to provide comfort and support for my own family on a scale that they, and I as a child in Alvington Crescent, could never have imagined. Particularly during my Magnet years, I made fascinating friends, and had enormous fun, along the way. And much, much more importantly, I have been blessed with wonderful children, and with a wife for whom even the word 'wonderful' is somehow insufficient. She, like my parents, has always helped me recognise that merely living well is not the same as living a good life – that what you take from life is in the end less important than what you put back. Or as she might prefer to put it, the phone calls from Downing Street matter a lot less than the millions raised, and thousands helped, through organisations like Jewish Care and CSV.

Even the years in politics, I still believe, gave me an opportunity to 'put something back' – and to work alongside remarkable men and women who were in the end driven by a desire to make Britain a better place. I have had critical words in this book – sometimes harsh ones – for Tony Blair, Gordon Brown and a number of other players on Britain's political stage. For myself, too. My aim has been to give an unvarnished account of events at the sharp end of politics, events which not only tested but I think also changed each of us. My own education in political life, something I had known only as a voter before my first meeting with Tony over dinner in 1994, was neither easy nor always pleasant, and I have tried to be honest with myself and others in describing it. Yet, in the end, I still think that it was an enormous privilege – if one which I am now greatly relieved to be writing about rather than still living.

As I was starting to work on the book, a journalist whom I know asked me 'off the record' to describe some of the key players at the heart of the 'cash for peerages' debacle: Tony, Jonathan Powell, Ruth Turner, and of course the 'Labour lenders'. As I began to do so, he suddenly broke in: 'They can't all be saints!' I laughed. 'Of course not,' I replied. 'They are human. They have flaws. Just like you. Just like me. But if there is one thing I've learned, it is that if you look for good qualities in people you almost always find them.' That was certainly true of the lenders: highly successful, highly ambitious, but also to a man genuinely charitable and determined to help improve the lives of others. And it was true, too, of Labour's inner circle: Ruth, who despite the misleading media coverage, never did anything during the long difficult months of 'cash for peerages' other than act honestly and tell the truth as she saw it; and Jonathan, who like me was almost obsessively determined not to discuss 'cash for peerages' in any detail once the investigation was under way but who managed to convey sympathy on a human level with Gilda's and my ordeal. And Tony himself, a much more complex figure than perhaps I and others recognised when he moved into Downing Street, and hugely frustrating at times, but in the end a really good man trying to do really good things for his country.

In fact, I can think of no better summary of my own experience of British politics than the one he gave when he finally said farewell in the House of Commons. The frustrated actor delivering his parting soliloquy, he declared: 'Some may belittle politics, but we know it is where people stand tall. And although I know it has its many harsh contentions, it is still the arena which sets the heart beating fast. It may sometimes be a place of low skulduggery, but it is more often a place for noble causes.' The key now – for all parties in a political system that has become too often overwhelmed by 'harsh contentions', and tainted by cynicism – is to remember and somehow to recapture that nobility.

My more immediate concern, however, is Gilda. She is at the door. We are late. And we have an appointment in Oxford – for lunch with Juliet and Phil.

Michael Levy

London, March 2008

Acknowledgements

My thanks first to Ned Temko – journalist, tennis partner, and friend – without whose invaluable help, talent and patience I could not have written this book; to Eddie Bell, my literary agent, for his advice and guidance throughout; and to Ian Chapman and all the team at Simon & Schuster for their encouragement and belief.

The writing of this book, however, would also not have been possible without the kindnesses, help and inspiration which I have received from many others in living the life which it records. Some are already present in its pages, some are not, but to all of them I am enormously grateful. I only wish that I could list every name, but that would require almost as much space as the book itself.

They include Jean Cobb and the late Pat Lilley, who at Magnet and in the years that have followed not only managed somehow to bring unfailing calm and order to my working life, but greatly to brighten it as well, and who between them put up with me for a total of 75 years. I am grateful, too, for the great times I shared with the other enormously gifted colleagues and friends at Magnet and M & G records, who made my years in the music business not only successful, but hugely enjoyable. And I am thankful as well for the opportunity I have been given to work with so many special people in the charitable and voluntary sector – at Jewish Care, CSV, JFS, UJIA and the other dedicated charities with which I remain involved.

In politics and public life, too, I have been fortunate to have worked alongside men and women of great talent, drive and personal generosity – Tony Blair, Jonathan Powell and many, many others both in government and the Labour Party; as well as the extraordinarily talented and dedicated team of diplomats and staff at the Foreign and Commonwealth Office.

Finally, another few words of thanks not only to Gilda and our children Daniel and Juliet, but to their own partners in love and life, Vally and Phil, and to the rest of what I came to think of as the 'inner circle' during the gruelling months of 'cash for peerages'. They included, of course, my extraordinarily able legal team: Neil O'May, Geoffrey Bindman, Roy Amlott and Mark Dennis. I am especially grateful to them because they are not just remarkable lawyers, but remarkable human beings. Also always there for me were Stephen, Ruth, Alan, and Judith; Michael Goldmeier; Jeff Shear; and many, many other family and friends. 'Thank you' somehow seems insufficient for the gratitude I feel.

Index

(the initials GL and ML refer to Gilda Levy and Michael Levy)